Collected Papers of
Martha Harris and Esther Bick

Martha Harris

COLLECTED PAPERS
OF
MARTHA HARRIS
AND
ESTHER BICK

THE CLUNIE PRESS, PERTHSHIRE, SCOTLAND
FOR
THE ROLAND HARRIS TRUST

First published 1987

British Library Cataloguing in Publication Data

Harris, Martha and Bick, Esther
   Collected papers of Martha Harris
   and Esther Bick

   I. Title
   000′.0   XX0000.X00

   ISBN 0-902965-24-7

Typeset by Action Typesetting Limited, Gloucester.
Printed and bound in Great Britain by
Billing and Sons Ltd., Worcester.
For Clunie Press, Old Ballechin, Strathtay, Perthshire,
Publisher to The Roland Harris Trust.

Table of Contents

TABLE OF CONTENTS

Acknowledgements are due to the following, in which these papers originally appeared:

[1] *Journal of Child Psychotherapy,* Vol.2, 1968
[2] *Journal of Child Psychotherapy,* Vol.1, 1966
[3] *Journal of Child Psychotherapy,* Vol.1, 1965
[4] *Journal of Child Psychotherapy,* Vol.3, 1973
[5] *International Journal of Psychoanalysis,* Vol.43 (1962), p.628
[6] *International Journal of Psychoanalysis,* Vol.49 (1968), p.484
[7] *Journal of Child Psychotherapy,* Vol.10, 1976
[8] *Journal of Child Psychotherapy,* Vol.4, 1970
[9] *New Society,* 15th June 1967
[10] *International Journal of Psychoanalysis,* Vol.45 (1964), p.558
[11] Previously published in *The Child Psychotherapist,* ed. Dilys Dawes and Mary Boston. Wildwood House: London, 1977.

Introduction

Portrait

She was tall and strongly built, even slightly masculine, if you didn't look at those arresting eyes. Heavy-lidded and deep-set, almost sleepy and yet penetratingly attentive, with a soft blue grey, 'the hills in my eyes' she would say. The strong facial bone structure of her father rather overshadowed the aspects of delicate beauty from her mother ('What wonderful big hats she wore', Mattie would say longingly.) Her gait in latter years was a bit stiff in the lower back which emphasized the fine, broad thorax. She looked particularly splendid in royal blue and purple and would have worn floral gowns for ever. Fine materials were a passion, and she could rapidly run up a dress, though never with the skill and patience of her mother. She always had too many irons in the fire, so that meals, lectures, the garden, sewing and reading tended to go on simultaneously in some mysterious economy. For days before giving a party for the students at the Old Rectory in Mersea the shopping and cooking would go on in the interstices of the day and night. And on the day amazing amounts in amazing varieties of meats and salads and sweets would emerge as if from nowhere. She had a particular way of talking that often seemed at first a stutter but was in fact a complicated process of accommodation between the complexity of her thought and the minute responses of her audience. A typescript from a tape looked terrible, but the effect on a listener was like standing well back from the brush-strokes of a Van Dyke, amazed to see that the mass of wiggly lines suddenly fused into silk and lace and jewels. The slight soft Scottish furriness of her voice tempered her vehemence in debate and her laugh chimed out in a most infectious way. While easily entertained by wit, she was not witty or entertaining herself, but her gaiety could fill a room and encourage the sallies of others, keen for her admiration. Her hands were strong and slightly gnarled later on, death to weeds and dexterous with needles. When the film was being made in India in the hysterical atmosphere of too little time and money and a plethora of prima donnas, Mattie's quiet and attentive knitting away soothed everyone, as a fascinating diagonal patterned pullover gradually emerged. She did not write easily but had to revise and revise. Her handwriting was the opposite of her mode of speech, for it looked lovely from a distance but was almost unreadable because she never took the pen from the paper. Everything was fused together, like Mrs. Bick's description of 'looping'. Animals did not attract or interest her much, despite her childhood on the farm, but the beauty of the landscape ravished her. The works of man made perhaps less impact, with the exception of literature, and there her knowledge and memory and comprehension often astonished. She read voluminously, but only very unwillingly of the psycho-analytic literature. Even Bion, whose supervision had been her great inspiration after Mrs. Klein's, she read half-heartedly. Though she'd been keen on sports in her youth (the broken front teeth came from the hockey field) games of any sort bored her. One couldn't imagine Mattie playing cards or chess, though Roland had been an enthusiast of the latter. But Scottish dancing – that was another matter. No reel was long enough for her. She was devoted to children, but I never saw her dote on a child, nor talk over his head, nor violate his privacy. Her warm reserve was almost paradoxical, charming without effort, generous without being indulgent. She seemed always to mean what she said, but never said all she meant and when something hurtful had to be spoken, she could 'tell the truth, but tell it slant', as Emily Dickinson would say.

Introduction

Mattie as an Educator

Mattie had a wonderful mind. She could reach deep into herself and use the richness and fluidity of her contact with her own emotional being to understand others. Her students were given a remarkable experience, for they were safely held by her breadth of attentiveness while being brought close to the exhilarating, frightening, exciting, beautiful, astonishing ways in which babies feel and begin to think. Mattie's love and enjoyment of children and life and her devotion to psychoanalytically inspired exploration of the early development of mind came together in a particularly faithful way in her teaching, and shaped a whole generation of child psychotherapists.

Seeing the lovely gardens she could create, a glorious blend of colour in which the relative wildness of herbaceous borders and free-growing shrubs concealed the very hard work and patient care of the gardener, was for me a source of perceiving how she worked at the Tavistock.

When she first took on the task of organizing the Tavistock child psychotherapy training, she was faced with sustaining a psychoanalytic conception of personality growth which Esther Bick had taught. Mrs Bick followed Melanie Klein's still developing thought closely, and was committed to an uncompromising purity of technique. Mattie had to find a way to continue this teaching in a context of considerable disagreement among senior colleagues over some fundamentals. In order to learn, students needed some protected space for grappling with the Kleinian paradigm but also to engage with the wider currents of child psychiatric practice and the Tavistock community mental health approach. The echoes of this creative tension are recurrent in ongoing thinking about training now, and Mattie's way of integrating relevant knowledge through intense concentration on the particular is a powerful model.

The study of the interaction between babies and their mothers, and indeed other members of the family, through the method of Infant Observation developed by Mrs Bick, was pivotal in Mattie's conception of a psychoanalytic education.

The careful regularity of weekly nonintrusive visits allowed access to the intimate interplay of emotional lives in the family nexus. Seminars for discussion of detailed descriptions of all that had been observed was the first experience most students had of Mattie's teaching. It was an astounding experience. Students would be bewildered by the wealth of unfamiliar detail and what could seem like shapeless chaos, and by the intensity of their own emotional engagement. Mattie's comments would draw together in a memorably meaningful way the available evidence about the states of mind and feeling of the family members, and would offer a language which sounded quite ordinary and down-to-earth for describing emotional events which most of us had never been able to notice before. The clarity and simplicity of the language reflected Mattie's steady concentration on the essential data. Readers of the present volume will enjoy the limpid style of her writing about the observation of infants.

She had a capacity to be profoundly interested and to share with the seminar her fascination in the unfolding of a baby's potentialities and with parents' experiences of coming to know their baby and new aspects of themselves too. At the same time, the students' emotional responses, their anxieties and development would be unobtrusively held in Mattie's mind. We felt ourselves very fully known to her through these seminars but also to trust her use of this knowledge because it was used with love and concern to facilitate our development as individuals and as potential therapists. So she showed us how to appreciate the privilege of coming close to the intimate interior of family lives, of becoming aware of the conscious and unconscious emotional patterns, of seeing how an infant's personality took shape. Particularly characteristic was her emphasis on the interplay of internal factors – the temperament of mother and baby, their individual capacities for tolerating anxieties, expressing emotions and so on – and the external and contingent factors – who was available to contain and support mother in the vulnerable early weeks; how had the confinement been experienced; what might disturb or help mother and baby in establishing the feeding relationship. The combination for many students of beginning Infant Observation and beginning analysis was a watershed over which Mattie presided with personal delicacy and kindness.

In the gradual evolution of the pre-clinical training of child psychotherapists to its present form in the Tavistock Observation Course, Mattie's other central plank was what she called a 'Work Discussion' seminar. A very unpretentious and even mundane name for what turned out to be a hugely creative conception. One of her own experiences which contributed to working out the basis for this sort of seminar is documented in her paper on 'A Consultation Project in a Comprehensive School'. Struck by how useful observation of children in a non-clinical context turned out to be to teachers, she gathered together a group of people wanting to train as child psycho-therapists and instituted a seminar to which they were invited to bring recorded observations of their experiences at work. The members were from a variety of professions and settings and had a lot to offer each other. The method was for the member presenting to read aloud the written material and to add thoughts as they occurred. The ensuing dialogue between presenter and seminar members elucidated many further details and allowed for the exploration of the emotional aspects of the work setting, both building a picture of the inner preoccupations of the child or children being studied and clarifying the conscious and un-conscious responses of the worker to the children's communications. The helpfulness of these seminars to people struggling with often very distressed and disturbed children was enormous; finding meaningful links which might render the children's behaviour understandable reduced the degree of confusion, anxiety and persecution and freed the workers' imagination and hopefulness. The Tavistock course for teachers on Counselling Aspects of the teacher's role grew from this same kernel, and work discussion seminars have become a standard component of many other courses. The concept now seems so obvious it is hard to imagine being without it, but it arose from Mattie's conviction that a psychoanalytic attitude was relevant not only in the consulting room but in all settings where the understanding and management of the anxieties and conflicts of adults and children were central to the developmental possi-bilities inherent in the situation. This starting point made all the relationships open to a growing child at home, at school and in the wider community worthy of close study.

Mattie's own enjoyment of teaching, which made her seminars

and supervisions pleasures to be intensely savoured, must have been an important factor in her decision to initiate a large expansion in the child psychotherapy training. In the early 1970s, changes in the organization of the National Health Service, an expanding interest in psychoanalysis and psycho-therapy, and an increasing number of suitably qualified and experienced applicants provided the opportunity for mobilizing the resources of the tiny profession to launch a much increased educational programme. A generation of those whose training had been deeply marked by Mattie's influence were gathered together to serve as teachers. The privileges of the teacher, in presiding over the personal and intellectual development of her students were particularly appreciated by Mattie. The seminars of the Observation Course offered access to the many-layered possibilities of being able to use psychoanalytic methods and knowledge in a broader context than the individual work of the consulting room. Students, their colleagues, the children they worked with and the children's families were all part of the seminar's experience. Democratic instincts, personal generosity, a capacity for phenomenal hard work, and a conviction that the unique value of psychoanalytic insight ought to be shared as much as was possible enabled Mattie to inspire her psychotherapist colleagues to take on this challenge. Her own courage and devotion to and happiness in the work under-pinned a colossal determination not to be hampered by a weight of bureaucratized organization, nor to pay too much heed to the cautious and in many ways traditionalistic assumptions of most psychoanalytic educators. In retrospect, this shift of gear still takes one's breath away.

Of course her example, because it was so transparently expressive of a whole grasp on life, was immensely influential. The impact she had on those she taught derived from her being as well as from the power of her presentation of psychoanalytic ideas. Her attitude to her students felicitously combined a depth of interest and a great deal of patience when she sensed that honest learning was taking place, with a firm conviction that anxieties must be faced and tolerated. She did not believe in reassurance, but helped her students to bear the rigours of psychoanalytic learning by her kindness and extra-ordinary capacity to hold in mind their individual vulnerabilities. One of her favourite theoretical references was to W.R. Bion's use of Keats' concept of 'Negative Capability', and her approach to teaching was a beautiful exemplification of Bion's ideas.

Many of her colleagues can bear witness to the subtlety of her judgements of people – and very many students benefited from her sensitive contact with the creative spark inside them which could elude other observers but which Mattie could seek out and nourish.

In the later part of her working life, she began to place more emphasis on the importance of writing, and struggled to make more space for writing work of her own. The value of writing also came to take up a larger place in the Tavistock Clinic psychotherapy training. This volume will be a more formal record of her outstanding contribution to thinking about psychoanalytic education for a wider public as well as a delightful re-encounter with her for old friends and students.

Margaret Rustin
March 1987

Section I

CLINICAL PAPERS ON PSYCHO-ANALYSIS OF CHILDREN AND ADULTS

1 The Therapeutic Process in the Psychoanalytic Treatment of the Child
c. 1968

As we know, children are referred for treatment for many reasons. In some cases a child's illness may be a symptom of disturbance within the family. By working in a family psychiatry setting we may be able to help him indirectly by influencing parental attitudes. We may nevertheless be left with a child who cannot respond adequately to a better climate, still unable to cope with the frustrations that even the best of environments must necessarily impose, and who may never have been able to make sufficient use of what was offered. Such children like the adults whom they would later become, all suffer from some impairment in their ability to function in the external world and in the inner world of thought, emotion and imagination — an impairment which may be attended with greater or lesser awareness of conflict, dissatisfaction with the self, or of impoverishment in the personality.

Therapy by the psychoanalytic technique involves the exploration of the patient's unconscious conflicts, essentially between love and hate: directed first toward the mother, later extended to father and a wider circle; his relationship with these objects as internalised within himself is continuously active, thus influencing his current experiences. Following Mrs. Klein and her school, I am assuming that the psychoanalytic treatment of children is essentially similar in principle to that of adults, and that any necessary modifications of technique occur in order to make communication easier for the child. Thus although we hope for, and encourage, verbal expression, we do also depend to a large extent on other modes such as drawing, play with toys or dramatic play; as well as the more intangible messages conveyed by posture, movements, facial expression, tone of voice. By providing a setting where the child is encouraged to freely associate in play, behaviour, and in words, without as far as possible any direction from the therapist through implied reassurance or criticism, we encourage him to convey to us in the course of his treatment the emotional fluctuations and conflicts

3

in his relationships, both internal and external. I use this technique and setting whether I am treating a child once, or up to five times a week.

I will try to focus in this paper upon the therapeutic process as one which develops communication between different aspects of the child and the therapist, and which also facilitates communications between the parts of the child's own mind as a result of insight gained through transference interpretations.

In the course of a sufficiently prolonged psychoanalytic treatment therapists represent at different times various aspects of all the important figures in his environment, past and present, as he perceives them; but basically his relationship to us stems from his very first experiences of outside reality in the arms of the mother and through the ingestion of food, comfort and frustration from this mother: experiences whose nature was moulded and still continues to be moulded by his own approach as well as by its reception. The understanding mother who is able not only to approach the infant with food and love, but who can also tolerate the feelings of anxiety of which he needs to rid himself, helps him to take these back as a less intolerable part of his personality. The mother's capacity to experience and to manage the infant's personality helps the child whose anxieties are not too overwhelming to build within himself an integrating and understanding figure.

At depth, and in clearer form as the treatment proceeds, the transference deepens. The psycho-analytic relationship repeats this model. Our child patients are infants, but they are also developing adults, able and eager to understand verbal communication in terms appropriate to their age and intelligence, and so we are able to convey to them in the form of words the unthinkable, unnameable anxieties which they project into us. To be able to do this effectively a reasonable background of psychoanalytical theory may be essential but it is not enough. We need to be sufficiently well analysed to be in touch with our own deepest emotions before we can experience the understanding and convey it to the child in an interpretation that fits his unique communication — interpretations without intuition, based only on theory, are sterile.

I have sometimes found that children who started treatment in an acute state of anxiety could be given early relief through interpretation of the nature and content of these anxieties: for instance, young children with sleeping difficulties. I would, however, like to give an example here of Walter, a severely disturbed ten-year-old boy who was referred by his mother for manifold and increasing fears which he was endeavouring unsuccessfully to keep at bay by ever more complicated obsessional rituals. These acute anxieties broke out upon the first anniversary of his father's death, and had been multiplying from that time till he was seen at the Clinic three months later and began treatment with me. I am giving an extremely condensed account of the trend of the first two sessions and for the sake of brevity cannot elaborate upon the details that led me to make the interpretations recounted here.

In his first session he poured forth an account of his worries as he called them — his fears of being poisoned by germs from the air, his mother's food, pretty women who became witches, ghosts and terrible fantasies at night which might become reality if he did not have the light switch by his bed to control them. In that session I had been able to interpret amid other things, his fear of germs and ghosts as fear of the dead German father assailing him from all quarters. His suspicion of me in the transference was of a pretty mother who might well turn into a witch and poison him with my words as food even as he feared his mother had poisoned his father. He left rather startled but thoughtful and calmer. Then on his way out was evidently assailed by suspicion and asked me in the waiting room 'Where was Dr S?' (the consultant who had seen him the week before). In his second session a week later he told me a dream after some initial reluctance — a torrent of talk between the announcement of the dream and its final recounting: *A shark had eaten one man and was about to eat him. It had open mouth and sharp teeth but Walter made a noise, flapped and shouted to frighten it away.* I interpreted that the shark was myself, the mother who had devoured one man, father, as he feared I had swallowed up Dr S., and he was now afraid that I would devour him — hence the flapping, shouting, the pressure of talk to keep me at bay. A great expression of relief came over his face: he confessed that he had been reluctant to come to the Clinic that day, told his mother he was bored by me. I took the 'bored' as a literal fear. He went on to tell a long story about a man who fell into the undergrowth from an aeroplane, became a monster and was there killed by another who had stolen the elixir of life. He followed this by reference to other monstrous tales. Interpretation of his fear that I would discover that this monster was really himself, hidden in the depths of his own mind, that he was the devouring shark and that I would punish him by death led to great lightening of his spirit. He said in astonishment 'I'm feeling better, much better, my worries are going . . .' then eagerly and quickly, 'but I've others I must tell you . . .' and began to recite them. It seemed that my interpretations, though far from complete, had yet conveyed to him sufficient understanding of his intolerable anxiety to relieve him and encourage him to seek further relief. In a later session he told me 'The worst of all was the feeling that I had to tell somebody everything in my mind or else no-one would even know it . . . but then I believed that thought is like a tape recorder, it goes on and on till it's all finished and then what happens.' Here he was able to express to me the despair of the child who cannot contain the violently unacceptable aspects of himself, is driven to continuously project them and is then terrified that with them go all his mental apparatus. I think he became able to verbalise this as a result of meeting in his treatment a therapist, an adult who could speak his own language, with whom he could share his fears, and with whom he could ally himself.

Transference to the therapist of the earliest and most primitive emotions tends to happen more quickly and more vehemently with children than with adults. We may have to endure long periods of sustained resistance sometimes, accompanied by contemptuous abuse and even physical violence that would be rare with adult patients. For this reason toughness, inner strength, are as important as sensitivity in a child therapist. The therapist's very ability to sustain such resistance and the massive projective identification accompanying it, without being overwhelmed and without abandonment of the analytic technique: the attempt to persevere in understanding the dynamics of the situation: is in itself therapeutic, even when the understanding is imperfect as it must always be. It is not possible, however, to go on tolerating indefinitely those emotions whose strength and occurrence are too much for the child: the over-greedy possessive love, the excessive hate; unless we do see some way of understanding them, and the pattern of the relationship their action and interaction creates with us. Our strength as therapists develops from familiarity with and success in attempting to cope with these emotions in ourselves, and also from every experience of working through difficult resistances against insight which are encountered in our patients. From such experiences we develop the confidence to persist in attempting to unravel obstinate difficulties which take on a new and different pattern.

I have in mind now a ten year old boy, Paul, whom I treated for just over three years. He was an engaging, friendly, considerate boy, much loved by his parents but doing consistently rather badly at school in the nicest possible way — inclined to be a little insipid. He started analysis with me in a very positive way, ready to turn it into the most special of all his special relationships and anticipating a move up to the top of the class without any effort on his part. To interpretations he listened with invariable politeness. This idealised relationship broke down before his first holiday and from then onwards we entered into a prolonged and increasingly violent period of resistance, hitherto unparalleled in my experience, during which he attacked me and specifically my interpretations both verbally and physically. 'Think!' he would say. 'You've no right to think, get down and sweep the floor, that's what women are for, to sweep up after men. You're quite young, you could have more babies but I'll smash up every one of them in you and you'll never be able to open your mouth again.' To avoid hearing the interpretations that provoked the envious attacks he would often build an elaborate house with the furniture, shut himself in, stuff up his ears and read books, listen to his pocket wireless or consume bags of sweets and throw the papers out at me. Many a time I was in despair, felt it was hopeless trying to wrestle with this violence, was infuriated by his contempt and discouraged by the apparent ineffectiveness of my interpretations: a state of mind which he was of course endeavouring to project into me, as I attempted to convey to him.

Recurrent working upon the theme of his envious and destructive attacks upon me as predominantly the feeding and creative mother, resented because I was not uniquely his possession, of the persecution and overwhelming guilt induced by these attacks, gradually loosened the resistance. In the last year of his treatment he gravitated spontaneously to the couch and began to associate like an adult. He returned recurrently and repentantly to this violent period, told me how sometimes when his hands were over his ears he was really listening, and would try to remember and write down at night what I had been saying. And he would curse himself for the rage that arose when I said things he felt were true: so puzzling, for he also wanted to hear them. By this time he had become very grateful to me, for not only had his school work improved markedly, but also his confidence and enjoyment in life. He became a much stronger personality, capable of grappling with frustrations instead of evading them by charm. As he said to me in one of his last sessions, 'Why should finding out that I'm such a bastard make me feel so much better. I wouldn't mind taking on Kruschev now, but perhaps it would be better to send him to you for analysis; that would give him something to think about!'

Paul was a boy who by his character structure, the exploitation of his good qualities to gain approval and affection and to placate possible persecutors, had managed to avoid an acute sense of suffering. One might wonder what is the motive for children like him to co-operate in psycho-analytic treatment — for co-operate he plainly did, as he so generously admitted later, even in his violently antagonistic period. And what is the motive for childen like Walter to continue with treatment after their most acute anxieties are allayed, as his were within the first six months? I think we can come nearer to explaining this if we consider Freud's 'Two Principles of Mental Functioning', and realise that even young children have, as well as a desire to experience pleasure and avoid pain, a need to understand the world as it is — which includes the reality of their own internal world. Starvation of truth, as Bion stated recently in his paper 'A Theory of Thinking', can be analogous to alimentary starvation, and induces a mental state of debility. Realisation of the truth of an unacceptable interpretation can bring with it a feeling of relief and strength that mitigates the unpleasantness.

I will instance here Jean, a thirteen-year-old girl whom I took on for weekly treatment after she had been having two years 2 – 3 times weekly supportive psychotherapy. This had included a good deal of reassurance and a relationship of social friendship with her therapist. I had some qualms about her reception of the new regime. She did find it difficult at first; was hostile about the reduced sessions, the change of therapist and the nature of the treatment. During one of these early, resentful sessions, however, she said, 'I'm comparing you and Mrs C. in my mind with my two English teachers at school. We used to have Mr A., who was terribly kind to us all and very encouraging about our work. He'd always find something good to say about my essays so I enjoyed doing them for him, but somehow I never knew where I was. Now Mr B., our new teacher, he's not so nice to us, he's much more interested in the work and he tells us what's wrong and makes us correct it. It's not nearly so easy with him — I don't like it but somehow I'm learning much more.'

As I see it then, in analytic treatment the therapist acts as supplementary ego. The child depends on us to receive his messages, to follow at depth the main thread in his transference relationship to us, and through interpretation of this, is led back into contact with the split-off and repressed aspects of his personality. By studying interaction in the transference, we have an opportunity to perceive the distortions and blockages that occur in the child's responses to the reality of our interpretations, and to bring them to his attention. By making an interpretation specifically and demonstrably based on his material, we can help the child to understand the work of analysis as a process of understanding relationships, in which he is able to play an active part. Greater understanding of the emotions provoked by the inevitable frustrations in the analytic situation, can then help him to deal with the frustrations of his environment in a more realistic way: to study and strive to adapt himself, or to alter it where necessary, instead of turning away or dealing with it by omnipotent distortion.

I am going to present material from two sessions in the analysis of a boy in the latency period. He was 9 when he made this first drawing[1] in the first few months of his analysis, and 10 when he made the second drawing a year later. I have had this second one reproduced at two stages: as it was before I made any interpretation, and as he finally completed it. I thought we might discuss indications of changes taking place within him during the year, suggested by comparison of the drawings and of his behaviour in the two sessions.

But first a brief account of my earliest acquaintance with

[1] *The reproductions of these drawings are not available.*

David. This occurred when he was just two years old and was brought by his mother to the Tavistock Clinic because of acute sleeping difficulties which refused to respond to ever-increasing sedatives. She was then in the seventh month of her next pregnancy. They were both pale, strained, exhausted, with huge circles under their eyes and in a pretty desperate state.

David had been a much wanted baby, born to professional parents in their 20's. The pregnancy had been normal but labour was very short, lasting only one and a half hours. At birth he weighed 6lbs., was very shocked and was given oxygen. The mother had plenty of milk, and fed David on demand, but although he sucked and throve well physically, he cried a great deal and was seldom contented unless receiving attention. By three months he was beginning to be more regular in his feeding and sleeping. Then when he was fourth months old his mother had influenza badly and I suspect was also depressed, and was unable to continue breast feeding. David refused to have anything to do with a bottle for either milk or orange juice, and had to be weaned straight onto a cup and spoon. He did not suck his finger either. From that time he began to sleep badly again by day and by night. The sleeping difficulties became particularly acute when he was 22 months old and his mother was two months pregnant; finding it extremely difficult to cope with him, she sent him to a little nursery school for an hour or two a day, to a neighbour in the same house. After a tearful beginning he settled down fairly well and appeared to enjoy it. At the same time without maternal pressure he quite suddenly became dry and clean by day. This step in his development was attended with increased anxiety, for he began to waken up more and more frequently and would work himself into a hysterical state unless perpetually comforted by his mother. She moved into his room and seldom got more than half an hour's sleep at a time.

This was the situation when they arrived at the clinic and when I took on David for emergency treatment. I saw him over five months for between 40 and 50 sessions in all. During this time his mother had her second child and was away in hospital for about two weeks.

David's sleeping troubles improved after the first few sessions, and cleared up more or less completely after several weeks — mainly as a result of interpretation of his anxiety about urinary and faecal attacks on his mother's body, attacks that were largely projected into the father's penis. His chief anxiety centered round the loss of his mother and his own destruction, which included castration by his father. A very warm attachment to and concern for his mother emerged, but also a clinging identification with her in an attempt to preclude envy. During the treatment not only did his sleeping improve, but he also became less anxious and clinging, more capable of amusing himself. This improvement was maintained over the period of his mother's absence and return with the new baby. At this time the father, who had at first been indifferent — if not negative — came to see me and became very co-operative, seeing that David continued to be brought for his sessions regularly. The relationship between the mother and new baby went well; David, assisted by extra attention from his father, was able to adjust to the new situation and even to enjoy the baby without being overwhelmed with jealousy. Treatment stopped for practical reasons, on the understanding that the parents would contact me again should further difficulties arise.

I did not hear from them again for seven years. They rang me up to say that David, who had hitherto been doing quite well at school, was falling behind, becoming anxious and sleepless at night. He was now the eldest of three boys. His attractive, vivacious mother had continued to be subject to the bouts of depression that had affected her from his birth onwards, and there were recurrent marital difficulties between the parents. The fall-off at school coincided with the arrival of a new Maths teacher: a brusque, loud-voiced man who made David's mind go blank when he asked questions. It turned out later that this blankness and confusion also tended to arise in games in which the father — an intelligent, ambitious writer — posed questions to his sons.

David himself was then a sensitive looking, handsome boy, but there was occasionally an evasive, repellent look in his eyes, the look of the vindictive underdog. He was apparently on good terms with his brothers and showed no rivalry with them, but tended to be over-protective. He had no close friends at school. His father thought he tended to form temporary relationships with bullies in order to placate them, and plainly feared he had homosexual tendencies. There was a brief period at the beginning of David's analysis when he talked about school life and work, was obviously anxious to establish a good relationship with me, and tended to look for an interpretation of any kind as reassurance that he was doing all right: becoming most anxious when none was forthcoming. This related to anxiety about me as a depressed, ill mother, absent in mind and in emotional response, if not in body. Interpretation of his feelings of responsibility for this, of his deep uncertainty of the genuineness of his co-operation with me and of the value of his gifts, tended to produce muddled and furtive evasion, under which lay fear of my penetrating further into his thoughts. Anxiety became stronger about a powerful, all-seeing, retributory penis-conscience into which he had projected his own hostility, and with which he did not know how to cope since it could be neither placated nor deceived. He almost stopped talking and playing with the toys, then began to draw: rather painful, restricted efforts, which were — however — a real attempt to communicate with me despite his fear. At this time he told his mother that the treatment was very difficult but was worth it.

The first drawing illustrates some of the themes on which we worked at this period of the treatment. It is of a greyhound race. David drew first the lines across the page, then the empty seats and the hut from which the greyhounds emerge. He put a cross through this and a criss-cross broken-up pattern over it. He then drew the greyhound with muzzle heavily outlined and tail stuck out stiffly behind. He became uncertain whether there should be another greyhound behind or not; twice one was drawn emerging from the box, then rubbed out messily, till finally the head and forelegs were allowed to remain. He then wrote upon the top lefthand seat: 'Reserved for Mr Jones'; started to write 'Reserved for . . .' on some others, which then dwindled to three wiggly lines on all the rest, and all the seats remained empty. He seemed at a loss. He could give me no information about Mr Jones (but this was not so long after Princess Margaret's wedding to Mr Armstrong-Jones). His response to my query about the other reserved seats was 'I don't know', in an agitated defensive way, and a hasty attempt to colour in the drawn shapes of the hut, in a way that suggested he felt criticised by me and was trying to cover up his misdemeanour.

I shall not go into details of my interpretation of this picture. In this session and at this stage in his treatment, David found it impossible to respond directly to interpretations. The analysis was for him so much an examination situation in which he feared discovery and punishment, and in which instinctual impulses had to be extensively denied. In this picture the lonely, wooden-looking greyhound is heavily muzzled, he has no eye; only the anal impulses are directly represented by the faecal tail. The rows of seats look down on him with the empty assertion of moral superiority, indicative of the inhuman super-ego formed from the emptied breasts, the penis and babies expunged from the mother's body. This was David's internal situation, projected into me in the session, through which my interpretations were experienced as pitiless criticism by the terrible father Jones, the Maths master, from whose hostility he had to hide and defend himself. The colouring of the shed was, I think, an attempt at reparation: to restore life to the cut-up body of the mother from whom the babies emerge; but an unsuccessful attempt based on flight from insight, avoidance of guilt.

Yet there was plainly a part of him that was able to co-operate in the analytic work, because he continued to bring himself and even expressed appreciation of me at home, although he could not do so to me directly.

Themes expressed in this session continued to be in the foreground of his treatment for some months. He continued to talk very little, to make few direct responses to interpretation; but his drawings developed, became more varied and eloquent. The recurrent houses, ships, bars, castles, chalets, often filled with blank windows, tended to become more ornate and detailed. Sometimes they were built up brick by coloured brick, or plank upon plank where even the nails were put in with meticulous details. I interpreted the omnipotent nature of this reparation which had to be done by him alone, and his continual denial of the fact that at depth in his analysis he realised the damage was being done by his inability to co-operate with me as a real external person, and to acknowledge what he was learning from me. His drawings began to include people but for months there was no female figure. One day he drew a landscape of hills, and an enormous boy with a pack on his back and a really nasty furtive look in his eye (a vivid representation this time, rather than a denial, of his own repellent expression). This boy was putting his huge foot on a hill in the foreground of the picture. David was impressed when I interpreted this as a representation of the way he was trampling on the breast, the mind that feeds him in his treatment: treating it as an inanimate object, part of the landscape and not connected with a living mother/analyst. From then onward women occasionally appeared in his drawings.

The 'island' drawing was done a year later. For the month or so before the Christmas holidays David had been talking more and responding more directly to interpretations. His Christmas holiday was two weeks longer than mine as he was abroad with his parents and in fact had a good time. When he returned, he gave me tantalising glimpses of this, designed to awaken curiosity and envy in me, and thus avoid experiencing these emotions in connection with the two weeks' analysis he had missed. He asked me at the end of the week if I would see him on Tuesday (his first session next week) fifteen minues later, so that he would have time to call at a Wimpy on his way from school. I wasn't able to do this, but on Tuesday he arrived a quarter of an hour late (having had, I assumed, his Wimpy), looking fed but furtive, and began to draw at great speed.

He told me it was an island with two areas of civilisation at each end, divided in the midst by a desert and rocky mountains. The civilisations are spreading gradually, he said, but they are quite independent and have not yet met to influence one another. In the mountains are savage tribes, head-hunters and cannibals who have no civilisation and fight among themselves. Sometimes they go into the desert along the trail to explore, look for food and camp at the oases, then they go back to their mountains. Sometimes people from the English civilisation go into the desert to look for a way to the mountains where there are valuable minerals which the savage tribes don't know how to use. But the English civilisation have not yet met any of the tribes in the desert, nor have they met anyone from the Russian civilisation there. At this point I interpreted his map as a statement of the situation between himself and me (he sits on the left, I on the right): the difficulty that two civilised selves have in meeting, owing to these savage emotions in between, connected with the desert — the holiday and weekend deprivation in which he is still wandering in search of some oasis, a good drinking

14

relationship with me; and where I also am made to wander and get lost looking for him. The warring tribes are on my side of the drawing, and it would seem that he is afraid of me, as representing the parents engaged in a headhunters' cannibalistic intercourse; afraid also that if we meet each other, this is the sort of intercourse we shall then have. Yet it is his civilisation that wants to meet these tribes, to get their valuable minerals?

Here he drew the four rivers flowing from their sources in the mountains to the two civilisations and to the two other coasts, saying that the civilisations need this water for their industries. I interpreted that from this savage intercourse there also sprang the source of life: that from our meetings, these four rivers — the four sessions — flowed the understanding needed to develop his civilisation. If we took the whole map as representing himself and his attempt to show me what is going on in different parts of himself, it would seem that he felt the sessions were civilising some areas but not others, and that the two civilised parts knew nothing about each other. He then made a railway between what he later labelled the English and the Russian civilisations, with four stations, and added grassland along this railway. This again I took as the four sessions which help to connect separate parts of his mind: the parents inside him in a civilised intercourse. He added more huts and mud buildings at the mouth of the eastern river nearest to the savage tribes. He said that was a sort of civilisation too, but not a proper one, because it was based on fishing and hunting, not on making things.

I interpreted this as the greedy parts of himself that dive into my mind, as the mummy's body, to get the food, babies, penises it contains, in order to consume them and not put anything back. This is the cannibal David who takes the Wimpy analysis-breast from me, consumes it in secret, thus stealing fifteen minues of our time all for himself and depriving me of the satisfaction of enjoying a good feeding relationship with him in the session.

Meanwhile, David finished drawing the savages' huts, saying that although they are near the Russian civilisation they don't have any connection with it, because savages fear strangers would be hostile and so build walls to keep them out. Eventually, as the Russian and English civilisations are joining along the coast, they must spread inland and will influence the cannibals and head-hunters. When most of the island belongs to them they

15

can probably reclaim the desert by irrigation and planting trees. I suggested that when he and I meet in mutual understanding and a common aim to develop this, then he becomes hopeful of including his greedy savage impulses, within himself and modifying them. This would mean that instead of feeling that he has me inside him as parents who fight and eat each other up and who obstruct communication between his mind and mine, and the different parts of his mind, he has me inside as the friendly parents who make babies together and who encourage him to learn to make things. There is hope that with these friendly parents inside him, even the desert — the holidays and weekends — will be less barren.

David left after this session excited and glowing. I found by chance from his mother a few days later that he had gone home and told her that Mrs Harris was very pleased with him, said he was talking more and getting much better at analysis.

One of the striking differences from the earlier drawing and session, is his ability to respond and ally himself with my interpretations. The savage cannibalistic tribes, although at first projected into me, are also acknowleged as part of himself, and are felt to contain something of value. The greedy, the black anal spoiling attacks are no longer felt to be irremediable, when they can be communicated more clearly and brought into contact with the civilised creative part of himself, for they contain the minerals necessary to enable the civilised parts to develop fully. The savages are more human figures than the ghastly blind muzzled dog, and they are regarded more kindly by his civilisation than the dog is by the empty tombstone-like seats and the lofty place of Mr Jones. His destructive impulses and the super-ego derived from them, have been humanised by their projection into the analyst, and their reintrojection in a less persecuting form as a result of interpretation. The deserted seats in the first picture have in the second picture become the desert, which does contain oases and is visited by both civilised and savage people, and has eventually some hope of being reclaimed.

In the first drawing there is an almost total denial of impulses. David gives a lifeless picture of his ego and instinctual life crushed beneath the gaze of an empty, persecuting super-ego. The first stage of the second drawing portrays the black canni- balistic parents in his unconscious, devouring and splitting his personality, cutting him off from himself and from contact with his external object. These are created by the projection and reversal of the oral and anal impulses that lead him to spoil and empty the breasts and parental intercourse. There is splitting and projection, but life and contents. In the second stage of this drawing, as a result of interpretation, he is able to establish a connection between his conscious and unconscious, through the contact with the external object. There is a lessening of projection, acknowledgement of the cannibal part as his own, and hope that this part, with the impulses it contains, can be valuable: the anal impulses find a useful expression in drawing, the oral impulses in talking.

The development of this second drawing suggests, I think, some advance towards integration. This progess within the analysis was accompanied by marked and steady improvement in school work, greater inventiveness in games, and more permanent friendships which were not based upon the need to placate.

Note: Some of this material appears in ''The Child Psychotherapist and the Patient's Family''.

2   The Child Psychotherapist and the Patient's Family

Those of us who work with children are more dependent on the co-operation of the patient's family than is the adult therapist as a rule. If the patient is a young child it is usually the mother, sometimes the father, who has to bring the child to treatment; the older child or adolescent still needs parental backing and encouragement at times to continue during difficult periods.

In this paper I am putting down some of my thoughts as a child psychotherapist and analyst who works with children in a clinic setting and also in private practice. For some years I have been working in the Department for Children and Parents at the Tavistock Clinic. In this Clinic we have a variety of approaches, so my reflections about work with children and their families must be taken as stemming from my own particular experience and practice and do not necessarily represent the views of other people there.

A common pattern in this Department is for the child to be treated once or twice, or up to five times weekly by a child psychotherapist or psychiatrist, while the mother is seen by a psychiatric social worker or social caseworker. In a fair number of cases the father is treated regularly as well, and occasionally treatment may be offered to some other member of the family too. In some cases, and these are likely to be the older children, neither parent receives regular treatment: it may be because they are receiving this elsewhere, e.g. analysis or group treatment.

Interviews with parents preparatory to starting treatment of their child

As a non-medical child psychotherapist I may not see my patient until he has been interviewed by the psychiatrist and has received psychological tests, until the problem has been investigated with the parents and some idea has been obtained of the role of the patient within the family, of the motivation of both parents and child in seeking treatment, and of their capacity to co-operate. This is usually determined in the case of the parents as a result of interviews with both psychiatrist and psychiatric social worker and further discussion with the psychologist and child psychotherapist involved. If regular analytic treatment seems the appropriate course of action, and I have agreed to take on the child, I ask to see both parents for a preliminary interview. I am assuming here that they will naturally wish to see, and hope to be able to place some confidence in, the person who is going to treat their child. For my part I find it illuminating to form a first-hand impression of the parents, to observe their interaction with each other and with me, and to hear from them an account of the difficulties in the child and their relationship with him. I do not, in this interview, try to probe into the psychopathology of the parents or attempt to interpret, and I am wary of giving advice. Sometimes one or both parents may have begun treatment already with a social worker or psychiatrist. One of my tasks in this situation is to form as clear a picture as I can of the child as seen through their eyes and to get the feel of how, as parents, both individually, and in their relationship with each other, they might seem to a child.

I do not structure this preliminary interview but try to answer as simply and as factually as possible any questions the parents may ask about the nature of the treatment the child will be receiving from me. This has usually, of course, been explained by the psychiatrist or social worker but very often I find that they wish to enquire further, or to have the same questions answered anew by the actual person giving the treatment. I tell them that the child will come and talk or play, because younger children cannot express themselves fully by words alone. By observing the child's play I shall hope to understand gradually some of the conflicts and anxieties that are interfering with his development; conflicts and anxieties of which he will, for the greater part, be unaware. By talking to him about these as they unfold in the treatment situation in relation to me, I may help him to understand them better and to be less ruled by them in his everyday life. I explain that the therapist becomes for the child an extremely important figure, an object both of devotion and hatred. It depends upon the child and the stage of treatment which emotion is most apparent at any given time. Because the child knows the therapist in the treatment situation only, and only as a person who is there to listen, to attempt to understand, and to convey understanding, he is likely to express himself more violently and more freely to her than he does in other situations.

19

Because it is essential for him to be able to express every aspect of himself, however unacceptable, in his treatment, in order to be given understanding and help in coping with those unacceptable parts, he must be able to feel that what goes on with his therapist is confidential. I tell the parents then that I shall not therefore be able to discuss with them what goes on during a treatment session. However, I make it clear that should they wish to make an appointment to see me or want to talk to me on the phone at any time, I shall be willing to do so. I usually mention that there may be times when the child is unwilling to come to his session, when he will belittle the treatment as boring and useless, and at these times I shall rely greatly upon the support of the parents to encourage him to come regularly to understand what it is in himself that he is averse to meeting and has to attribute to the treatment situation.

Ongoing relationship with the parents of a child in treatment

If it is a clinic case where the mother is being seen regularly by a social worker or caseworker, I find that in practice I usually have very little to do with the parents after the initial interview. The mother has the opportunity of discussing her anxieties about her relationship to the child and the rest of the family with her own worker and can ask this worker to convey any message she wishes to reach me about the child. In such cases I very seldom wish to take the initiative in suggesting an interview with the parents after treatment has begun. In times of family crisis, due to acting out by the child or other causes, I find it very useful to be alerted by the caseworker to the parents' view of the situation. But I seldom find it necessary to attempt to advise or to alter the home situation directly. I leave it to the caseworker to help the parents to reach as good an understanding of the situation as they can and to act accordingly. If it is not a clinic case and there is nobody else working with the parents, I am available in a supportive role when necessary.

When it does seem advisable to see the parents I do not ordinarily tell the child or ask his permission, even if he is adolescent, and I usually prefer the parents not to tell him, so that the ongoing transference relation is not unduly disturbed. As parents, however, are not always able to be discreet, I do look out for indications in the child's session that he had become aware of the meeting between us. If he indicates that he is aware of the meeting, I acknowledge the fact, and try to understand and to interpret his reactions to it. There may be, especially with adolescents, occasions when a meeting between parents and therapist is likely to jeopardize the whole future of the treatment. This I would then indicate to the parents and make the strongest recommendation that they discuss the current difficulties with their worker, or, if they have none, with a colleague suggested by me. The obvious person would then very likely be the psychiatrist who has taken medical responsibility for the case.

Private clarification of the therapist's role vis à vis the parents

I find it useful to remind myself what my role with the child is vis à vis the parents. As I see him one or at the most five hours a week, I cannot possibly assume parental responsibility for the management of his contemporary life. Experience has led me, like many other therapists, to become increasingly hesitant about giving advice. Some time ago, for instance, I treated a little boy who was due to go from his preparatory school to a fairly tough public day school of high academic standard. Although he was an intelligent boy I was doubtful whether he would make the grade in this school, as he had been extremely indulged and undisciplined at home, unused to many other children and had terrorized the family helps, who were then dismissed as 'useless'. I expressed my doubts very forcefully to the parents but made no headway; this school was in the family tradition and the little boy was sent there. He had a rough time for the first two terms, but treatment continued and the boy's difficulties with teachers and work at school opened the parents' eyes to the need for firmer discipline at home, and this, together with the insight I was able to develop within him, about the greedy and ruthless omnipotence which made him unable to tolerate rivals, resulted in his making a very good adjustment to the school. I mention this case because it was one where at first I felt I had failed badly in not being able to persuade the parents to send him to a school that made less demands upon him. In fact the more demanding situation brought his difficulties more into the open and it was possible to work through them in psychotherapy.

When parents seek treatment for their child at a clinic or privately, however well informed they may be, they come with an unconscious fear of punishment and a deep sense of guilt which, even when acknowledged, is only partially conscious and based on reality. Somewhere in every parent still exists the little girl and boy who are convinced that they can never become a proper mother or father. When things go wrong, this little girl in the mother feels found out and projects upon the therapist her super-ego picture of her own internal mother who is going to blame her and take the child away because of her presumption and bad management. It is important for us as therapists to gain, through our own analysis, enough insight into our own motives, to be in touch with the part of ourselves that does tend to compete with the mother and may unconsciously want to take the child away. If we respect the role of the parents as one of responsibility for the management of the child's life, one which whatever their own difficulties, they alone can fill, we can convey reassurance to them by our attitude that the treatment will not be a battle for the possession of the child: thus we may mitigate the paranoid fears of many parents that the child and the therapist will be getting together behind their backs to criticise or commiserate. On the other hand, the therapist can, through criticism which she may think justified, or by her unconscious attitude, confirm the parents in their fear and lead them to break off treatment, or to develop an unhelpful dependence beneath which lurks hostility which may jeopardize the analytic work at critical moments.

Or too strong an unconscious rivalry with the parents can make the therapist over-dependent upon them and their approval, and thereby interfere with her treatment of the child who is bound to sense this. If the therapist identifies too strongly with the child and unconsciously blames the parents for all his difficulties she becomes more vulnerable to their blame, to any attempts of theirs during the treatment to project their own feelings of guilt upon her. She can then feel so totally downcast and responsible for every set-back or spell of acting out on the child's part, that her ability to understand and tease out with him in his treatment the facts involved becomes seriously affected.

My experience has tended to make me increasingly convinced that as the therapist treating the child, I can help the parents best, and can often encourage more favourable attitudes in them towards the child, by analysing as fully as possible the transference relationship (Bick 1962; Boston 1967). By trying to preserve as regular and reliable a treatment framework as possible, protected from outside interference, I hope to be able to function with the receptivity that will enable the child to bring into the transference the alien split-off aspects of his personality, the conflicts and anxieties engendered by these which impair his relationships, and prevent him from making the best of whatever his family is able to provide.

Initial improvements when child transfers anxieties to the therapist

Young children will transfer and express these anxieties very quickly. Sometimes they may be given so much initial relief through feeling that they are understood and can be contained by their therapist, that the resulting easing of difficulties at home may give the parents sufficient confidence in the treatment to enable them to take with greater calm difficult patches later on; as, for instance, occasions when the child is fighting against re-integrating and assuming responsibility for living with painful insights and unacceptable parts of himself, and acts out his conflicts at home.

In states of acute anxiety which result in symptoms like night terrors, excessive clinging, eating phobias or school phobias, I have sometimes found that the child is terrified that his real parents and the everyday familiar situation will completely disappear and that the parents and world of his bad dreams, the witches and magicians of fairy tales, will take over. I shall give a brief illustration here of such a case with some indication of the psychoanalytic technique employed to enable the child to gradually transfer these anxieties to the therapist and the treatment situation, where he can be helped to face them.

Walter was a severely disturbed ten-year-old boy referred to the Clinic for manifold and increasing fears which he was endeavouring to keep at bay by ever more complicated rituals. These acute anxieties had first been noticed upon the anniversary of his father's death and had been multiplying from that time till he was seen by a male consultant three months later and began treatment with me. His most troublesome symptom was an inability to eat any food prepared by his mother whom he feared was poisoning him. In his first session he poured forth an account of his worries, as he called them, his fears of being poisoned by germs from the air, by his mother's food, of pretty women who became witches, of Hamlet's father's ghost and terrible phantasies at night that might become reality if he did not have the light switch by his bed to control them. In this first session I had been able to interpret, among other things his fear of germs and ghosts as fears of his dead German father assailing him from all quarters; his suspicion of me as a pretty woman mother who might turn into a witch and poison him with my words as food, as he feared his mother had poisoned his father. I drew his attention to the way in which he was continually and suspiciously gazing round the room, and returning to me; I said that he was using his eyes like the light switch to keep me under control. He left that session very thoughtful and calmer but asked me suddenly and accusingly, on his way out, what had happened to the doctor who saw him first.

In his next session a week later he was a little reluctant at first to come with me. Then he told me when he was in the playroom that he had a terrible dream, plunged into a torrent of confused talk, before finally after five to ten minutes managing to tell me the dream. It was that *a shark had eaten one man and was about to eat him. It had an open mouth and sharp teeth, but Walter made noises, flapped and shouted and frightened it away*. I interpreted that the shark was myself, the mother who had devoured one man, father, as he feared I had swallowed Doctor S. whom he first met at the Clinic. He was now afraid that I would devour him, hence the flapping and shouting, the great pressure of talk to keep me at bay. A great expression of relief came over his face; he confessed that he had been reluctant to come to the Clinic that day, told Mother he was bored by me. I took the 'bored' as a literal fear. He went on to tell a long story about a man who fell into the undergrowth from an aeoplane, became a monster, and was there killed by another who had stolen the elixir of life. He followed this by other monstrous tales. Interpretation of his fear that I would discover that this monster was really himself, a part of himself hidden in the depths of his mind, that I would find out that he was really the devouring shark and would punish him by death, led to a great lightening of his spirit. He said in astonishment: 'I am feeling better, much better, my worries are going . . .' then eagerly and

24

quickly, 'but I have others I must tell you,' and began to recite them.

In those first sessions with Walter a transference relation was established in which I represented very terrifying aspects of his parents: the witch shark mother, and the ghostly monster father, parents who had been formed and pictured thus in the depths of his mind from the projection of greedy, omnipotent infantile aspects of himself that he was unable to accept and to integrate within his personality. These split off and violently repudiated aspects of himself were continually threatening to overthrow his perception of external reality, his saner relationship with his mother and his school. His conviction of the omnipotence of his destructive wishes had been, of course, intensified by his father's death, and he was therefore also terrified that his hostile thoughts might actually kill his mother too. When, in his treatment, he met a therapist, an adult who spoke his language, who took seriously this primitive, crazy part of himself, he was relieved to be alone with it no longer. By demonstrating to him that I was prepared to tolerate those projections of his destructiveness I enabled him to focus them more and more in the treatment situation. I became the bad parent of the fairy tales, the recipient of these monstrous terrifying parts of himself, and his relationship with his family became much easier: he was able to go on at school, to eat his mother's food again, the world outside became a less terrifying place and his manifold fears decreased. It would have been useless my saying to him that he had not killed his father, that his mother was not going to die. His mother had already tried to reassure him in this way. With the healthy part of his mind he was quite aware of this himself, as he said to me: 'I know that my mother's food is alright but when she hands it to me I cannot help feeling that there is poison on the plate.' But this same part of himself with its capacity to perceive and to be modified by external reality, was in danger of being completely overthrown by the confused and helpless infantile aspects, threatened by the return of his own projected omnipotence and destructiveness.

Walter's mother was seen regularly each week by a psychiatric social worker. After her initial anxieties about Walter decreased, her treatment focussed around her mourning for her husband to whom she had been devoted, whom she had idealized and upon whom she had depended as an escape from her own family. The relief she obtained from working through her mourning undoubtedly contributed to the eventual success of Walter's treatment, and to the re-establishment of friendliness between mother and son.

Through the therapist's ability to accept the projection of the violently split off parts of the child, she can help him to cope by understanding the anxiety engendered by these. (As a little three-year-old patient of mine said to her parents: 'I don't have bad dreams at home any more, I have them with Mrs Harris, she takes my bad dreams away.') This does not interfere with the child's normal healthy dependence on his parents, relative to his age. On the contrary, his capacity to love and to learn from them is freed, when the negative relationship stemming from the omnipotent unmodified infantile projections is taken care of in the treatment. A more loving and trusting attitude on the child's part is then likely to increase the parents' confidence in themselves and therefore to help them to be better parents.

Work in the transference, centering round an adolescent's projections into the parents

I shall now give a brief summary of some aspects of two years' work with an adolescent girl of sixteen, which resulted in some improvement in her relationship with very disturbed parents. She began to have a less totally dependent relationship with her mother who functioned for her as an idealized doormat, and a less selfrighteous and persecuted relationship with a father who was blamed for all the family's misfortunes. In this case I met the parents before beginning Marion's treatment and had virtually no contact with them during the two years. They had both been having irregular spells of psychotherapy themselves for a number of years.

Marion was the only child of a very unhappy marriage. Her father, although intelligent and reasonably successful by worldly standards, was not happy in his profession. Her mother, an intelligent housewife, tried to compensate for the failure of her marriage by becoming a social success. Marion herself was talented, discontented at school which she despised, and where she was erratically successful in certain subjects where she did not need to work. She was outwardly poised and sophisticated beyond her years but inwardly very uncertain, dependent on flattery and, as she put it, a fake. In the parental quarrels which often centered round her, she supported her mother and was both terrified of and provocative towards her father. At school there were recurrent rows which involved her parents. She would complain of being victimized by a teacher, or of being ostracized by the other girls. Her mother, and on one occasion at least her father, had identified wholeheartedly with her grievances, and had stirred up trouble among the staff at school. It was an uncontainable family situation in which one member was always feeling persecuted by the other, and where they combined occasionally to feel persecuted by the world outside.

When I began analytic therapy with Marion I expected that a considerable degree of acting out would occur at home, with attempts to cause trouble between me and her parents, as she had done between them and the school. This did come to pass but it gradually became possible to reduce Marion's need to provoke, and to be provoked by, her external parents by analysing her relationship to the internal parents, as it emerged and became transferred to me in the treatment situation. Her growing awareness of the part played by her own projections in the family difficulties enabled her to begin to have a fitfully better appreciation and tolerance of her parents as real people, her mother became less idealized and her father less black.

In her first few sessions with me anxieties emerged that I was going to pursue and to reprove what she called the 'show-off little Marion': a tiresome part of herself from which she had been running away all her life, which continued to operate, to act out, but about which she always put off thinking until tomorrow. She decided that I was quite unlike Mrs O., one of her teachers whom she liked very much, who was always encouraging, and always gave good marks, but 'somehow you never know where you are or whether what you've written is any good.' She thought that I was more like the History teacher, fresh from college, who cared more for her subject than for making the pupils happy: 'She tells you all your mistakes, and expects you to work, which isn't pleasant, but I'm learning a lot more.'

The first teacher was seen rather as she saw her mother: kindly, permissive and too identified with the bossy show-off little Marion (who pretended to know it all, and who could not bear her vanity to be hurt) to help the Marion who really wanted to grow, to have her mistakes pointed out and to learn from experience. The second had elements of a more positive picture of her father, stern and demanding that she should struggle with the omniscient aspects of herself, the omnipotent greedy little Marion who substituted ambitious self-important phantasies for real effort. From this teacher, however, she felt that she could learn; from her father she could not. Her relationship with her father, a person who did in fact seem to be demanding , touchy and self-important, but nevertheless concerned that his daughter should develop to make something of her gifts and of her life, was distorted by her excessive projective identification (Klein 1946): by the attribution to him of the contempt for femininity which she was unable to apprehend in herself. To the father, to the male, she attributed all possibility of intellect and creativity which enabled her to have a non-rivalrous twin-sister relationship with a mother whose life revolved solely around her, but to whom as a result she was inextricably and guiltily bound.

In her treatment Marion constantly attempted to reproduce the relationship with me as the first teacher: the mother who was kindly, comforting and admiring, but unperceptive, placating and secretly despised. When it was difficult to maintain this, when I made an interpretation that impressed her as illuminating, she would rapidly transfer authorship from me as the mother, to some father source. 'You didn't of course think of that yourself, you must have got it from one of your psychoanalytical books.' Or she would spoil it by attributing to me her own motivating vanity, suggesting that I was much more interested in finding occasion to make clever remarks than in sympathizing with the hard life that she led. Or else she would find that she just hadn't heard what I said: her mind had gone elsewhere. It took some time before she perceived and acknowledged these absences, which were first indicated by a sudden onset of silence, but once they were acknowledged we were alerted to looking out for their occurrence and made some headway.

We found that these absences occured when I had said anything that excited feelings of envy, or threatened to put her in touch with an envious part of herself which she had projected into someone else, and by which she was being persecuted. It became clear that envy was the salient feature in this precocious little Marion part of herself, with which she could not work: the experience of which she constantly tried to avoid by evoking it in other people, thereby antagonizing possible friends and making herself a prey to insecurity. In our work it was easier to give her some conviction of how she projected into me, and therefore felt envied and attacked by me, as the father. It was more difficult to put her in touch with the subtler nature of the projecting distortion of me as the mother, the breast, the primary source of comfort and life separate from her, and not of her own making, whose individuality was then denied to become a doormat for her, a twin sister to herself.

Her mother did in fact play in with this, and even tell Marion how much more important to her was her daughter than her husband. This was an external reality frequently brought in as factual evidence to resist the recognition of the operation and projection of her own divisive contemptuous parts, the recognition of the degree to which she had to foster the ill-assorted relationship between parents, in order to avoid feeling the odd one out.

As she became more able to understand the projective identification of her alien and spoiling aspects into me in the transference, she became less totally dependent on the good opinion of friends. She began to have hopes of becoming less of a fake, of developing a personality of her own, and of marrying one day a man for what he was and not just for what she could get out of him, and to please her mother. In order to achieve these hopes, a great deal more work will be necessary to get a better grip of the forces within her that recurrently split off newly established insights. There are indications however that she is establishing with her father a relationship that is less implacable and self-righteously persecuted, and with her mother one that is less idealised and homo-sexual. Her parents, especially the mother, have been able to appreciate this, and although there is evidence to suggest that appreciation is tempered on their part by an intermittently grudging and obstructive attitude towards the flowering of her adolescent hopefulness, this is not to a degree that necessarily blocks further progress.

Consultation with parents and child together

I would like now to give some account of the more direct role which, as a child psychotherapist, I sometimes play with the parents in cases where I do *not* anticipate taking the child on for regular treatment. These may be infants or young children who are referred for consultation in an emergency situation (Carr and Harris 1966) when, for instance, the child may be suffering from acute sleeping or eating difficulties. Usually in such cases I *see both parents and child together for an initial consultation,* during which I encourage them to give as fully as possible an account of the nature and the onset of the difficulties and to contribute their ideas about possible causes. As we discuss the child I try to observe his behaviour in the interview and to match what I see with their account. I do not attempt to interpret in the transference deeply unconscious material, even if I were to think that I had enough evidence to do so. My contribution lies in helping them to express as freely as possible their anxieties about the child, in trying to link together different aspects of the situation as they see it in a way that may enable them to look at if afresh and enlarge their view of it. If I can draw their attention to anything in the child's behaviour that might illuminate our discussion I do so.

The following is a brief account of an interview with a young couple, Mr and Mrs R. referred by their general practitioner because their younger child John, aged fourteen months, was keeping them awake all night with head banging and constant demands for attention. The general practitioner who sent them warned me that they, father in particular, resented the Clinic and they were afraid that the child was going 'bonkers'. It was only despair about the situation and the uselessness of drugs that finally drove them to ask for advice. Mr R. was a quiet, large, intelligent looking man, his wife, some years younger, was attractive and laconic, but depressed and anxious beneath her composed facade. John was a delicate-featured white-faced little boy with his father's large forehead and intelligent eyes and with the sensitive expression and distant composure of the mother.

Both parents showed considerable anxiety about my initial reaction to John, as if to say: 'Well, here he is, tell us the worst,' but gradually relaxed and let him play beside his mother on the couch with the car and the dog I gave him. Mrs R. began by saying that she could not think why this had happened to John, as she always said he had the nicest nature in the family, nicer than anyone she knew. As a baby he had fed well, was much less demanding than his sister Stella, and easily satisfied, until three or four months ago when he had begun to waken two or three times in the night. At the time they had not troubled much, thought this phase would pass, but it had grown worse. 'He gets up and refuses to go back and it is getting everybody down.'

Enquiry into possible reasons for the onset of the problem and any antecedent symptoms produced quite a complicated story. Mrs R. did most of the talking, turning to her husband now and then for help in remembering. It appeared that she had looked after both her children from birth owards with the help of au pair girls and various temporary helps. There had been two changes of au pair girls, one when John was eight months old, the next when he was eleven months. John had been very attached to both girls but the mother did not think this head banging and sleeplessness could be connected with their disappearance, as it had begun a month before the second girl, a Spaniard, left, and John was now very attached to his new nursemaid, a little English girl. Stella had shown that she was upset at each change, but had recovered quickly; John had not seemed to notice. Further enquiry elicited that when John's sleeplessness and head banging began during the last month of the Spaniard's stay. This girl, who had been particularly devoted to the children, was in a very hysterical state owing to an unhappy love affair; the parents then wondered whether her state of mind could have had an un-fortunate effect on John. I asked how he had reacted to other changes in his life before this: to new food, for instance? Mrs R. started at this question, said that she had forgotten to mention that he is now extremely difficult about food, which he never used to be. He had been bottle fed from the start as she had no milk and had been unable to feed any of her children; had fed and slept well, and always seemed a strong, happy baby. When John was five or six months old they had had extra help for two afternoons a week from a nursery nurse who was very keen to wean him from the bottle and fed him from a spoon and cup. Mother thought at the time that she was too impatient because John had shut his mouth when the spoon approached and when he finally opened it to protest she popped the food in. However, as this nurse was used to children, John soon ceased to protest and accepted the food. Mrs R. then thought it must be alright and allowed the nurse to persuade her to wean him from the bottle at six months. He did not seem to mind giving it up at the time and took solid foods very well. 'But now of course,' his mother said, 'he gets a bottle whenever he likes.' I asked how this compared with Stella's way of feeding. 'Stella was a more restless child,' said the mother, 'and of course the first baby died. He was a boy too.' At this point she became extremely depressed and far away. I did not enquire further about the first baby, thinking it better to wait, but also because John created a diversion at this point.

Earlier on he had left the divan, clambered on to his father's knee and then set about exploring the room tentatively, at first crawling back now and then to father or mother, but keeping his distance from me. His mother and father had both been very much aware of his activities throughout and very careful lest he should hurt himself or get too dirty. Mr R had asked John for the dustpan he discovered under my seat; John gave it up quite willingly at once. He crawled then to the wastepaper basket between me and his mother, was investigating it and then pulled it violently towards himself banging his upper lip hard. Mother, who had just mentioned the dead baby, and seemed so far away, at once rushed forward to comfort him. John, however did not cry, as I expected, took a deep breath, closed his lips firmly and for a few seconds rubbed his forehead in a distressed, anxious way. I asked if he was usually so brave when he hurt himself. 'Yes,' said Mrs R., 'perhaps too brave.' I suggested that this seemed rather like the reaction they had described to the pain of parting from the au pair girls he was so fond of and to the loss of his bottle at six months: that unlike Stella, he keeps a stiff upper lip and hugs the painful feelings to himself. But this could mean that they piled up until they became unendurable and he had to have a violent outlet like the crying in the night and the head banging, which would suggest he felt he had a very nasty experience in his head.

Mr R. said that this was plainly so, particularly a few weeks ago when he was quite cruel to himself and bashed his forehead till it was black and blue; and this seemed to occur mostly when he felt frustrated. Mrs R. remembered that this had coincided with his becoming increasingly fussy about his food. She said that he was now liable to turn against any kind of food and to refuse to feed from anybody. Yesterday he had flung a banana three times across the room before he finally ate it. I asked if he could feed himself from a spoon. Mrs R. said that he would, 'but more is dropped on to the floor than goes into his mouth'. I said that he might need to refuse several times, and feel that he was allowed to have some control over what he took into himself, since this appeared to have been denied to him earlier when the nanny popped food in without his consent.

Meantime John had started exploring again and came back to the wastepaper basket, dividing his attention between it and me. He found a half-smoked cigarette, looked as if he would put it in his mouth, occasioning alarm in his parents. I held out my hand and said 'ta'. He gave it to me readily, looking solemn but friendly. He then fished out two burned matches which he handed to me with a pious air. After this he started to explore beneath the divan. Mother considered this was too dirty and encouraged him back beside her on the couch. As he climbed up he banged his head very slightly, then sat back against the wall, banging it monotonously and repeatedly, the same set expression on his face as when he had banged the wastepaper basket.

The parents said despairingly 'This is what he does, but it is mild for him,' became agitated and appealed to me to say what they should do: 'trying to stop him does not work.' I said I thought it would be a matter of giving him time to get over it, opportunity to express and work through the anxieties aroused no doubt by the various changes among other things, to help him to feel that he could show his anxiety and anger and have it tolerated; for instance, he must have felt better when his mother let him fling the banana from him twice, as he ate it the third time it was offered. I suggested that the head banging and sleeplessness seemed to be connected with suspicion of food and were likely to improve when he felt better about eating. As they had described him and as far as I had observed him, he was plainly sensitive to atmosphere, and for that reason it would be important to arrange things practically so that mother and the family were under as little a strain as possible. We then discussed practical measures about feeding and sleeping. Mr R. ended the

33

interview saying that he felt considerably relieved, the whole business made more sense to him now and confirmed his hope that John was not just being naughty, changing into a depraved character. We left it that John and Mrs R. would come again in a fortnight's time unless she felt she must get in touch with me sooner.

She did come again in a fortnight's time, during which the situation had improved considerably. Both mother and child looked more lively and happier. John related to me much earlier in the interview, was freer in his explorations, dividing his attention between mother and myself, and chatting away in indecipherable phases (he had been quite silent during the first interview). Mrs R. said to me in a pleased tone: 'He likes you, I can see that! He does not take to everybody so quickly.' She was rather disconcerted when John began to play a game with me in which I had to offer him cars and bricks: he then spurned them, hitting them back at me or on the floor. When she realized however, that I was not wounded by this and that John was deriving great satisfaction from the game, she stopped remonstrating and let it continue while she went on talking to me.

I saw Mrs R. and John twice more at fortnightly and three-weekly intervals, interviews during which I had further opportunity to observe his extreme sensitivity to atmosphere. On their third interview, when Mrs R. was describing how the first baby had died, strangled by the cord round his neck and how John himself had narrowly escaped asphyxiation in the same way, John who had been playing with me evidently sensed the sadness in her voice and something of the meaning of her words, because he suddenly left me, crawled along the divan to his mother, put his arms round her neck and emitted strangulated distressed little cries. That was the only time I heard him cry during the four interviews. He continued to play with me each time (his knocking down, projecting game), with great pleasure and slight variations. He evidently sensed that I was a person to whom both he and his mother could safely show their anxieties and be understood. In her fourth interview Mrs R. reported that John was sleeping well throughout the night, eating well, and that the head banging had almost completely ceased. She was by this time talking of him in different terms, not just as the nicest natured child she knew, but as a charming little boy with a most determined nature and a fierce temper, who would be quite a problem to rear, a problem she appeared to be facing with interest and more confidence.

In this kind of consultation my role with both parents and child is perhaps not so different after all from that of the child psychotherapist, as I have outlined it, with the parents of the child who is going to be treated by psychoanalytical therapy. It is that of a sympathetic observer, a therapeutic person who is capable and trained to consider all aspects of the problem as presented by the parents and child, who is there to help the parents to think around the problem and to follow the implications of their own understanding and intuition, to utilize the unrivalled experience which they have with their own child. I did give some advice in these interviews, but I am always cautious of doing so and offer it in a tentative manner, preferably when I can see that it is likely to come, not just as a pronouncement from authority, but as a strengthening of perceptions that are already available to the parents.

In the initial interviews I have with the parents of a child I am going to treat, and in subsequent interviews with them during the course of the child's treatment, I employ a similar technique with the parents, although in these cases the child is not present.

Observation of the development of infants in families

The therapeutic role of an interested and sensitive observer has been brought home to me many times from weekly observations made of the development of babies throughout their first year in an ordinary family setting, and from listening to such observations reported by students and colleagues. Those weekly observations and discussions were instituted at the Tavistock Clinic some thirteen years ago by Esther Bick for child psychotherapy students, and have since become part of the training for students in all disciplines at this Clinic (Bick 1964). The object of this exercise is not a therapeutic one; we are allowed into those ordinary 'normal' families to learn, to observe in detail the interaction between mother and baby and any other members of the family who may be present, and to form as clear a picture as we can of the way in which these relationships develop. Such systematic observation has proved a revelation to many of the

people who have undertaken it; over and over again I have heard
social caseworkers say they had never realised before how much
the mother-infant relationship is affected by the contribution the
baby makes, or the degree of the stresses under which a mother
with a new baby làbours — whether it is a first baby or whether
there are older children to be cared for too. At such times the
nature of the parents' relationships to their own parents, both
external and internal, emerges very clearly. For instance, if the
father's relationship with his own mother is a good one, he can be
a great support to his wife in her role as a mother, can help her to
find confidence and maturity in this if she is not too disturbed a
person. This kind of support can also be given by the sympathetic
observer who is interested in all the members of the family, and
concerned that they should find their own method of working
together and thriving.

I had the opportunity of making observations in a family with a
first baby. The mother was unwell with constant diarrhoea
during her pregnancy which was unplanned. By the time the
baby was due, she was apprehensive but looking forward like a
little girl to having a 'doll' baby with ribbons and the very best of
trappings which she and her husband could buy. The baby was
born very quickly: a big, vigorous, hungry boy. Both parents
were immensely proud. The mother consciously wanted to feed
him herself, but it soon became plain that anxieties in both baby
and mother would rapidly bring this to an end. He was on the
bottle wholly when he was seven weeks old. It would not have
been helpful to encourage her to continue breast-feeding; she
was too deeply uncertain of the nature of this liquid from her
body which she was giving the baby. Pressure would have
intensified her guilt. This mother certainly cared for the baby
and did the best she could. Yet it took her several months to
develop a really maternal love which could tolerate and respond
comfortingly to his distress. In the first months she would plod on
mechanically and apparently unfeelingly, conscientiously dressing, bathing or whatever she was doing, when he was screaming
his head off. But underneath this apparent callousness of hers hid
a terrified little girl. Later on when things were going better she
told me that when other girls at school had talked of getting
married and having babies she had thought to herself, 'Married
maybe, but never a baby, I am sure I should let it die.' The

gradual and great development that took place in her ability to love and enjoy the baby came largely through her confidence in, and support from her husband, who had no doubt that she was the right person to look after his child and was prepared to do all he could to help her with this.

Experience derived from making and discussing such observations, has greatly influenced my attitude and technique in dealing with the parents of the children I treat; it has made me chary of attempting to take responsibility for the management of the child's life outside the treatment room, and has led me to believe that as a child psychotherapist the best thing I can do for the parents of my patient is to allow them and to help them to function as parents, in so far as they are capable of doing so.

REFERENCES

BICK, E. (1962) 'Child Analysis Today', *Int. J. Psycho-Anal.*, Vol. 43.

BICK, E. (1964) 'Notes of Infant Observation in Psychoanalytic Training', *Int. J Psycho-Anal.*, Vol. 45.

BOSTON, M. (1967) 'Some Effects of External Circumstances on the Inner Experience of Two-Child Patients', *This Journal* Vol. 2, no.1.

CARR, H. and HARRIS, M. (1966) 'Therapeutic Consultations', *This Journal* Vol. 1, no. 4.

KLEIN, M. (1946) 'Notes on some Schizoid Mechanisms', *Developments in Psycho-analysis*. London: Hogarth, 1952.

From the *Journal of Child Psychotherapy*, Vol. 2, 1968. (Some of this material appears in 'The Therapeutic Process in the Psychoanalytic Treatment of the Child').

Introduction

Many, possibly most, child psychotherapists are engaged for the greater part of their professional time in more or less long-term treatment of children for between one and five times a week. When so much of our time is given to the few, some of us have been concerned also with working out ways of making effective use of the insights derived from our analytical work, with a wider population and within a more limited time: for instance in dealing with or helping others to deal with urgent situations.

It is in this context that the following paper was read and discussed at a meeting of the Association of Child Psychotherapists presented as a method of approaching crisis situations centering around a young child.

First Consultation

Willie, aged 22 months, was referred for consultation by his family doctor. He had been restless, fretful and wakeful since birth. Paediatric examinations had yielded no evidence of organic abnormality; sedatives had been tried without avail. His mother was overwrought and the situation rather than improving with time seemed to be growing worse.

In the Clinic waiting room, my first impression of Mrs T. was of a slight, weary, chronically depressed and anxious young woman in her late twenties, who might have been pretty had she had the spirit. Mr T. was a tallish, pleasant-looking man of about the same age, also thin, but with a healthy outdoor look. Willie was small, slight, very fair, wiry but delicate-looking. He was climbing upon the furniture at the other side of the room from his parents. He came when called, ignored me completely when introduced by his mother, ran ahead of us upstairs and into my room when he had ascertained where we were going. As soon as we were all inside and the door shut, he screamed and ran to try to open it. Mrs T. sighed and said, 'He always does this, he can't bear to be shut in.' She hesitated whether to open the door, but as I made no move she sat down and left his father to cope with him. Mr T. distracted him by rolling to him a lorry taken from the drawer of toys which I had placed on the floor. Willie took this lorry and, holding it, or pushing it along in front of him, followed it, and in this way explored the room. Throughout the interview he was almost ceaselessly active; running, sometimes taking one or two other vehicles from the drawer, pushing them singly or together. He showed signs of being acutely aware of car noises in the street and of sounds outside the room, but completely ignored me and any conversation between his parents and myself.

Mrs T. readily began to give me an account of the situation, helped out from time to time by her husband. She was anxious at first but became increasingly confident as the interview proceeded, reassured that I didn't mind what Willie was doing in the room — that he couldn't do or come to much harm — and moreover, that his father was keeping an eye on him.

She said that the main trouble was that he didn't sleep at all during the day and only very uneasily at night. He always had been wakeful and banged his head if she didn't go to him. He had what the doctors called 'three months colic', would draw up his knees and writhe. The paediatrician said that he was the worst case he had ever seen. No, there had never been any problem about food. He had never been breastfed but he had taken evaporated milk easily and soon added solids. He still had a bottle but liked to chew foods. He was a great eater and took twice as much as his sister Lyn who was ten years old. 'Where does it all go?' his mother wondered. Here she assured me that he was a very happy child (a remark that was reiterated at least twice during the interview) 'if you don't frustrate him, for he can't put up with any check'. For instance, he hated to be indoors, he liked everything new, quickly tired of being in the same place for long. He climbed, constantly trying to go elsewhere or get at something else. When out shopping he would insist on walking and pushing the pram himself and would get fed up sitting in it. Then when taken indoors he would scream and all day long clamour to get out of the flat. This was on the first floor of a three-storey house, and his mother couldn't let him out of the door on his own as he wasn't safe on the stairs. He often fell and hurt himself but never seemed to notice, too busy to stop. He never came to be comforted. Although he was always on the go during the day, at night he refused to sleep, and screamed if made to stay in bed. As bedtime approached he became more active. They had tried leaving him till midnight to see if it would tire him out, but he wouldn't go even then without a struggle. He slept lightly, and kept waking or crying to get up. Mother wearily said she hadn't had a full night's rest or an evening out since the day he was born. If she left him when he wakened he would go on banging his head until she came.

He had always been an active baby, even before he was born, quite unlike Lyn. In the last two months of her pregnancy he had kept pushing himself out this way and that. She couldn't get comfortable in bed and sometimes had to sleep in a chair. He was born very quickly — in a quarter of an hour. Right from the start he had not been a cuddly baby, again unlike Lyn, and had been more easily quietened in the pram than in her arms. He still didn't like to be cuddled or held, screamed when dressed or undressed and if put on the potty. 'He understands alright', his mother indicated to me apologetically 'but it's not worth the trouble of forcing him'.

When she felt desperately tired she had taken him to the doctor who gave him sedatives. 'If he is given enough he is knocked out for a time but you can see that he is fighting them, and afterwards is much more fretful and irritable', so she did not like to do it too often. Mr T. joined in at this point to agree about the sedatives, to emphasise the strain on his wife, for there was no-one with whom Willie could be left except himself and his hours were long; he was doing extra work in the evening to try to save up to buy a house. At weekends in the summer the whole family would go to the cricket field where Willie could wander around freely and mother could relax. She was unable to do this in the park as Willie would just wander away and had twice got lost. On the cricket ground there was always someone around to bring him back. When they travelled there, however, they had to go by bus as Willie screamed in the underground. He didn't like the bus much either so mother seldom took him on one unless father was there to help her with him.

This in brief was the parents' account given mainly by Mrs T. with increasing freedom, and corroborated by Mr. T. whose attention was divided between Willie, his wife and myself. Mrs T. related principally to me, concerned to get her story over. I said very little beyond asking an occasional question or prompting her to clarify. Meantime I also observed the child.

Willie continued to be ceaselessly on the move. He explored the room, shifting from place to place, interested only in the vehicles in the drawer of toys put on the floor for him. These he ran along the floor, following them but making no attempt to engage anyone in a game with him. He made no sound, ignoring me utterly despite one or two slight overtures on my part as he passed by my chair. It was not the shyness that one might expect initially from a child of his age. He appeared to notice neither me as a person nor anything about me. He tried all the cupboard doors in the room, and the drawers which were locked. Again and again he would pull at the doorknob to try to open the door but he didn't scream again, neither did he look at his parents to appeal for help. He climbed on the furniture, the chairs, the divan, the desk: he looked out of the window. He stopped momentarily to listen to sounds from the street or the corridor outside but he showed no signs of interest in his parents' conversation, neither did he indicate any awareness that he was the subject of it.

Then, well on in the latter half of the interview Mr T. lit a cigarette. Willie made an indistinguishable little sound, his first since the initial scream. He pounced on the packet. Father teased him, pretending to take it away from him, but said (to mother and me), 'It's alright, he can keep it — it's empty — I knew he would want it'. Willie clutched it in both hands in a determined fashion, made a little grunt and a half smile, climbed on to his mother's knee where he settled back firmly, holding tight to the box looking obstinately at his father but with a glint of mischief in his eye. Mother said sadly, 'Oh, it's alright now, you want me when you think I'll protect you, but you don't usually like to sit on my lap', and then to me, 'You'll see he won't give up that box, not for anything.' The game continued a little longer, father pretending to get it. Willie clutching firmly, mostly in dead earnest, but a little in fun. Mrs T. then said to me, 'Now watch what he'll do if I say "Go to bye-byes now"', although he's tired, he must be for he's been on the go since six o'clock this morning'. Willie heard her, sat bolt upright, protesting, then climbed down from her knee. He returned to the vehicles, still clutching his cigarette box. As he passed his mother's bag he took out a feeding

41

bottle, sucked rapidly for a few moments consuming at least two ounces, walked about with it for a little while longer, then put it back.

The interview ended shortly after this. Towards the end of the hour Willie became increasingly restless, pulled at the door-handle again and again but this time he kept returning to his father's knee, climbed on it, took his hand and tried to pull him up. He did all this without crying or speaking, but making effortful little sounds and then banging his head both against his father and against the door. As he did this his mother said to me, 'Perhaps he'll get better when he learns to talk. It must be very frustrating not to be able to say what he wants.'

In this interview I had given no advice, no interpretations. My comments and questions had been directed towards getting as full a picture of the situation as possible but allowing the parents to go on associating freely as the details of their story came to them. I had shown that I was interested also in Willie as he was actually presenting himself and relating to them and to me.

At the end Mrs T said to me anxiously, 'Well what do you think?', as if she feared my verdict but also had a slender hope of some magical and as yet unthought-of formula. I told them both that I had no easy solution for their problem, but that I thought that further attempts to talk and to gain a better understanding could prove helpful in time. I fully appreciated how wearing it must be to Mrs T. to have had such broken sleep for so long, so little time to relax, and that it must indeed make her at times feel quite murderous towards Willie — a state of mind that she had implied rather guiltily at some points in her recital. I encouraged both parents to consider that it was most important to think of taking any practical steps that might give her a rest. I said that plainly those weekend cricket expeditions when Mr T. took charge of Willie on the journey and where Willie had freedom to run around, must give Mrs T. and Willie a much needed break from each other — indeed they had had this to some extent in my room that morning when father was keeping an eye on Willie. As father had difficulty in getting off work I arranged to see mother again with Willie in a week's time.

The Second Interview

This was in fact three weeks later as Mrs T. cancelled the next appointment and a Whitsun holiday came in the following week.

In the waiting room I was startled by Mrs T's changed appearance. Her hair had been newly washed and set, she looked fresher, healthier, prettier. She greeted me warmly and called Willie who, to my astonishment, smiled and made contact with me immediately as if I had been an old acquaintance. Upstairs in my room Mrs T. said, 'Well, he's better — I don't understand it, but he is'.

When I asked her in what ways he was better she pointed to him and said that surely I could see for myself — did I not think that he looked so different, more peaceful and less on edge? That was in fact so, but to me the most marked change was in Willie's relationship to the two of us. He went to the drawer as before and took out two cars to add to the one that he had brought with him, but he continued to be interested in his mother and in me, appeared to be listening to us and to be understanding what we were saying. He rolled a car along the floor in my direction and when I sent it back towards him he looked at me brightly, and after a few moments' hesitation sent it back again. For a few minutes we had a little game with the cars, sending them to and from each other while his mother related developments since their last visit.

She told me that he had had two particularly bad nights after that; the first she attributed to the ride in the bus which, she said, always upset him, the second to a thunderstorm. But she said that she and her husband had gone on discussing their visit to the clinic. They remembered how I had asked them at one point whether there was anything that Willie liked especially that might help him to settle down more easily when he was put to bed. Then they recalled that when a little cousin with a cradle had slept in their house some months ago Willie had been fascinated by that. So father had made Willie a swing, and fixed it in the kitchen, and mother had started to put Willie in it after every meal and before his bedtime. There he would remain for three quarters of an hour, swinging himself after he had become used to it. So mother had begun to have some peace during the day for the first time, and he was in a much better frame of mind when it

43

came to bedtime. She said that he had become more amenable about this and had begun to drop off fairly easily if she would lie down beside him for fifteen minutes. They had given him a little bed instead of a cot. Although he still continued to wake at times in the night he would go back more readily, and on two or three occasions he had had a good night's sleep without interruptions. And so, added mother, had she, and for the very first time since Willie's birth she had had a night out with a friend. Father had had to babysit but, nevertheless, it had made all the difference in the world. 'He's not perfect yet by any means', she said with a smile, 'but you can put up with a bit of trouble when you know that it won't be for always.'

She thought that he had also been helped by learning to go up and down the stairs of the house on his own. She had spent two whole days with him on the stairs teaching him how to come down backwards. When she was fairly satisfied that he was safe she had decided to let him go out of the flat door on his own. That meant that he could now go downstairs into the little back garden to play and come back when he liked, so that she didn't always have to accompany him. She thought that because of this he had become better in the park. She didn't have to worry any more that he would run away and not come back. She could sit down there herself and relax. He had also become much more friendly to people. Formerly it was as if he hadn't had any time to notice them. In fact the other day a neighbour had said to her, 'What's happened to Willie? He's become quite a different sociable little boy.'

Willie had meantime continued to play with the cars, first sending them to me; then pushing one under the sofa, under the desk, into corners, and following it. He began to climb on the furniture as he had done on his previous visit. He got on to an armchair by the window and looked outside. He pulled the cushion off the chair, stood on the springs, then fell and knocked his head against the corner of the desk. He roared with pain and anger and ran to his mother's knee. When she picked him up he settled back, looked at me accusingly and handed me back the car of mine which he was still holding. Mother became flustered, rubbed his forehead quickly and reached for his bottle from her bag. He cuffed the sore place on his forehead, eagerly sucked the bottle and stopped crying at once. I had the impression that his mother's anxiety was more about the noise he was making and about my reaction to it than about his hurt. When he stopped she seemed quickly relieved, was pleased when he nestled back into her lap, then laughed when he turned round and hit her breast several times while still sucking the bottle.

She began to talk to him, asking him who he had been looking for out of the window. She told me that he would often look out for his father and for Lyn coming home. As he heard her say this he looked at me and said 'Daddy?' enquiringly. He got down rapidly and rashly from his mother's knee, recovered the car which he had returned to me, and began to run it along the floor again. Mrs T. said to me, 'He knows what you're saying now and he'll talk to you. You try him,' then to Willie, 'Where's Lyn?'. He stopped his activities, thought a moment, then said, 'Lyn a cool.' Mother translated, 'Lyn at school,' and prompted me again to try. I said, 'Where's Daddy?' He said, 'Daddy?', looked at the door, and ran to the window. I said 'Daddy at school?' He shook his head firmly and said 'No, Lyn a cool' as if I were quite silly. We had a little more conversation (which I do not now recall), greatly to the satisfaction of himself and of his mother who enjoyed showing him off.

Mrs T. said 'He must feel much better now that he can talk — I think that was the trouble perhaps — he was frustrated because he couldn't make himself understood. Also he doesn't eat nearly so much. That began in the hot weather, he lost his appetite a bit, but he got out of the habit of eating so much, and so he doesn't have to burn up so much energy in running around.' She went on to speculate that, nevertheless, he was always likely to be very active: it was his nature: he took after her husband who did two jobs and was always on the go.

While she was telling me about her husband's work, Willie, who had been busy with the cars but listening, seemed to feel left out. He banged his head deliberately, but very slightly against the divan, whimpered in a self-pitying 'look-at-me' way and ran, pointing to the hurt place. Mother rubbed and kissed it to his great satisfaction and to hers, and he returned to his game. She drew my attention to this, and said it was new. He had become quite cuddly and would now sometimes come to her for a cuddle and a sit on her lap as she remembered Lyn used to do.

At the end of the hour as she rose to go she said, 'The real

45

difference is that I can get through to him now — I never did before.'

Willie did not want to go, but finally went out of the room holding on to my car. His mother said 'He won't want to part with it', but when at the street door I asked for it firmly, saying that he could play with it next time he came, he looked hard at my face to see if I really meant it, evidently decided that I did, relinquished it with a good grace and said 'Bye bye'. (However, this parting evidently rankled a little for on his next and final visit to the Clinic, although he greeted me in a friendly way, he went straight for this car in my drawer, put it in his mother's handbag, shut it up firmly and wanted to be off at once!)

Third Interview two weeks later

This had been arranged for a fortnight later and there was no cancellation this time. I do not propose to go into any details of this interview. The picture was very similar to that of the second visit. Mrs T. reported continued improvement with the sleeping problem. She said that she was getting much more rest and was less tied to Willie during the day as he would play by himself for a great deal of the time. He was beginning to want his bottle less and this time she hadn't brought it with her. The head banging had stopped.

As for Willie, he played in my room as before. He talked to us both (despite his grudge against me for not giving him the car), and twice came up to his mother for a cuddle and brief attention.

Mrs T. began to go into details of her pregnancies and disappointment at being unable to breast feed either of her children. I had the impression that she very probably had been depressed for some time after Lyn's birth but as Lyn seemed to have been a much less overtly demanding and restless baby than Willie, she had been more able to cope. She had evidently not wished to have another baby; her pregnancy with Willie nine years later had come as an unwelcome surprise, although she was hasty to add that she soon got used to the idea and would never for a moment have dreamed of parting with him once he had arrived.

At the end of this interview she elected not to come again unless matters took a turn for the worse. She had spoken this time about a neighbour with a difficult withdrawn young adolescent boy who had suddenly started refusing to go to school, and Mrs T. had said that she should come to the Clinic to get help for him.

Mrs T. was congratulating herself that they had come about Willie before matters had gone too far and thought that since he had become so much more friendly to strangers they wouldn't have any problem about his going to school. It was plain that she was reassuring herself about this and was responsive to my comment that it was conceivable that this might be a time when she would feel like coming to consult me again. This time has not yet arrived. From later reports from the G.P. no further crises have arisen.

Discussion of the Material and of the Changes that have taken place

In such cases where the worker sees the child and parents for a few interviews only, it is inevitable that many questions are posed which cannot be answered. Much vitally relevant information remains unknown and the degree or nature of changes may remain more or less obscure. After my first interview with Willie and his parents I had no firm expectation that the situation would improve so dramatically or so soon. My impression was that the relationship between the parents was basically an affectionate one, that despite Mrs T's resentment they were fond of Willie and genuinely concerned about him. I remained quite uncertain as to the degree and extent of Willie's illness, of how much it was a reaction to his mother's depression and how much it was the cause of this depression. Her account of him and my observation of his behaviour, especially the ignoring of myself and for the most part of his parents, suggested a serious degree of emotional and intellectual impairment. On the other hand the twinkle in his eye and the playful little struggle with his father indicated that he was much more observant and in touch than had at first appeared. His behaviour in the following interview confirmed this second impression.

In speculating upon what had happened in the three weeks between the first and second interview I think it is helpful to remember Mrs T's words, 'The real difference is that I can get through to him now — I never could before', and to ask briefly why she managed to get through.

I would suggest that this became possible for her after she had an experience of getting through to me in that first interview, and possibly also to her husband in a way that she had not done before. It was important that the parents had come together, jointly responsible for their son, and that they were enabled to express their problem, their feelings of helplessness as parents, to an 'expert' who was supposed to have some experience in dealing with these problems. But not an expert, who from the height of superior knowledge, treated them as helpless children, instructing them in what to do, or in what they should not have done, thereby confirming their own childish fears of being discovered to be inadequate and fraudulent parents incapable of responsibility and dependent therefore upon some higher authority. The helpful expert in such a situation is the one who can have a role analogous to that of the understanding mother with the distressed baby, who receives the projection of the infant's anxiety, is *with* it, and enables it to cope better with the pain because it no longer feels alone. A child who does not thrive and respond to the mother's efforts to alleviate his distress, evokes all her own infantile helplessness and loneliness. Such a mother can easily lose touch with the experience that she has acquired, and lose faith in the defence she has built up against her inadequacy.

It seemed to me that I came through to the parents as someone who was interested in them both and in Willie, and also as someone who had no magical expertise which would solve their problems for them, but who gave them the hope that talking together and attempting to understand would help in time. This encouraged them to go on working upon the problem, to draw upon their own observations and intuitions, their unique knowledge of themselves and of the child, in order to find new methods of coping. They had been encouraged apparently by my question as to whether Willie liked anything especially, to re-examine and to try to understand his feelings better: they remembered the cradle, and then it was father's intuition that hit on the idea of the swing.

In the first interview I had formed the impression that Mr T.'s attitude to his wife was supportive and concerned, but that clearly, with two jobs, he could not be at home very much. He might have been told that for the sake of his family it would be advisable to give up one of the jobs to be at home more, but no doubt it was largely for the sake of his family that he was trying to earn the extra money to buy a house. It would be presumptuous indeed upon such short acquaintance to give such advice. By being invited to come with his wife and Willie, and I hope also by my attitude, he was confirmed in his important role as Willie's father and mother's partner, and encouraged to use his ingenuity to help her. The extra support and attention from her husband, ensuing upon this interview, may have been one of the important factors in helping to give Mrs T. new life and hope, the comfort that her helplessness was being taken seriously — that she was not being blamed for it, and the extra strength, therefore, to give more of herself to Willie. Had Mr T. not been involved in this first interview, and had he not been capable of responding to his family's need, I doubt whether the situation could have improved so rapidly.

What was the specific significance of the swing for Willie and why did it — according to his mother's account — play such an important role in settling and in diminishing his hyper-activity? I would like to make some tentative interpretations about this based on my experience of child psychotherapy and on opportunities to make more detailed continuous observations of the development of mother-infant interactions (Bick 1964). A restless active infant like Willie often needs a great deal of attention, to be held frequently, but not too closely or too long. He becomes readily claustrophobic. We had plenty of evidence of Willie's claustrophobia, not only from the parents' reports but from his behaviour in my room. A mother needs confidence and peace within herself to be able to tolerate and quieten such an infant. If she is anxious although she may be aware of his needs, they are felt as demands and while she tries to meet them she is likely at the same time to stiffen up and keep him out. (Mrs T. had indicated that she was already tense and sleepless in the last months of her pregnancy with Willie). The mother's woodenness and depression intensifies the child's anxiety and need to evoke some reassuring sign of life within her, to get into her and get something out of her. The violence and the determination of his projection of himself into the mother brings concomitant fears of being caught and shut inside an object that contains and is coloured by his own hostile grabbing impulses. (Recall that on the first occasion Willie had run ahead into my room — fearlessly

49

exploring, it might have seemed, had he not begun to scream in distress when the door was shut, apparently feeling trapped inside).

The swing would be to Willie a holding object that he can put life into, that he can make go, a reassurance against a wooden dead mother that he carries within him and that he is continually trying to escape from. Mrs T. indicated her intuitive appreciation of Willie's frame of mind by putting him in the swing after meals, when a voracious eater such as Willie is likely to suffer, if not from indigestion, then from feelings of anxiety about the nature of what he has just taken into himself.

As basically the food comes from the mother, an infant needs reassurance from a mother with continuing life and care for him undepleted by his ruthless taking. This Mrs T. had evidently found it difficult to convey to him from her arms. Her attempts to comfort and reassure by giving the bottle instead of herself, although possibly apparently effective at the moment of crisis, were likely to intensify in the long run his anxiety about containing a depleted, exhausted, ill-used internal object.

For Willie then I would suggest that the swing played the part of a containing mother responding with movement to his need for life, one from which he could escape and which did not threaten him with suffocation. For Mrs T. the swing would also be a substitute for herself which afforded her the satisfaction of being able to comfort him, but a much needed respite in which to recover herself and feel less invaded. This break from each other then seemed to make it possible for them to approach each other more closely in a loving way and to get greater pleasure from phsyical contact. With less demands on her Mrs T. felt that she could put up with it, if it was not for ever, could give herself more, and have a more personal, richer relationship with Willie as a whole person. The situation had become more contained in her mind, more able to be thought about. She could take the time and trouble to allow Willie to learn how to negotiate the stairs, to extend his explorations there with her permission.

The experience of a more receptive relationship from his mother probably led to the sudden blossoming of Willie's speech. It would become more worth his while to talk when he felt greater confidence in being understood: with his anxiety diminished by his mother's increased capacity to contain and respond to the total needs, he does not have to flee so fast from himself and his experience. He too can contain it better, think about it long enough to make some sense of it. try to convey his thought in the hope that it will be appreciated. He can derive from the greater rapport with his mother, the increased sociability which was commented on by the neighbour, and evident in his approach to me, as well as the greater confidence in expressing feelings of anger, pain and affection. As he expresses himself more intelligibly, appropriately and endearingly he is in turn likely to evoke more appropriate and friendly responses. The vicious circle of being misunderstood, of feeling persecuted, and being persecuting is broken. It then becomes easier for him to relax, to close his eyes on a day of happier experiences that linger within to comfort him.

These comments are by no means exhaustive. Other workers with experience of such therapeutic consultations may use a different frame of reference to explain the processes that take place. In any case these are interpretations after the event, none of them conveyed to Willie or his parents in the actual interviews. For this reason I believe that this kind of interview is one which can be conducted by workers without training in psycho-analytic psychotherapy and with varying degrees of sophistication in mental health work and concepts.

The essential requirement of the interviewer, is I think, a capacity to be interested in, to encompass the total situation without taking sides; to be able to encourage the parents to follow their perceptions, and to use their latent resources without increasing their feeling of helplessness, dependence and failure. Ability to refrain from giving useless advice, to distinguish between helpful advice and interference can come through bitter experience, but it can be taught and encouraged to some extent. I have noticed it developing in students making weekly observations in a family of the development of a mother's relationship with her baby throughout the first one or two years. I have noticed it in making such studies myself and in listening to the presentations of others. I have been struck (in a number of cases) by. the therapeutic effect of the observer who is genuinely interested in both the mother and the baby. Such an observer respects their attempts to develop a relationship with each other, and is not prevented by undue rivalry and condemnation from tolerating the mother's anxieties and grumbles. This can greatly strengthen the young parent's faith in herself and in the value of the work she is doing in rearing her child.

Undoubtedly there must exist in the parents themselves, in their relationship with each other and with the child, the potential strength and understanding to be reached by such measures. There are of course many cases where parents and/or child may be too ill to derive any benefit at all from the kind of consultation which I have described. However, I suspect that there are many others where timely contact with a worker can encourage them to make use of their unique opportunities of getting to know each other and can foster the hope that it is worth while going on trying, thereby helping them to find a better modus vivendi for themselves.

From a joint paper with Helen Carr in the *Journal of Child Psychotherapy,* Vol. 1, 1966.

4   Depression and the Depressive Position in an Adolescent Boy

Introduction

The clinical material in this paper will be centred around a dream, reported by a boy of 15½ after some 3½ years of analysis. In its context the dream, which was an important and vivid experience for him, typically conveys, I think, the picture of a patient struggling against those aspects of himself that perpetuate depression and inanition. He struggles to be able to face the conflict of ambivalence and the guilt it entails, and to maintain the depressive position, i.e. a state of integration, of responsibility for the conflicting emotions and parts of himself in relation to valued objects.

I am assuming that pathological depression ensues from an inability to face pain and to work through the depressive anxiety occasioned by some experience of loss or disappointment. This inability then leads to failure to rehabilitate the lost object or the object which has betrayed one, within the personality. In the course of treatment, early anxieties about loss and defences against experiencing these, come to be re-lived in the transference relationship at every break, and in the case of patients who are seen four or five times a week, at every week-end. The material which I would like to discuss in detail was stimulated by a forthcoming holiday.

First, however, I shall give a very brief account of Malcolm, although I do not propose to go into details of his history and of possible environmental factors in the aetiology of his depression. He is a highly intelligent boy with considerable artistic gifts, who has been able to use his intellect and talents fairly well. He was referred for analysis by unusually perceptive parents because of recurrent bronchial and catarrhal colds, behaviour that was a little too good, and a certain flatness of affect that convinced them he was not able to enjoy life as fully as he should have done.

In his analysis, he was from the start reliable and meticulously co-operative. He appeared to be appreciative and he provided interesting material, though somehow never so interesting in actuality as it could have been. We came to realise that his associations were less spontaneous and less responsive to my interpretations than they seemed to be, that they were carefully edited and controlled, or appreciated by him as much more important than anything I could say about them. They were regarded as works of art to which I made little contribution. I was necessary to him as a repository for his worries, a place in which to examine and to sort out his own thoughts. His analysis was seldom appreciated at the time, although he took away and made use of my interpretations in later sessions to understand himself — they were all grist to his mill.

He gradually became more aware that he was missing something, in his analysis and in life generally. He felt that his parents were able and willing to offer him more than he was able to accept. Of his mother he said he had always known that she was a good mother, but somehow not for him, something always stood between them. He watched his young brother's friendly confiding relationship with her and envied its spontaneity. He became more aware of his own subliminal depression as it began to thaw, as the world outside his narcissistic preoccupations seemed a warmer and more exciting place. As in the analysis I became more of a person and less of a repository, he began to feel badly about his boringness, his lack of generosity in giving himself. He said he now realised what a help analysis could be if he could only learn how to keep contact with me. When a more enjoyable working/feeding relationship with me had been established, it was soon again attacked and destroyed in order to avoid oedipal jealousy, which was stimulated by any signs of my private life or other professional commitments, and recurrently by breaks in the analysis. In earlier stages, his adolescent self had usually managed to split off any experience of infantile jealousy of the parental intercourse by maintaining that his parents, like myself, were now passé and dull, whereas all the glamour of life was before him. As he became more aware of, and therefore more able to contain, his infantile jealousy and attacks upon me as the parental couple, his psychosomatic symptoms, resulting from the intrusion of objects attacked and damaged by his projections, diminished. He became worried at realising his dependence on the analysis. As he was learning more, he became afraid that if he had to stop all the benefit he had received would disappear. At week-ends he became depressed and resentful about this reluctant dependence, as he once put it, feeling that he was so small and I was so important. His infantile resentment which, when projected, created paraniod fear of me as a self-important father who kept mother and her breasts for himself, recurrently interfered with a learning/feeding relationship with me as the mother in the sessions.

After some months of working on this, he became much more confident that he was able to keep inside himself as a permanent possession what he had learned about himself from analysis. He thought he should stop shortly. He felt badly about being such an expense to his parents; also, no doubt, I had other patients waiting for me.

A little investigation revealed the unconscious hypocrisy in this apparently reparative urge, deflected as it was from the object to which it should primarily have been directed, from myself as the analyst, the breast that had fed him, to whom gratitude and reparation were due. His improvement was seized upon by an omnipotent part of himself which wanted to make off with it to enjoy it on its own.

The dream gives us some information about this part of himself. He dreamed it shortly before a holiday which he was facing with mixed feelings. He was depressed about the break from analysis, but he also wanted to use it as an occasion to test out his progress, to see whether he could engage upon some fruitful enterprise with his friends. He said he was aware that his parents were allowing him freedom. They were not insisting that he should go with them and do what they did, but inwardly he did not feel free to choose.

He came to the Thursday session saying that he had had a vivid dream the night before. It remained as a bad taste in his mouth but he hesitated to tell me in case he was just trying to get rid of it all. It was a long dream: *He was going to a farm with Rhoda to buy a barn or a building. The farm belonged to a man who was terribly hard-up; and rather horrible, perhaps a madman. This man told them about a scheme he had for getting more money to make his fortune. This was to do with injecting stuff into girls to give them bigger busts, and he was anxious to know how he could advertise this. He asked Malcolm if any of the girls he went out with would be interested in the idea. Malcolm was going to say that all the girls he knew were well-developed. He thought that the*

55

idea was disgusting and unsafe, and he told the man that the hormone pills which were used for this were unsafe, so his idea must be even more dangerous. Rhoda was very taken aback by the man and withdrew. Malcolm went with her to protect her. The man suddenly became wild and rushed down his little hill shouting 'Everything that I can see is mine!' Malcolm thought this terribly pathetic, he had so little, just a measly few fields and a small little hill. He went away with Rhoda leaving him to his poverty. Later on, however, the man followed them to town with a cartload of old coats to sell.

Rhoda is a young married friend of his mother's and of the family in general, who was expecting a baby and looking for a house. She had frequently appeared in the analysis as a somewhat idealised version of his mother and myself, but a really good person, the kind of girl whom he would like to marry.

Malcom's first association to this dream was that the crazy man was distinct and familiar, he could not say just who he was like. As he elaborated his description, it was clearly that of Malcolm himself, but with a sallow jaundiced complexion. He described the few fields in the dream as somewhat sickly looking too, muddy and waterlogged. The little hill on which the man was sitting was muddy too.

I suggested to him that his initial hesitation in telling me the dream was due to anxiety lest it came from the crazy man, the mad part of himself which maintained that by injecting me with its flatus it was thereby filling my breasts. By blowing it all into me he would get rid of the bad taste in his mouth caused by awareness of this crazy part and the food it poisoned. He said that in the dream he had enormously resented this man's implications that girls needed to have their breasts made bigger; they were all right as they were. Agreeing to my interpretation that this man was a part of himself, Malcolm said that he seemed to be timeless, to have no regard for time, as if this were some aspect of himself that had been with him always and would never change.

Malcolm himself in the dream had felt that the things this man was satisfied with, that he called 'all mine', were so basically bad because they were puffed up to be more than they were. It seemed absurd that he was not repairing his barn and cultivating his fields which were really a potential source of wealth, instead of indulging in this crazy scheme of expanding breasts. There was such a distinct division between the crazy man and himself with his friend that he felt it was no wonder the man was so furious and susceptible to being got rid of, because he must feel so isolated, although when he ran down the hill he seemed to be going to a wife in the valley. She was not an active person or helpful but someone just like himself and content to do as he did. Malcolm himself, the 'I' in the dream as he said, knew the difference between good and bad but he was too weak to do anything about it; he did not know how to talk to the crazy man who did have the power and the ability to improve his poverty if he could only see it for what it was. There was no one to tell him; his wife was as blind as he was.

This madman is the most complete delineation we have had in the analysis so far of a homosexual part of himself that attempts to acquire power and wealth by omnipotently entering and controlling the breasts with his own flatus and using them as sexually enticing objects. It operates in his relations with girls, where the girls are sometimes evaluated as desirable in so far as they increase his status with other boys. Similarly in his analysis, he has in the past often collected sessions and interpretations to puff up secretly into works of his own designing in order to enlarge his self-importance. Malcolm indicates that it is madness to use the breasts thus, as masturbatory objects into which to enter to void his sexual envy and jealousy thereby making them unpalatable to a saner baby part of himself which needs to feed from them and to develop, to really learn from his analysis. This baby part is represented in the dream by the pregnancy of Rhoda, the mother whom he protects from the dangerous seducer. It is his omnipotent infantile masturbatory self which has a wife in the bottom of the valley, which seeks comfort from its own bottom when frustrated. Thus in his analysis he has often sat upon my interpretations, made them his own, playing with them and cogitating upon them privately, while withholding from me his spontaneous reactions, which could have enabled me to feed him with subtler understanding.

This masturbatory part is without insight and difficult to talk to because it is cut off from the Malcolm who knows the difference between good and bad. It becomes wild when it feels rejected and isolated but he cannot finally get rid of it. It follows him with a cartload of old coats, the worn out objects that have been used to clothe its projections, the recipients of its masturbation, and with which it persists in trying to eke out a living for itself. It is nevertheless a part of him which has strength and potential real wealth if the strength can be employed in reparation, in rebuilding the barns and planting the fields. Malcolm said that he knew in the dream that the barn and buildings had to be restored first before the fields could be dug and planted; that is, that the internal containing breast mother, who has been damaged by masturbation must be restored before he has a secure basis for genital potency. But the problem is to bring the Malcom with insight into contact with the real strength which is obscured by the omnipotence. In his analysis reparation can be consolidated and omnipotence diminished by acknowledgement of what he does learn from me and by recognition that it is harmful and unnecessary to blow it up into something bigger than life.

When the dream had been interpreted in these terms, Malcolm said that on further thought when the madman said 'All that I can see is mine' he was really implying that his possessions were restricted by his vision. If he could only see more he could have more. This reminded him of the previous week-end, when at a party he had a long talk with a friend's father who is a great opponent of psycho-analysis. Malcolm had been telling this man how much he himself had benefited from analysis. He thought that he was making quite an impression on him, but later he was terribly hurt to overhear him passing derogatory remarks both about himself and about psycho-analysis. He now realised that he must have been behaving in a subtly superior way, like the man on his little hill, smug about himself and his possessions, without realising how much he was antagonising his friend's father. He thought it must be this disguised superiority that prevents him at times from getting on easily with people, rather than shyness. He agreed to my suggestion that this was a way of evoking envy in others, by flaunting his possessions of esoteric knowledge, or symbolically, the idealised analytic breast which he had appropriated in order to avoid experiencing envy in himself at having to leave it behind with me at the week-end, for me to share with my party, my husband and children.

Some time later in the session he said that the ramshackle buildings on the farm had not in fact been sordid, that they were lighter and warmer inside than outside. He had noticed this

58

when he stood inside them at one point. I took this as yet another indication — we had had many others before this — that he felt there were reserves of warmth and understanding inside himself, a lifegiving breast at the core of his being, which could not yet be fully utilised because his omnipotent self-importance was impeding the work of reparation.

Discussion

This brief but richly condensed material of Malcolm's throws some light on the forces that cause and perpetuate his depression. He had said he knew his mother was a good mother but something came between them, i.e. he realised he had a good object although he could not always reach it. He saw that his young brother could appreciate his mother. He knew from the occasions when the appreciative baby part of himself was able to accept the understanding I could offer him that there was a good analytic breast available when it could be approached in the right way. The madman in the dream is the destructive part of himself which threatens his good object — Rhoda representing the mother — the baby part of himself that needs to be fed from an uncontaminated breast.

This madman can also be seen as a father who holds domain over mother, who spoils the breast for Malcolm by injecting poisonous sexuality, and who is a threat to the maturer protecting relationship which he tries to have with women. The madman is not the real father whom Malcolm currently experiences as encouraging him to enjoy his friends and to have a life of his own and whom he now visualises as having an interesting and worthwhile relationship with his mother. It is a lofty archaic superego figure, formed from his own projections, in alliance with his id (the wife in the valley) and equally out of touch with his ego.

Malcolm himself, his ego, is in between. He tries in the dream to recover something from this possessive crushing superego, but is defeated. On former occasions when for instance I seemed so big to him and he so small, this superego had been projected into me in the transference, had made him feel persecuted by me so that he had to go away, to retreat from contact. In this session he was, however, able to ally himself with me as a support to his ego and to acknowledge the crazy superego as part of himself. He was also able to link it with his superior behaviour, an idealising and possessive way of using the analysis, which does disservice both to himself and to his good object, apparently puffing it up to be so marvellous, but in fact sitting on it as the man does on his muddy little hill, the pot full of faeces.

On the other hand, we have seen that this superego controls potentially valuable objects — Malcolm goes to the farmer to buy a barn, and this barn though ramshackle has light and warmth inside. He needs the co-operation of the farmer, this controlling paternal superego, to recover good life-giving parts of himself which through projection remain unavailable to him, in order to have a rehabilitated internal object as a basis for developing, making a happy marriage and a home for himself and his future family. (Rhoda, if you remember, was looking for a house). His ego needs to recover the power of the aggression which is encapsulated in the superego, reintrojected there after it has been split off and projected into the father's penis. Without that power he remains relatively impotent though not entirely, because he does protect Rhoda. His superego, deprived of insight, is grandiose, restrictive, and liable to degenerate into a blind expression of id impulses — the rushing downhill. (The games field had hitherto provided for him one of the few constructive channels for the expression of this violent instinctual force. This was, however, to a large extent an expression of a split-off part of himself, rather than an insightful experience of this part of his nature. The fear of this force caused inhibition in other spheres, as for example in his relationship with girls).

I would suggest that it is the crushing weight of this blind omnipotent superior superego which is causing the weakening, the depressing, and the general impoverishment of his personality. Formed by the projection into the father's penis of an envious omnipotent part of himself which is felt to be threatening to his primary good object, the breast mother, it thereby creates for him an internal mother who is constantly menaced by a bad intercourse. In identification with the oppressed and denigrated internal mother, the passive wife in the valley, he is depressed and impotent; he is also depressed about his inability to make full use of himself, of his potential strength which becomes unavailable through projection and encapsulation within this superior paternal part of himself. In the dream, however, and in the working through of the dream, Malcolm is making an effort to integrate this destructive and powerful figure as a part of himself, although he does not like to swallow it, it leaves a bad taste in his mouth. In trying to take responsibility for it and for the harm it has caused and to use it in the service of repairing his good objects, to further the analysis, he is attempting to use depressive anxieties in a creative way. He attempts to maintain and work through the depressive position as fully as possible. That this must be a gradual process one can see from Malcolm's statement that this mad part is timeless, has always been with him, and from his fear that it will never change.

There were in his earlier history certain situations of actual deprivation and loss, which were, however, well within the ordinary range of children's experiences. His family circumstances and relationships are more than averagely good, and to a great extent he has been able to benefit from them and to develop on favourable lines, as he has always been able to benefit from his analysis to a certain degree. He cannot, however, fully realise the richness of his personality and of his creative capacity until he is able to consolidate insight into this mad and destructive part of himself, and the devious ways in which it expresses itself, how it interferes with good relationships with people outside and with his internal objects. By this interference it recurrently brings about experiences of loss.

Malcolm may be right that there is an unalterable core to this aspect of himself. If, however, he can accept this as belonging to himself — remember that the man in the dream became so wild because he was so isolated — if his saner self can learn how to talk to his mad part, to direct it better, to limit its distortion of good objects, then he will have a lesser load of unconscious guilt to carry, be less identified with destroyed objects, and therefore less incapacitated by depression.

Conclusion

In conclusion, a few comments on some of the features which Malcolm has in common with Mrs Lush's patient Lilian,[1] features which have been mentioned by a number of psychoanalytical writers on depression (Rosenfeld, 1959).

In both patients there is impoverishment of the ego due to the introjection of and identification with a denigrated object (Freud, 1917) as a result of the overemployment of the mechanism described by Melanie Klein (1946) as projective identification. She uses this term to describe a process whereby parts of the self are split off and projected into objects which become identified with the projected self. The denigrated object is thus created by the projection of destructive and spoiling parts of the self.

In both patients there is marked idealisation. In Malcolm this derives from a narcissistic overvaluation of his own products, but this narcissistic aspect exists in him alongside a more normal object-orientated self (Rosefeld, 1964). There is in him awareness not only of idealisation with concomitant anxiety about the persecution which is being defended against, but of a really good object and good parts of the self which are not fully repaired and maintained because of his ambivalent attitude to them. Lilian's ego appears to be altogether weaker than Malcolm's, less capable of standing up to pain and frustration. More extensive projection and loss of both good and bad parts of herself result in extreme dependence and need for reassurance. Her longing for an ideal object appears as a more desperate defence against her feelings of persecution and inner emptiness.

The feeling of superiority, which together with that of inferiority, Abraham noted as characteristic of melancholics, is clearly illustrated in Malcolm's dream. This derives from the severe superego mentioned by so many analysts from Freud onwards, and is manifest in both patients. We can see how in Malcolm, under the meticulous superego that kept him up to the mark, underlies the early archaic superego formed from the projection of primitive destructive emotions and parts of the self (Klein, 1933). In Lilian's material thus far, the superiority is less obvious (although it is there, e.g. in the gloves incident) and inferiority and helplessness are more apparent. The demands of her superego cripple her — she feels she ought to go to school but she cannot. In Lilian's case there are indications that there was as a precipitating factor in her first marked depressive illness, a narcissistic injury (Abraham) — the birth of her younger sister. In Malcom's case where the depression manifested itself as a dampening of affect rather than as a flagrant illness, there were no signs of such a precipitating factor. His depression was perpetuated rather by the omnipotent possessive part of himself which could not face the envy entailed in feeling dependent on a good object and allowing it to keep its integrity. Through resorting to its own self-created idealised objects and self-image, this narcissistic part of himself made him recurrently lose contact with good objects, both external and internal. There are also indications in Lilian's material (the gloves incident again, for instance) that she has similar difficulties in appreciating and valuing help from a separate external object.

REFERENCES

ABRAHAM, K. (1911) 'Notes on the Psycho-Analytic Investigation and Treatment of Manic-Depressive Insanity and Allied Conditions'.

ABRAHAM, K. (1924) 'A Short Study of the Development of the Libido', in *Selected Papers on Psycho-Analysis*. London, Hogarth.

FREUD, S. (1917) 'Mourning and Melancholia', Standard Edition, Vol.14. London, Hogarth.

KLEIN, M. (1933) 'The Early Development of Conscience in the Child'.

KLEIN, M. (1935) 'A Contribution to the Psycho-genesis of Manic-Depressive States'.

KLEIN, M. (1935) 'Mourning and its Relation to Manic-Depressive States', in *Contributions to Psycho-Analysis*. London: Hogarth, 1948.

KLEIN, M. (1946) 'Notes on Some Schizoid Mechanisms', *Developments in Psycho-Analysis*. London: Hogarth, 1952.

ROSENFELD, H. (1959) 'An Investigation into the Psycho-Analytic Theory of Depression', *Int. J. Psycho-Anal.*, Vol. 40: 105-129.

ROSENFELD, H. (1964) 'On the Psychopathology of Narcissism', *Int. J. Psycho-Anal.*, Vol 45: 332-337.

[1] This paper is extracted from one written jointly with Mrs. Lush, in the *Journal of Child Psychotherapy*, Vol. 1, No. 33 (1965).

5　　　Depressive, Paranoid and Narcissistic
　　　　Features in the Analysis of a Woman
　　　　following the Birth of her First Child,
　　　　and the Death of her own Mother.
　　　c. 1960

Mrs G. was 32 years old when she began analysis with me for five
sessions a week, a month after the birth of her first child, a boy.
She had been persuaded to take this course by her husband, then
in the second year of his own analysis, because of her acute hypochondriacal and paranoid anxieties during this pregnancy, and
depression following the birth. The medical analyst who referred
her alerted me to the possibility of suicide. Other symptoms
which emerged were immoderate jealousy and fear of being
abandoned, also phobic anxieties.

History

This summary of the patient's history is derived from material
given in the course of two years' analysis.

　　She was born in South America where her childhood was spent
in the country within travelling distance of a university town.
Her father was a wealthy doctor, her mother had been a school-
teacher and was an enthusiastic amateur painter. Both parents
had 'advanced' ideas on child upbringing and believed that total
lack of frustration would preclude complexes and promote
mental health.

　　She was breastfed for nine months, slept in a cot beside her
mother in the parents' bedroom, until, when she was nineteen
months old, her brother was born and she was put in a room of
her own. She then showed such jealousy that he was kept out of
her sight as much as possible. She continued to resent and to
bully him throughout her childhood, to feel that her mother had
an unfair preference for him because he was a boy, good-looking,
and of a mild disposition. Later on, she began to feel guilty about
his inability to stand up for himself, his 'zombie' character, and
to blame her parents for not protecting him from her violence.

　　Throughout her childhood she was intensely and possessively
attached to her mother, and remembers at a very early age standing by an upstairs window sobbing bitterly while her mother

drove out to go for her weekly painting lesson, one of the few occasions upon which they were parted for a few hours. For as far back as she could recollect she resented her father as coming between her and her mother, and as the years went on she became increasingly critical of him. She remembered him as exploiting and deceiving her on many occasions, and persuading her mother to connive at this. A recurrent grievance was made of the occasion upon which he led her, as a ten year old child to sell the old pony to which she had been greatly attached, in favour of a fine Arab mare. It then turned out that the Arab mare was not to be her own, but a loan which had to be returned to the rightful owner after 18 months, when she was left with nothing.

She and her brother led a wild outdoor life, seeing few other children, and with few restrictions. The family was treated with deference by other members of the village. Her father in turn admired and deferred to his elder brother who ran an artists' colony some miles away, where he lived sometimes with his wife, sometimes with mistresses. His children both legitimate and illegitimate, named after famous poets, were the childhood companions of Mrs G. Following his brother's example her father started to have mistresses whom he brought home. These were the occasion of regular cataclysmic rows between the parents, remembered as occurring mainly at meal times, from the time she was about five years old. Unable to bear them she used to carry her food out and eat alone. Her brother remained but developed feeding difficulties.

When it was time for her to go to school, her mother equipped beautifully one of the larger rooms of the house as a schoolroom. There she taught her own two children and one or two others. Mrs G. enjoyed this and learned easily, but as the other children left and travelled to larger schools, she longed to go too and for years waged a surly intermittent battle, which finally succeeded when she was 15 years old. Her two years at school were the happiest of her life, gauche and shy though she was. She had been well taught and was among the best pupils there. Her brother wanted to come too but could put up no fight so never managed to get to school.

She blamed her father bitterly for keeping her at home on the pretence that she would receive a better education there, and then for his meanness in refusing to pay university fees for her.

She solved the problem by getting a scholarship, and took great satisfaction in refusing to study medicine as her father then suggested, and specialised brilliantly in mathematics.

She met her husband, a fellow student, some years older than herself, and married him when she was 21 with the approval of her mother but not her father. He was her first and only boy-friend although she had been secretly and romantically attached to others. They came to England when she was 25 on a post graduate fellowship, after which the marriage became increasingly unhappy owing to his impotence, increasingly troublesome perversion phantasies and her ungovernable jealousy of other women, and fear of his unpredictable tempers. The husband began analysis after getting into social difficulties when accused of exposing himself to a charwoman. A year after this they conceived their first child.

Two months before this, Mrs G.'s mother had died of cancer of the breast. Her father had taken elaborate precautions to conceal the nature of the illness from his wife and relatives. Mrs G. had not forgiven him for failing to inform her and giving her an opportunity to see her mother again before she died. From the time of her mother's death she was unable to do any creative work with her subject, and feared that she was quite finished academically. When she sought analysis neither she nor her husband had a university post and little prospect of obtaining one in this country, although the prospects at home were good. As they had little money they were eager to get well enough to return home as soon as possible. The husband had a part-time job; they had no help and he was to look after the baby when she came for her sessions.

Account of the Analysis

When I saw Mrs G. for a preliminary interview she made a bizarre impression. She is a tall bony woman with basically fine handsome features and was at that time thin in the face and lumpy in the body. She entered the house suspiciously, with a sidelong shambling gait, eyes averted, and sat down with a sullen apathetic expression. Her dress was at variance with her manner and physique: white ankle socks, a brilliant blue coat and discordantly brassy-coloured short cropped hair. She looked both garish and dilapidated. Within the first week of the analysis the coat, ankle socks, and dyed hair disappeared. She reverted to her natural shade of hair, a soft brown and wore the more unobtrusive slightly untidy clothes consonant with the not so smart intellectual.

During her first session she was surly and depressed, lay down reluctantly and again had great difficulty in talking. The gist of her first halting remarks was that she had been trying to make up her mind whether she really needed analysis or not. Her friends, her husband, and the analyst whom she had consulted all said that she did, but she did not know whether the difficulties that they diagnosed for her were serious ones or not, and anyway how did they know any better than she did how she felt. She had no opinion about herself. Did analysis really change anyone and if so was it necessarily for the better? She had just received a letter from her father, telling her not to let anyone monkey with her mind as it would damage her creativity (this said defiantly).

The first moment of contact I made with her in this session was by saying that she seemed to be conveying to me that although she had let herself be persuaded to try analysis, whatever that might be, she was warning me that she had no intention of being changed and was going to resent it if I found out what was going on in her mind before she knew it herself. She exclaimed: 'Surely not! It would be crazy to undertake analysis and then work against it.' She then mentioned friends of hers who had been in analysis for years and showed no signs of being able to stop, in her opinion two years should suffice and would in fact have to do as she intended to go home after that time. I suggested she was afraid of being trapped, of my using knowledge about her to keep her dependent upon me, that I had the impression that the moment she came in my door she became afraid she would not get out again. She then said that she had really come because her husband nagged her so; he said that unless she had analysis she would prevent him from making any progress in his. What finally made her accede to his pressure was her mad behaviour to the doctors at the antenatal clinic and during her confinement — she had behaved shockingly badly for no particular reason, because they were in fact well disposed towards her and reasonably competent. I said that this mad behaviour towards the doctors showed signs of being repeated here with me to whom she had been sent as well disposed and reasonably competent, but through her father she was expressing her own suspicions that I would damage her creativity as she feared the doctors would damage her baby. This parallel struck her.

In her second session she was more relaxed and began to talk with greater ease giving a detailed account of her difficulties in hospital during pregnancy; unreasonable demands, paroxysms of rage at having to wait, suspicion of every move and final wild alarm at being confronted with a psychoanalyst. It appeared that the doctor with whom she had got on worst was about ten years older than herself, recognised as knowledgeable and successful and envied for his self-confidence. She was on the other hand also uneasy with the younger doctor whom she could rattle and plunge into a state of indecision, who was overawed by her brilliance. Her associations linked this doctor with her brother whom she now feared would realise that he too needed analysis, would get her father to pay for him and thereby reduce her chances of financial help. On the other hand she thought her brother would surely need analysis more than she did, as she had bullied him so as a child.

Thus we had the first delineation of a recurrent quandary: if I were the older doctor, a helpful competent parent who had something to give her, she feared dependence, became envious and did everything she could to shake my equanimity and pleasure in my work; if she triumphed by reducing me to the level of the zombie brother, I became an ineffective analyst who needed help more than she did and loaded her with a resented burden of guilt.

In the first few weeks of the analysis she made a point of arriving promptly, telling me that if she were late it would be her husband's fault. There gradually emerged a picture of a jeering triumphant male figure, always lurking to find fault with her, to come between her and happiness: the doctor at the post-natal examination who was just waiting for her and the baby to make an exhibition of themselves to prove his point that she needed psychiatric treatment; the father who had illtreated her mother throughout her life and who had isolated her during her mortal illness: the father who had delayed answering her request for money to pay for her analysis. These angry accusations tended to arise at any experience of restriction of the analysis: the weekend, traffic delays, waiting for her husband to return so that she could come out and leave the baby, the first bill. They were interpreted as a transference experience of the analyst as the purse-proud controlling father object who used his power to bully and keep the needy infant part of herself from the nourishment and comfort contained in the analysis as a breast.

For the first month there was a notable omission of any reference to her own baby. The resentfully needy infant in herself occupied the couch for the greater part of the time, eager to have this analytic nourishment, taking in interpretations greedily, but suspicious of what they were doing to her, and of the payment that would be exacted were she to swallow them. Attempts to clarify the confusion that seemed to exist between her relationship with her actual baby with the baby part of herself, and with a needy internal object which sometimes seemed to be the brother, resulted after five weeks analysis in a brief dream, told with great anxiety, but also greeted with some relief as a hopeful sign of some creative inner life.

The dream was of *two babies, one healthy and bonny, and the other puny, starved and apathetic, she thought about to die. Either or neither belonged to her.* She associated that the healthy baby was in fact very like her own son, but also like photographs of her brother in infancy, sweet-natured, admired by all and stimulating ferocious jealousy in her. In response to my query about the puny starved one, she muttered in low-voiced distress that she feared she would have to give up breast-feeding her baby. She had never had enough milk for him, but over the past weeks it had been getting less. Her husband had accused her of wanting to transfer him completely to the bottle so that she need never miss an analytic session in order to stay and feed him (he was demand-fed, and not always regular in his demands).

This dream was interpreted that in so far as her baby was her mother's baby, her little brother, and was felt to be a competitor for the breast, for the analysis, she was distressed because her greed would make her place herself first at his expense. She had already voiced her conviction that she was my only patient, an omnipotent way of annihilating the other children. She justified this by her own need as the apathetic infant who started analysis with nothing inside her, no idea about herself. The acting out of her own infantile need and greed she then feared would actually transform her healthy child into the puny dying infant, as she in phantasy was starving my other patient-babies by keeping them from analysis.

These interpretations were digested thoughtfully. On the next session, a Monday, she came with pains in her arms, which she connected with holding the baby, but also with the cancerous secondaries which developed in her mother's neck and arms. Her father had deceived everyone into believing that these were merely arthritis. It was then possible to connect the dying baby in the dream with the dying mother, the internal hungry cancerous breast, into which was projected her own infantile greed, which claimed her milk, needed for her own infant.

She then broke into a flood of tears; despair and love for the baby; self-reproach that she who had been breast-fed for nine months would not be able to do this for her own child. I took this as grief at being unable to keep alive in her the goodness she had received from the breast, and currently from the analysis, to protect this from being eaten up by an internalised analytic breast distorted by the projection of the greedy controlling infantile parts of herself. Her grief continued and by the end of the week I was led to believe that her milk had completely gone.

During the next Monday session, 6 weeks after starting analysis, she noticed for the first time a tall cylindrical pot on the mantlepiece, where it had always stood, renewed from time to time with fresh flowers. She rose from the couch with anger and alarm, convinced that this was a pot made by a friend and compatriot of hers, whom therefore I must know. She had already discovered that I was acquainted with some other friends of hers, therefore the situation was quite untenable. She would probably find I knew all her friends and therefore she had no-one in England of her own. The tirade of persecution continued during which she threatened to break off the analysis. My attempts to account for and to interpret this in terms of jealousy at being confronted with a flower (baby-giving) penis in me after the week-end did not seem to calm her sufficiently. Later in the week, in response to an erroneous interpretation of mine about her increased envy of me as a fertile feeding mother because of her own inability to breast-feed, she mentioned casually that she was still feeding the baby, that the milk unaccountably had begun to return and was now more plentiful than it had ever been. The tirade then seemed more understandable as a reaction against being helped by me as an external separate person, fear of dependence on a mother who could take the breast away, and who preferred to have a renewing intercourse with father at the week-end, her night-time. Recognition of dependence on an outside mother was a threat to her omnipotence, to her belief that unaccountably she was curing herself. The helpful external mother-analyst, distorted by the projections of the threatened omnipotent part of herself was then taken in as a grudging controlling object which would allow her no life of her own.

Following the analysis of this intensely persecuted phase the sessions went more smoothly for a time. She seemed to be more collected and in possession of herself. Work centred largely round her need for the analysis — surlily acknowledged — as a kind of drug, which was seldom enjoyed at the time, but avidly ingested to keep her going and to slake an immoderately greedy infantile aspect of herself which became violent as soon as it was denied. This was often projected into me in the mother trans-ference, the cancerous breast which was hungry for her material and which doled out interpretations of dubious value, designed she feared to make her into a drug addict, a mere infant bereft of all independence. The one good thing in her life was the baby who she feared might turn against her if she were unable to feed and to satisfy all his needs. Her husband was necessary to earn an inadequate living in order to leave her free to care for the baby and to come to analysis, her analyst necessary as a receptacle for anxieties and grumbles, a breast from which she could take away supplies with which to feed the baby, supplies that were often felt to be inadequate, a poor quota of the wealth which was locked away and seemed to be located in the parental intercourse. At week-ends and before the summer holidays she talked of frequenting pubs with her husband, stating that they were the only places where she could feel friendly and enjoy herself. The pubs came to be understood as the whore-mummy, both idealised and denigrated, into which she could enter freely, via a sexual relationship with the penis, thus obviating the necessity of facing payment in terms of facing the frustration of being an outside baby, and of being a little girl without a penis.

Hypochondriacal fears particularly of cancer, tended to recur, especially after week-ends, alternating with obsessional pre-cautions against her husband leaving on the gas, or hurting the baby while she was away for her session, according to whether the analyst was internalised as a damaged denigrated object, or whether the destructive part of herself was projected into the husband and controlled there. At other times in the transference, but more fleetingly than I gave her credit for, I appeared to be experienced as the mother who fed her for nine months, who had taught her well, whom she had loved, and for whom she still grieved.

The approach of the first summer break evoked angry sorrow. Dreams of her mother dying tormented her, and there were occasional renewed outbursts of anger against her father, who appeared currently to be an apt vehicle to carry the projection of her own neglectfulness and evasion: so much so that I was seduced at times by sympathy with what appeared to be a trying reality situation. At such times I was unable to follow closely and point out to her how the domineering envious megalomanic father was being created in the transference and experienced as the cause of every interruption in the analysis. Her conscious experience of me was of a conscientious pedestrian kindly analyst who did her best but often seemed downtrodden and weary at seeing her. My interpretations she declared were sometimes helpful and threw new light upon her relationship with her father and her husband, but there could be no hope of a radical change in her life unless they themselves altered. Myself, as the down-trodden analyst who did not like her, I linked with the dying mother who accused her in dreams of making her lead this joyless drudging life. (On seeing the patient who preceded her she had spoken one day with sympathy for the lives of analysts who existed as dustbins for the troubles of others, a sympathy that cloaked the envious distorting of my work, the dustbin promiscuous parental intercourse).

Just before the summer holidays outbursts of rage and dis-appointment about her husband's suspected pornographic interests, were interpreted as the repudiation and hatred of that part of herself which was split off and projected into the husband — the dirtying distorting prying interference with the parental intercourse, aroused by the approach of my holiday.

She then dreamt that she was accused of sending an unkind letter to her mother when she was dying. This shocked her, she was in tears and could give no associations to the dream. There had however been an account earlier in the week about her poisonously vituperative letter to her father accusing him of meanly holding on to all his money and doing nothing to help her to get well. In this context I interpreted the dream as partial acceptance of my previous interpretations, experienced as a conscience which accused her of torturing the loved mother, the healing analyst, already doomed by the invasion of her greedy infant parts (the cancer) by poisoning the intercourse by the unkind letter. She then acknowledged that she was terrified of becoming a prey to 'phobias' in the summer holidays, said that she was now able to go out freely on her own and to do her shopping which had hitherto been a great ordeal. She appeared to accept my interpretation that this panic arose from her fear of being unable to preserve during the forthcoming separation the progress she had made; that masturbatory attacks upon me as the night-time sexual mother would be so strong that this internal nightmare world would spill into her daylight experience, distort her sense of the familiar external world and impede her movement in it.

She returned from the summer holidays pleased at managing so well, but it soon became evident that this was on the basis of avoiding any painful feelings resulting from awareness of separation and exclusion from the analysts sexual intercourse, by intruding into this intercourse by denigratory masturbatory attacks, both verbal and physical, in collusion with her husband/brother and sister acting out dirty jokes about the parental intercourse. I was regaled with instalments, both witty and amusing, of a saga they had composed about Dusty Harris, a dwarf dustman who was consumed with envy because his wife was a psycho-analyst. Concurrently however she began to panic lest she had become pregnant, and guilty about what this would do to her baby before he had even been weaned, afraid that he would turn against her.

Her infantile self, dependent and desolate at being weaned and turned out of the parental bedroom upon the birth of the brother (the holiday) was projected into her own baby, and pitied there. The nature of the turning against the mother was interpreted in the details of her attacks on the analyst's holiday intercourse: the attempt to entertain and seduce her into a homosexual alliance which excluded and diminished the father into the impotent dirty dwarf baby: the attempt to deceive this psycho-analyst mother, seductive entertainment to overlook that she was being used as a dustbin: her babies, her creativity both dirtied and pulverised, allowed intercourse only with a penis shovel which cleared out the rubbish and left her empty to receive another load.

The autumn term after this first holiday was disturbed by the need to change to a late night session once a week owing to alterations in her husband's work. This was experienced as a recurrent weaning threat, the intrusion of a tantalising parental intercourse, and led to increased suspicion and fighting against involvement in the analysis. During this period her breast milk was diminishing and she had to face the prospect of weaning her baby. Into him she continued to project and through him to experience the anxieties about weaning that she had evidently been unable to contain during her own infancy, and which she was unable to contain in the current analytic situation. She continued to agonise that he had never been properly breast fed, that he would hold it against her for the rest of her life, that his grudge would make him into a delinquent or a sexual pervert, She felt she could never have another baby and expose him to the terrible jealousy that she had suffered because of her brother.

Her way of experiencing weaning and the threat of other babies is illustrated in the following dream which she had shortly after her baby was weaned (at nearly 8 months old) and at the beginning of November when her own Christmas holiday was already being anticipated: *An old man, shabby and scruffy, but some-how with a good face, not petty, was teaching her with a class of children to do exercises at which she was no good. During them she was watched critically and snubbed by a girl called Barbara. Her feelings were hurt but the old man was somehow comforting. She then found herself with her brother, Barbara, and her husband in her mother's house which became that of the crazy aunt. Her husband then became the son of the crazy aunt. He complained to her bitterly because her mother preferred her brother to himself and in revenge he began to flirt with Barbara, She suddenly felt quite alone and desperate. Her brother has disappeared. Then a stranger, a man of forty appeared and was willing to flirt with her. She did not respond but he too was nice and comforting.*

Her first association was that she often had inadequacy and jealousy dreams but this was the first time that anyone had come to her rescue, the first hope that she had that she might find another man if her husband did desert her. Barbara was a good-looking girlhood acquaintance who had been immured in a convent by her parents in an unsuccessful attempt to prevent her from having premature sexual relationships with boys. She had last seen Barbara when she finally parted from her mother.

The old man gave rise to a spate of associations about her greatly admired paternal grandfather, an explorer and hero of the sea, unhappily married and under-rated by his wife and family. He died when she was a small child and she had seen him seldom. Although she had thought of him very often when she was a child he had not been in her mind for years now. The stranger of 40 had something familiar about him, perhaps some-body that she had met in a book. Later in the session after she had been talking of her wish to have a secret little hoard of money unknown to her husband so that she need not be accountable to him for all her spending, she went on to talk of reading Ernest Jones's biography of Freud. She accepted my suggestion that the stranger of 40 was Freud and believed that he was around that age when he wrote 'The Interpretation of Dreams'.

The crazy aunt had figured several times before in the sessions as a distorted version of the analyst: a woman doctor, married to her megalomanic faithless artist uncle. As a result of reading Freud this woman forsook medicine and her family to put up a plate and practise as a psycho analyst. Her son who lost his eye as a result of a childhood accident was rather retarded mentally, and bore the same name as Mrs G.'s husband.

This dream begins by expressing her inadequacy in dealing with being one among many other children, one of a number of patients in analysis, of containing both the envy and jealousy provoked by this experience, but expresses also her ability to find within herself a comforting father person.

Both the old man and the stranger of 40 had elements of the analyst: the age of the latter, the association with Freud, the old man teaching the class of children (she knew I was a child analyst) his association with the sea (she had rung up one week-end and been told that I was away sailing).

Barbara who takes away her husband and who snubs her also represents the mother analyst who deserts her for sexual relations with father; where weaning is felt as humiliating, a reduction to infantile clumsiness, disturbing her omnipotent illusion of having the breast inside as her private possession (immured in the convent) and also of having a penis — the husband — enabling her to move freely and enter into mother's body.

But the Barbara mother is created through the projective identification of a distorting precociously sexual and envious part of herself. When she goes with this Barbara part of herself into the mother's house-body, mother becomes the crazy aunt. The projection of her jealousy as well as her envy into the brother also removes her insight — the one-eyed defective son — and leaves her bereft and desolate, deserted not only by her objects but by parts of herself so massively projected.

Nevertheless she indicates that through analysis she has recovered an internal object which does come to her rescue: the old man seems to be a displacement on to a father-person of the maternal qualities of the analyst (her mother was also her teacher for a long time), for whose shabby treatment she does not take responsibility herself; he seems also to represent her admiration for the courage of the analyst as a man in navigating and exploring the unknown seas of her emotions, what is going on in her crazy internal world.

The stranger of 40 can be seen as the Freud father penis in the mother analyst which makes her flirt with the idea of acquiring in an omnipotent and delinquent way, from reading, the means of analysing her own dreams, of feeding herself, instead of having to go through the painful experience of being analysed like other patients and of accounting to me for the use of my interpretations. I thought that this dream also suggested some early experience of a better relationship with her father than she had previously indicated, a turning to him and finding comfort from him at her own weaning or at the birth of the brother. Interpretation on these lines was strongly repudiated, yet further evidence came in later dreams — also in her consistent realisation of the importance of his father to her own little boy. There was also a rapprochement between her father and herself after this which led to his contributing a certain amount towards her analysis.

After she had been in analysis for over a year the regular pattern of the sessions was disturbed for more than two months. Her husband had to fly home unexpectedly to see his father who was seriously ill and who finally died. She had difficulty in obtaining baby-sitters for both real and neurotic reasons. I altered the sessions where I could in view of the real difficulties, but there were a number of times when she had to miss sessions because of her arrangements falling through at the last moment. The uncertainty made her wildly anxious, more so than before previous breaks or changes of time, especially as this trip meant a serious depletion of the small amount of capital they had left and the money which her father sent irregularly paid for only part of her analysis. She thought of giving up analysis altogether for the time being until her husband came back. She over-ate and started smoking again, although she had given this up almost two years before, in order to deaden her appetite for food. She then became obsessed with the fear that she had carcinoma of the lungs, wanted an X-ray to check upon this but feared that the X-ray might cause the cancer even if it were not already there. She turned to reading psycho-analytic literature, and thought of applying for training as an analyst, but feared that she would be controlled by patients, like Ferenczi, who she declared had allowed himself to be analysed by them and finally driven crazy in the end.

She dealt with her anxiety initially by increased and more fragmented projecting mechanisms. She became, however, enormously reassured to find as the weeks went by that she could cope better on her own than she had anticipated, and that she was now relieved of the feeling of obsessive jealousy of her husband that had plagued her before. She had her hair permed and took on a new lease of life, began to contemplate the possibility of managing to live without analysis without collapsing. She seemed to be co-operative, provided extremely interesting material, often in the form of dreams, to which sometimes she offered such detailed associations that I had difficulty in selecting and finding an opportunity to make relevant interpretations, which did not seem to bother her in the slightest. When I did manage to get through to her the sabotaging that was concealed in this apparent co-operation, she became persecuted and objected that I was never pleased: if I thought she was a hopeless patient why didn't I say so and have done with it?

She became intensely involved in a feminist cause, full of self-righteous indignation about men who envied women their intellects and their production of babies, who would just like to keep them drudging away at housework. My interpretation of how she was splitting off and projecting into me an envious anti-mother part of herself which was in fact ensuring that my work in analysing her was repetitive drudgery, did not seem to get through. She then had the following dream: *People she knew had fallen into the hands of Nazis in the Argentine. The Nazis knocked them about in a cellar or murdered them for holding radical opinions, probably for being C.N.D. or Jews. They mutilated them with awful wounds. She had an intense personal fear that this would happen to her, so kept quiet feeling extremely cowardly and saying to herself angrily that this was what came of having principles, your life was endangered and there was no government to protect you. If they were to start on her should she knuckle under and renounce her principles? She couldn't be blamed for it for no government took responsibility for dealing with these criminals.*

This dream she said was extraordinarily painful, presented her with a very poor view of herself, but it went on to something quite different: *She was swimming in a lake with some people and some pets. It was pleasant and warm, then they came across a peculiar undertow. She was dragged under in a state of panic, unable to breathe, fought her way out and decided that there must be in the lake a deep narrow passage leading into the centre of the earth and that water flowing into it created a downward current. She did not know whether it was possible to swim to the other side; they decided to send a person attached to a wire. She was chosen to go first but was afraid of choking and losing consciousness so they all decided to send one of the pets, an animal, not something human, which seemed a happy solution.* This dream was much less horrific than the first one.

Her first association was that after the trial of Eichmann she heard that some Nazis in her country had mutilated a young girl by cutting off her nipples and carving a swastika on her breast. In the dream itself details of the tortures and of the people involved were extremely vague. The lake she thought might be the one in which the Nazis were supposed to have put their treasures after their defeat. Further associations to Eichmann, who seemed to her such an ordinary little man, led to her amused recollection of a brawl at a party between her husband and a friend because of some joking play on his Christian name which is similar to that of a prominent Nazi leader.

She continued to elaborate on this story in a witty amusing way that seemed to be leading further away from the dream. I broke in and interpreted the amusement and detailed account of this brawl as an attempt to deny the painful insight in the dream and to divert what she feared would be the further pain of coming to understand it more closely; also to lead away from any connection between herself and Eichmann by the familiar device of saying: 'It's my husband who's the Nazi, not me.' She received this interpretation rather truculently and waited for me to continue. I suggested that the difficulty of maintaining her principles, protecting her good internal object, derived from the continual projection of the Nazi parts of herself into me as the parents and keeping the good reforming life-giving ones for herself, the good feeding breasts experienced in the analysis as her own creation. She then felt hopelessly bereft of support from me in dealing with the criminal parts of herself which tried to get back at her. The absence of harmonious internal government derived from parents who are not allowed to come together in a constructive way, made it difficult for her to be strong enough to take into herself and to fight those criminal parts, which she feared would overwhelm her.

As on previous occasions she objected angrily that it was impossible for her to have united parents within her as her parents had in fact got on shockingly badly, I should know that by now. I suggested that whatever may have been the situation with her actual parents, we could study the repeated way in which she had to prevent a close understanding relationship between herself and me during the sessions: the tantalizing or torturing way of presenting rich material in the form of dreams and associations, which if it were defended and worked upon with my help, could probably lead to radical progress in the analysis. In the dream there was an acknowledgement of cowardice which distressed her greatly, and it would be important to investigate just how difficult this cowardice is operating in the session. It would seem that her sadistically critical conscience was attributed to me, and that she feared my interpretations as an attack from which she had to retreat to protect herself.

After some further truculent cogitations she then said: What about the second part of the dream? Was this a way of dealing with the painfulness of the first part? This remained as shame rather than terror. The second part had also become very frightening but seemed to end more satisfactorily she thought. Again she had no picture of the identity of any of the people or pets in this part of the dream. The pets were small things, rodents perhaps. I suggested that this part of the dream began as an escape from the frightening isolation of the first part, with the experience of being inside the mother and at one with her: the vagueness of the others hardly distinguished them from herself. This was a situation to which I had drawn her attention several times of late, created in the sessions by her reluctance to admit my separate existence as the analyst, by swimming along on her own free associations and failing to clarify what contributions came from herself and what from me, a comfortable situation which she hoped to maintain till she got through to the other side and finished analysis. But the cellar experience cropped up again to disturb this happy situation, in the deep narrow passage where the undertow was created by the water flowing in. This came from the apparently helpful but destructive urinary pouring of associations into myself. This created a vacuum, did not help the baby part of herself that was hungry for contact to find its way to my mouth as an effective nipple, or allow interpretations like babies to be fruitfully conceived. It was the Nazi part of herself that maintained she was depositing treasure in me thus; whereas her associations could only be of value in furthering her journey in the analysis, if she were prepared to follow them and find where they led. But this was a frightening exploration because it led to the castrated analytic breast without a nipple, kept in the cellar, in her bottom, a repository for and victim of her greedy and enviously sadistic parts.

As she appeared to be thinking about this, I suggested that the deep narrow passage that threatened to suck her down was reminiscent of a small child's anxiety about being sucked down the plughole with the bathwater. She exclaimed involuntarily that that was clever of me. She had been afraid of the swirl as a small child and wondered where all the dirty water went to. I suggested that this was how she now wondered what I, as the bath lavatory, now did with all the projected gnawing faecal parts of herself, masquerading as pets, or obliging babies that could be treated as expendable. It was the fear of my defaecating these faeces back into her that had made her on previous occasions have to reassure herself that I was not one of those 'projecting forceful analysts', and which made it difficult to allow me to really get inside her with my words, either as a feeding nipple or as a potent penis. Nevertheless my understanding her childhood fear I thought had momentarily made her hopeful that closer contact need not necessarily mean either being sucked into me or invaded and taken over by me.

After this session it was possible to make occasional but very fleeting contact with this invading Nazi part of herself, sometimes referred to as 'crazy', 'schizophrenic', also criminal, and with the despair which she felt about it ever being cured, the years of analysis it needed, which she could not afford. Her delinquent behaviour during the sessions continued to manifest itself mainly in concealing reactions to interpretations, both from me and from herself, so that often I did not know whether she had heard me or not. A session or so later, however, it might become evident that she had taken in something and had been working on it by herself, a re-enactment of her childhood eating on her own. Frequently however, and usually under pressure of greater than usual anxiety occasioned by any impingement on the analytic routine, this part of herself was projected into me, and she would react to attempts to understand it as if I were an envious ignorant analyst trying to rob her of her valuable productions (Bion 1962).

During the next few months she began to study again in her subject and to investigate University posts that she knew were likely to come up within the next year. She began to write papers that she kept hidden in a drawer away from her husband. This was further acting out of the transference situation where she was concealing from me what she was secretly stealing and making from my interpretations, in order to project her own suspicion and envy of what was hidden in my drawers. As her second Christmas holiday approached she had been 19 months in analysis. Her brother had been born when she was 19 months old, and her envy and rivalry with me as the pregnant sexual mother — when not manipulated by projection — alternated with periods of despair when she felt that she must be schizophrenic and incurable.

· Instead of the downtrodden careworn analyst I figured more often as someone with a lively social and sexual life. She began to agonise for another baby, felt bitter about her husband's impotence. It seemed that nothing but another baby could rescue her from having to face infantile feelings of jealousy and inadequacy, from the intolerable fear of being supplanted by another child because of her own incurable misuse of the breast. She took to reading psycho-analytic literature in an organised and thorough way, saying that as the time she could remain in analysis was limited she had better supplement it. She had grandiose ideas of doing some research to reconcile the Kleinians and the Freudians. She did not seem to be able to hold more than momentary insight into how this so-called reconciliatory research was in fact used to prevent a living and working relationship with me, that she was so busy intruding upon and manipulating the parental intercourse that the needy infant part of herself was prevented from getting any nourishment.

She did in fact become pregnant nearly 21 months after she began analysis. This pregnancy was concealed from me (and to begin with from herself) for nearly three months, as she concealed from her husband the papers in her drawers.

The analysis finally terminated rather abruptly in May, after two years. Her husband had obtained a full-time post and could no longer look after their son while she attended her sessions. Onto the part-time help whom she obtained were displaced her paranoid fears of the analyst as a defrauded mother, envious of her pregnancy whom she feared would turn her little boy against her; and so this woman was sacked. Into her son was projected her own infantile jealousy of her mother's pregnancy, and her demands that mother should be with her all the time. It was not possible for me to give her times that would coincide with her husband's periods at home, so she elected to spend her afternoons with her son and to give up analysis, on the understanding that should she find it impossible to manage without, I would try to fit her in later on.

She was afraid that her 'phobias' of hospitals, shops, and of cancer, might return; knew that she needed much more analysis; but was grateful for the improvement in confidence and general well-being that she perceived in herself. She also wanted to test out this improvement before going to her home country where it would be impossible for her to have analysis.

Discussion of Case

In the early months of her analysis Mrs G. evinced many of the features mentioned in the literature on depression and melancholia (she referred to herself as a melancholiac): the diminution of self-regard, severe super-ego, impoverishment of the ego, aggressive id impulses, the narcissistic identification with a denigrated, debased object. (Freud 1917, 1923,1926; Abraham 1916, 1924). Her loss of self-regard resulted not only from the identification with a destroyed internal object — the dead mother, the cancerous breast, whom she had been unable to mourn fully — but also through projecting into the lost idealised mother the baby within her, the idealised part of herself (Klein 1934, 1940).

During pregnancy she then had paranoid suspicions that this idealised internal possession would be attacked or stolen by the doctors, penises into which she had projected the sadistic parts of herself (Klein 1946), originally directed against her pregnant mother. Hence when the baby was born it seemed to be experienced as the loss of this idealised part of herself: as a creative person she felt that 'she was finished', and her fear was that she was left with nothing but a destroyed internal world. She could now live only for her child but was uncertain of having any milk or goodness to give him.

The general agreement, with the exception of Jacobson and Kanzer, that the fundamental depressive situation has to be looked for in the first years of life (Rosenfeld), was, I think, borne out in her case, where ruthless oral greed became speedily such a marked feature in the analysis, reactivated by every threat of weaning.

The penis envy which Helene Deutsch mentions as being at the root of depressive conflict as well as oral envy, was very marked throughout. The penis was seen as having unlimited access to mother's body and all its contents, and for this it was coveted in a homosexual fashion (one aspect of the fear of sexual perversion projected into her child at weaning). There was also evidence to suggest that the penis envy derived from earlier envy of the breast (Klein 1957), strongly activated like the greed by any threat of loss; this led her to turn away from the analysis as a breast-feeding experience, distorted by her spoiling projections, and to attribute the benefit she had derived from it to an idealised penis preserved as her exclusive possession (the unappreciated heroic grandfather). But this attribution to the idealised penis of the strength and creativity of the breast, increased her rivalry with it and with men in general, and increased her castrating attacks upon them.

Her marriage to an impotent and extremely envious man whom she allowed to bully her, and to some extent to act as a severe super-ego for her, could be seen as a pathological union on the basis of projective identification with a powerful and destructive part of herself, initially projected into the father. Her lack of insight into this Nazi part of herself had blinded her to the extent of her husband's psychopathology. On the other hand, in so far as she tried and was able to help her husband with his work, and to some extent with his impotence, there was a reparative drive in this choice of partner (to rehabilitate the zombie younger brother) — but reparation of a manic kind, not based on insight and acknowledgement of guilt. Moreover as her husband depended on her stimulation before they could have intercourse, as the analyst depended on her associations before making fruitful interpretations, she told herself that she created and conrolled the penis that made her pregnant.

The acute feelings of depression and unworthiness with which she entered analysis and which were preventing her from feeding and enjoying her baby, from being able to give the 'primary maternal preoccupation' described by Winnicott (1956), were relieved within the first few months, largely through working upon her identification with and possession by a damaged or dead internal object. The feeling of having a better internal object and a better external one in the baby, on to whom she also displaced her experience of goodness from the analyst, brought to the fore more acutely at times paranoid anxieties of being robbed and defrauded of her due, experienced often in relation to her father and her husband.

As this persecution was interpreted as resulting from the projection and displacement of her own transference hostility and stealing, she began to give more direct expression to her own impulses, first of all in dreams, in fears of harming the baby or of her husband harming him. She began to distinguish between the baby as an external person, and her experience of him as the internal breast, constantly in peril. With some diminution of projective identification she began to have some 'idea' of herself, to find herself as a mother, and, it seemed, to meet the baby's real needs. As the analyst was able to accept and to interpret her projection of the dead internal mother, she was able to mourn her mother's death more fully, and to draw upon her experience of a mother who had actually given her a great deal, but whose death had revived her childhood separation anxieties. (Klein 1934)

The gradual restoration of her internal world and of her capacity to enjoy life led to a phase when manic mechanisms predominated, when instead of being persecuted by a severe superego she was more at one with her ego ideal. Her ideal self was a scholar, a patient seeker after truth, champion of the weak and oppressed, of the rights and equality of women, and seemed to be formed from perceptions of her mother and of her heroic grandfather, the man who saved her from humiliation in the dream following the baby's weaning. The most obdurate and persecuted phases in the analysis recurred when I attempted to analyse the area of hypocrisy in the view of herself, as shown, for instance, in the Nazi dream.

I became increasingly aware of the narcissistic quality of her relationship to me as she improved and was threatened by having to acknowledge the value of the analysis. (The term narcissism I use as it is employed to describe a clinical condition by Rosenfeld (1964), designated as primary love by Balint (1960).) At such times she appeared to be identified with me as an omnipotently incorporated object which was used to obviate aggressive feelings caused by frustration and any awareness of envy. Flight into this narcissistic state, inability to allow herself to experience dependence upon me as a separate external object, loved and respected, was increased by the uncertainty of her external circumstances, by practical difficulties in remaining in this country. Nevertheless it was clear that we were dealing with a basic character defect, a major defence against paranoid anxiety.

It was forecast, I think, in the first session when, although she had told me that she sought analysis because she felt that her creative life was at an end, she expressed fear that analysis would damage her creativity. It gradually became more apparent to me that it was the omnipotent narcissistic infantile part of herself, overvaluing its own anal and urethral products (Abraham 1920), which felt endangered by the existence of a good external breast not created by itself. There was evidence to suggest that her early upbringing overstimulated her infantile sexuality and masturbation, and the free expression of aggression to all and sundry; therefore giving her little help in differentiating, evaluating, and integrating the various aspects of herself and of her objects — on the contrary, encouraging and idealising projective mechanisms.

The converse of her narcissistic state in the analysis was one of great anxiety and fear of disintegration, full of doubts about herself and the stabilty of a good internal object. In the last weeks during her second pregnancy, there was rapid fluctuation between these two states of mind and fleeting insight into the connection between them.

Her fear of the analysis as a claustrum, the dreaded interior of the mother's body (Jones, Ferenczi, Klein (1932), Lewin (1935)) was indicated in the first session. She did not report claustrophobic fears (and the converse agoraphobic) until just before her first holiday, when they had been greatly alleviated and when she was afraid of their returning. The alleviation seemed to be due to a lessening of anxiety and therefore of the need for the violent splitting and projective identificaton of destructive parts of herself; these, internalised, resulted in the hypochondriacal phantasy of the cancerous breast (Rosenfeld 1958), which when projected outward were bound in the external situation of the shop: the breast which excited her greed and envy, and distorted by them, threatened to enclose her (Segal 1954). Throughout the rest of the analysis the claustrophobia remained latent, appearing mostly in dreams, as the Nazi dream, and was not I think sufficiently analysed by me. Her fear of her 'phobias' returning alerted me to this in the final weeks, and I could then see the extent to which her projections made the analysis into the phobic object.

Although she left expressing surprise and unwontedly heartfelt gratitude for the relief and the confidence she had obtained from analysis, there was no real integration between her omnipotent narcissistic self and the needy baby one, genuinely capable of love and hungry for truth; this had not been allowed sufficient time to learn to feed from, to internalise the analyst as a good external mother, and to develop a better heterosexual approach to the Oedipal situation by taking full responsibility for the Nazi aspects, instead of projecting them into the father.

The vulnerable, still deprived infant in her, was to a great extent projected into her son to whom she devoted herself whole-heartedly so that he need not suffer through jealousy of the new baby.

From subsequent letters from her, and from reports I understand that her pregnancy went well, that she was able to feed the new baby and to enjoy her two sons. Both she and her husband obtained the University posts which they had coveted and went back to their own country shortly after the birth of the second baby.

REFERENCES

1. ABRAHAM, K. (1916) 'The Influence of Oral Erotism in Character Formation'.
   (1920) 'The Narcissistic Evaluation of Excretory Processes in Dreams'.
   (1924) 'A Short Study of the Development of the Libido Viewed in the Light of Mental Disorders', in *Selected Papers*. London: Hogarth, 1927.
2. BALINT, M. (1960) 'Primary Narcissism or Primary Love', in *Psychoanalytic Quarterly*, Vol. 29.
3. BION, W. (1962) *Learning from Experience*, Chapter 28. London, Heinemann.
4. FERENCZI, S.(1927) *Further Contributions to the Technique of Psycho-analysis*, Chap LXI. London, Hogarth.
5. FREUD, S. (1917) 'Mourning and Melancholia'. Standard Edition, Vol. 14.
   (1923) 'The Ego and the Id.' Standard Edition, Vol. 19.
   (1926) 'Inhibitions, Symptoms and Anxiety'. Standard Edition, Vol. 20.
6. JONES, E. (1912) *Papers on Psycho-analysis*, Chapter XI. London: Bailliere, Tindall and Cox Ltd.
   (1932) 'The Psycho-analysis of Children'.
7. KLEIN, M. (1934) 'A Contribution to the Psycho-genesis of Manic-Depressive States', in *Contributions to Psycho-analysis*. London: Hogarth, 1948.

(1940) 'Mourning: Its Relation to Manic-Depressive States', in *Conributions to Psycho-analysis,* London : Hogarth, 1948.

(1946) 'Notes on Some Schizoid Mechanisms', in *Contributions to Psycho-analysis*. London: Hogarth, 1948.

(1957) *Envy and Gratitude*. London: Tavistock.

8. LEWIN, K. (1935) 'Claustrophobia', in *Psychoanalytic Quarterly,* Vol. 4.

9. ROSENFELD, H. (1958) 'Some Observations on the Psycho-pathology of Hypochondriasis', *I.J.P.A.,* Vol. 39.

(1959) 'An Investigation into the Psycho-analytic Theory of Depression', *I.J.P.A.,* Vol. 40.

(1964) 'The Psycho-pathology of Narcissism: A Clinical Approach', *I.J.P.A.*

10. SEGAL, H. (1954) 'A Note on Schizoid Mechanisms Underlying Phobia Formation', *I.J.P.A.,* Vol. 35.

11. WINNICOTT, D.W. (1956) 'Primary Maternal Preoccupation', in *Collected Papers*. London: Tavistock, 1958.

6   The Complexity of Mental Pain seen in a Six-Year-Old Child Following Sudden Bereavement

This paper is centred round a summary of seven sessions with a six-year-old boy three months after the death of his father. An attempt will be made to indicate from work done in these sessions the complicated nature of the emotions with which he was struggling in his bereavement. Some attention will be given to the confusion which could have opened up the way to a regressive illness, but also to the factors in his personality, his relationship to his external and internal objects which indicated the possibility of working through his mourning without further analytic help. I have used the word 'analytic' advisedly, because the technique used in these sessions was that of following the child's communications, trying to clarify them in the transference, although with a limited number of sessions in view. Some of his material will pinpoint that aspect of mental pain which is heightened by the suffering of the surviving loved objects who share the mourning for the lost person.

Mrs J. consulted me about her son James, at the instigation of a friend of his teacher. She was a plump, small, capable-looking and attractive young woman in her early thirties, white-faced and struggling with strong emotions. In my room she began by saying, 'Ah, the sun at last. I thought it would never shine again'.

She then launched into an account of the troubles she was having with James since her husband's death three months before. She had two sons, Julian and James, aged eight and six respectively. James was more difficult in temperament: forceful, aggressive, intelligent and passionate, very attached to herself. He had not always got on so well with his father because they were too much alike. When father shouted at James, then James shouted back. Between Julian and his father there had been a more peacefully loving relationship and when her husband had died suddenly, she had expected that it would affect Julian much more adversely. On the contrary, Julian had wept and continued to weep a good deal, but it had brought him and his mother much closer together. His grief appeared to be healing; but James, instead of grieving, had become angry, unmanageable and a torment. When told of his father's death he had said to his mother, 'You'll have to get married again at once . . . no, not at once, after my gym display'.

From being affectionate and intimate with his mother he had become touchy and persecuted, could not stand to see her or his brother looking sad and blamed her, saying, 'You are no good! You can't keep people alive'. Julian had asked her in bewilderment, 'What's the matter with James? Why does he always try to make me cry?' 'It's as if Julian and I had to do all his crying for him', she said. At school, which he had formerly enjoyed, both in his work and play with other children, he had now become grumpy and inattentive; he was always picking quarrels with other children. When, after a tantrum with her one day he had broken down and said, 'I'm horrible, but I don't know why', she thought it was time to seek some advice. Mrs J. felt that she would be able to cope eventually with her husband's sudden, tragic and untimely death because theirs had been a very happy marriage, and because she had good friends, were it not for the pain and bewilderment at this unexpected estrangement from James.

We had arranged that she would bring him to me for a few sessions, and that she herself should see a psychiatrist. She would tell James that she was taking him to see a lady who might help him to understand why he felt so horrible ever since his father's death.

James presented himself as a minute, vivid, poised little boy who separated readily from his mother and immediately dived into the open toy drawer on the floor of my room. He rummaged in a purposeful way through its contents, dropped a wax crayon in disgust as if it were dirty saying repeatedly and thoughtfully, 'A lot of toys — no, not so many toys'. After a minute or two I said that he seemed to be looking for something in particular, did he know what it was? 'Yes', he said at once, looked as if he would go on to say what it was, then shook his head as though he could not remember and returned to rummage in the drawer. He stopped once more with a puzzled air. I then asked him if he was looking for daddy? 'Yes', he replied immediately and sat back, looking through me rather than at me.

He then began to talk — an outpouring which continued throughout the rest of the session, with pauses when he would listen intently to what I said to him, thinking hard and then proceeding further. He listened to me as if I were a voice that came from inside him, as if it were of the utmost importance that he should get it straight. Throughout the session a theme recurred: that he was in a muddle and under great pressure to sort out this muddle. I can summarise only what I recalled as the main themes.

He started by saying: 'Yes, my father's dead and I'd like to see him. I don't know where he's gone. Yes I know where he is, he's in heaven'. (This was a typically contradictory statement — part of the muddle.) 'I know he's in heaven and not in hell'. He sat back on the floor, fingering a small pamphlet about the Beatles which he had brought with him to the session, absent mindedly pushing it under the drawer from time to time, and thinking aloud, accepting my comments and queries as further aids to his thoughts, or rather, very muddled outpourings.

Recurrent was his emphasis that father was in heaven, that he did not believe in hell, but wondered what heaven was like. I said that he wanted to believe that his father was somewhere in a good place, happy and not suffering. He agreed with this intensely and then asked me in a rather muddled way whether if you got on a plane to go somewhere — from Paris to London, for example — could someone else who was on the plane somewhere else — say Rome — manage to stop you? I wondered whether he felt the person who might stop him was the dead daddy of whose whereabouts he was uncertain? He repeated again, 'But I know where he is . . . but I would like to see him again . . . sometimes I think I must commit suicide and go to see my father'. I asked him how he thought of doing that. 'With a sharp knife, or get very ill and then die . . .', and then continued further in a muddled and confused way.

I said he seemed to be in a terrible muddle when he thought about daddy, as to what he really felt about him; he didn't want to think of a cross daddy looking down on him, stopping him from doing things and maybe telling him that he must kill himself, that he had no right to stay alive. On the other hand, when he thought of a nice daddy whom he loved, and whom he was afraid had gone to hell, a bad place, he wanted to kill himself in grief. When

91

I said this last, he looked at me full in the face, saying emphatically, 'One thing I know just three words I would like to say . . . "I — loved — him"'.

I suggested he was telling himself this, as well as me, because he felt that it was true but perhaps not all of the truth. Maybe there were times when he did not love daddy? . . . He then said, 'I wish he hadn't shouted at me . . . I shouted back at him'. When I asked him if he thought that his shouting could have made daddy ill, he looked at me very intensely and said, 'When you're little you're very, very strong and when you're old, even if you can shout loud, you get weaker and weaker and then you die'. I underlined the implications of this — he was feeling that although he *knows* he is little, he *feels* that when he is angry he gets big and powerful and with his strong shouts, able to make a big man like daddy disappear.

He then said sadly: 'Sometimes I forget what he looks like . . . I try to think of him and he's not there'. I took up with him his worry about not being able to keep a true picture in his mind of a daddy whom he loved. He said, 'I've got two pictures of him in my room . . . in one of them he's not smiling . . . I don't like that . . . I like the one when he is smiling . . .' I suggested that the not-smiling daddy was the one he was afraid of, the one who would stop him doing things, the one who was angry about being shouted at.

He then said again that he was sure his daddy was in heaven. I asked him what he thought heaven was, what was it like. He began a very confused description, the gist of which was that heaven was full of caves, all dark inside, with little animals in them, and not everybody allowed in them. I suggested that his picture of heaven sounded like his picture of the mysterious night-time daddy and mummy in the dark and in bed, the daddy somewhere in the cave of the night-time mummy's body. He was startled by this, stopped, looked at me accusingly and said, as he looked at the drawer beneath which he was continuing to poke his pamphlet from time to time: 'Your drawer's in a muddle, you should clear it up . . . everyone should clear up their own muddle . . .' He then went on immediately, as if to laugh it off, to tell me about a friend of his; how silly he was, and the muddles he got into; how on one day when somebody was talking about 'Henrietta Barnanaco' (and here James became very tongue-tied) the friend thought they were talking about 'Henrietta Banana', Ha-ha-ha! ... at the same time plainly aware of his own lack of success in putting this over as a joke. I said he felt that I was blaming him for his muddle, and that was why he had to tell me I was in a muddle to say that his friend was the one who was in a muddle — because he felt it so hard to sort out his own. He then said that he was in a muddle, his family was in a muddle ... then, no, that he was not but his family was.

Realising that the unpronounceable name was Henrietta Barnett, the name of a well-known girls' school, I took the friend who called it 'Banana' as himself, who felt to blame for the muddle mummy was in; the school full of children like a mummy with babies inside her, maybe girl babies that would never be born because of daddy's death. I then commented on how he had been pushing this pamphlet in and out beneath the drawer and suggested he was preoccupied with that part of daddy that went in and out of mummy's body in the night ... what did he call it? He told me he called it 'Willie'. I said that he was afraid that in his shouting he put mess and muddle from his willie into daddy's willie, and that he was afraid that not only might it have made daddy become ill and die, but that this mess was also inside mummy. In pushing under my drawer, he was pushing as if with his willie all the mess and muddle of the dead daddy and his feelings about the dead daddy ... (as indeed he was the one who had muddled my drawer) ... so his muddle was in me for me to clear up and he was afraid I could not do it. Likewise he was afraid that mummy would not be able to sort out the muddle the family was in without the help of a live daddy.

Seated on the floor he listened quietly to all this as I was trying to think it out and clarify it step by step with him, and when I had finished he said fervently, 'Sometimes you're not in a muddle ... I don't want to commit suicide ... no, I'll commit suicide with all my family and then we can all be with daddy'. Before he had said this he had begun to push the Beatle pamphlet beneath his own bottom instead of beneath the drawer.

I said that as I was talking he felt that I was really beginning to help him to straighten out his muddles, as if I were a helpful daddy; and that he was taking my words into himself as if into his body, which he was showing by pushing the paper beneath his own bottom. He felt, I said, that he was taking in a kind of helpful

93

daddy that would keep the family together. He then replied, 'I don't talk about bodies, makes me think of blood'.

Just after this it was nearly time to go, which I told him, but said that he could see me the same time next week and we could go on talking. He was rebuffed, and tried to hide it by rapidly saying that he didn't want to come again. He got up and sat in the armchair. I suggested that maybe he was now being daddy telling me what he wanted to arrange; and that his wanting to be the one who made the arrangements might have led to some of the trouble between himself and his daddy when they shouted at each other. 'Yes', said he, 'and that's the trouble with Julian now because he wants to be daddy too'.

At some point in the session when, in relation to his muddle inside and his forgetting of father, I had been trying to clarify the difference between the loss of his father externally and internally, and had used the phrase 'two ways of dying', James had hastily interposed as if to go one better. 'I can think of three ways of dying — dead outside, dead inside, dead both outside and inside . . . there are others, I forget; people told me but I forget'. Here also, I felt, entered that hint of competitiveness, the having to know best, a factor in the shouting matches with his father.

Apparently after this first session, James had started to talk about his father to his mother, to ask for details about his illness, and to say he would like to go and visit his grave. He had spent a much easier week with her and with his brother. He had not wanted to come back to see me the next week, but she had said to him, 'We told Mrs Harris you would be coming and you can't let her down'. 'Oh, no, I can't let her down', he said and turned up for his session quite eagerly.

I do not propose to go into details of the next or of any of the subsequent sessions — seven in all — but intend to pick up some themes which followed on from the first, and which may help to clarify it. During this first session I had hardly seemed to exist for him as an external object until I told him that it was time to go. From the second session onwards it was fairly clear that he had transferred to me, quite strongly, passionate, possessive, infantile feelings accompanied by resentment of separation, together with the hope and expectation of being understood. In the sessions that followed I thought it was important to bear in mind that we had a limited period to work together and to look for an appropriate time to stop.

On his second visit he came upstairs very readily with the air of one revisiting an old friend; sat down on the big chair and after surveying the room in a leisurely fashion, went to the drawer. He looked under the paper and picked out a crayon which he had rejected last time as if it were dirty and said accusingly, 'You were hiding this last week'. He began to draw a picture of large Mrs Harris with a flower by her feet, playing football with an elf, whom he agreed was himself. He said he had some nasty things to tell me about himself, and printed on a piece of paper, 'I am a pig — I am a horror — I am a lizard . . .' When I asked him to tell me more about those parts of himself, he replied the pig part says 'You are a pig' — pointing at me dramatically. When I spelt out this projection with him a little, he then said, 'Julian says "You are a pig"; I'm not guilty'. (His introduction of this word, not mine.) 'Julian is guilty . . . Julian says to me "You will die"'. He then drew a big mouth and teeth, said that this was my mouth; that I put my big mouth into his little one, and made him shout. When I linked this with a frightening dead daddy, he said pathetically, 'I don't sleep very well. I get into a muddle with indside and outside'. We spent a little while trying to clarify how, when he didn't feel able to think about his shouting and his greediness inside himself because it made him feel so badly, it got pushed out into Julian or into his daddy who got back at him in the night-time, — a sort of biting conscience.

In the next session there was some complicated play further illuminated by drawings which seemed to indicated a series of 'tip and run' stinging and kicking attacks, quickly shifted away from or covered over by a flowery joke (a cut up football that became a flower; a funny story about a baby in a pram behind a man reading a newspaper. The baby tore a bit of paper and the man shot up startled, 'Oh, goodness me, I've split my pants'). When I told him that he seemed to be trying to tell me about his baby self attacking from behind from the bottom in various ways, my daddy man who was allowed to find out my news, the daddy who was interested in mummy and in particular the daddy and mummy in the night, he looked at me knowingly and said, 'You mean like these ones?', took a tiger and a lion and made them bite each other, growling furiously.

He continued from there to elaborate expressively the details of a very mutually destructive wild animal parental intercourse, with mounting manic excitement and activity in the room until he tripped up through catching his foot in the armchair into which he had jumped. He looked utterly terrified and claustrophobic for a brief moment, scared of me. I suggested that for a moment I had become a sort of biting daddy inside the night-time mummy who had caught and was just about to eat him up for trespassing. He quietened down, rather thoughtfully, at that, and after a little lay down on the couch saying that he was lazy, that he was being the lizard . . . lazy lizard. The lazy lizard would rather stay at home in bed than go to school where he had to eat nasty greens for his dinner. I said that it was maybe the James who wanted to be the lizard who felt green about being expected to be the outside baby who had to work and learn to make an effort to feed from mummy's breast instead of staying inside and being waited upon. He felt that daddy had with his willie a special way of being able to get into mummy in the night-time, that maybe he was inside her now, like a baby. 'Yes', he said, pensively, 'I'd like to stay inside mummy, but my mummy can't stay at home, she's got to go to work . . .'. Then very sadly, 'My daddy could do hard work. He could pay for things, mend the kitchen draining board and drive the car. I can't do these things and mummy has to do them now . . . mummy will maybe marry again but not this year even if she meets someone. Maybe she will have more babies. After all, the Queen has four babies'. The session ended this way with James thoughtful and pensive but trying, as it were, to raise his spirits.

In the next session — the fourth — he seemed to carry on straight from where he had left off, showing his ambivalence as to the kind of baby he wished on mummy-me in the transference. He produced roguishly from his pocket 'A present for you . . .' (a monkey puppet) '. . . to bite you. It's hungry. It likes human flesh but not grown-up's flesh, children's flesh', turning to bite himself. While I was talking about this puppet monkey as a greedy part of himself which he did not want to own but projected into father's penis, the monkey ran amuck, biting up everything in the room, and finally taking up the original dirty crayon and writing 'pig'. He then settled more quietly to write lists of words and their opposites, stopping reflectively to say, 'My father's not dead, unless my mother's not lying ... Julian says he's not dead'. He became again very confused, and then when I tried to get him to show me what he thought, drew a great, fat, pre-historic animal, called a stegosaurus, coloured brown with huge feet and teeth, said it was a female one and crumpled it up. He rushed on as I tried to describe this as his baby-picture of a fearsome mummy who was filled up with poohs, the debris of the babies and the daddy she had eaten up. I suggested that this picture was one that got in the way of seeing mummy as he really knew her in the world outside — and was what he meant when he said he was afraid his daddy was in hell.

In the fifth session I had to tell him that we could not use the lift (since an edict about this had been issued to all users of the first floor). He chatted brightly about how he preferred the lift, but he'd like to have one that went sideways as well as up and down. Then when I said he was telling me again how he'd like to be the baby living inside mummy, carried all the time, he corrected me saying that, on the contrary, he'd like to be a man and just travel everywhere in a lift.

By this time, I was beginning to feel that we had to consider ending the sessions soon. I knew from the mother that she felt that their former close relationship had been re-established. I thought that a deepening of the transference relationship with me was likely to lead to encouragement of infantile dependence that was bound to get very disappointed if we were not going to embark on a more prolonged period of analytic treatment.

So when, in this session he became involved with a more latency kind of game of schools, in which he became the teacher, giving me sums to do which he then did and corrected with relish, I suggested that it looked as if his enjoyment in school had returned. Perhaps it might be time now for us to think whether he needed to come and see me for many more times. He reacted instantaneously by crashing his paper over my head — an immediate hit back of the blow which he felt that I had given to his head, his baby hopes of remaining forever inside. A little later in the session, however, he returned to the idea spontaneously himself, and said that he felt a little better but he could feel himself much worse. He said that he still said 'pig', forgot that he must not do so because his nana said she would smack him if he did it any more. He then became involved in further manic jokey

97

games about Fanny Craddock-Haddock, which seemed to be about spoiling the food of the breast for the other babies, the children that would follow him and be given food for thought by me. Then at the end of the session, he said very seriously as he left, 'I feel a little better but I'd like to be fully better before I stop. Am I the only child you see here? My mother might not have any more babies . . . she's after all got two mothers — sons, I mean'

In the sixth and penultimate session he was pre-occupied with the question of stopping. I myself never raised the question with him again, but tried to follow his struggles to decide when.

He began by brightly asking for the lift, but then stopped himself, saying that it might be needed for the floors above. As he passed the top of the stairs he sniffed, saying that the smell of cooking was still the same — nice — but added that he'd had a good dinner at school the day before except for the spinach, and made a mock groan as he mentioned that. He then lay on the couch for a few minutes before rousing himself to draw something which he concealed from me until he had finished it. He said it was a man thinking of a house he wanted to buy — could he afford it? James then said he was thinking of how his family would afford to pay for the summer holiday . . . he couldn't do anything about it, but grandpa would, and they would go by aeroplane — adding confidingly '. . . and you know how I like aeroplanes'.

He lay back on the couch again a little later, saying how he loved to be lazy, but once again aroused himself to draw. This time it was a man with a little man inside him, 'a Chinese picture'. The man had eaten the one inside. The man inside was dead, but no, he wasn't really. Then James suddenly burst out 'I'm big because daddy is inside me'. Turning the paper over he drew something which he asked me to guess, said it was Hebrew lettering. When I said it looked like Christ on the Cross, he exclaimed, 'How clever of you to guess!' Under Christ he drew nails like teeth then two angels — a girl angel who was sad at the death of Christ and another one unspecified who was cross instead of sad. He flung down the paper and said, 'Christ was stupid, can I go now?' I said that he wanted to go at once and leave behind all the muddle about the death of daddy that he found so difficult to solve, the muddle about his greediness to take daddy's place, his sadness about this, his loss and his mummy's loss because he knew he could never take daddy's place. Then he felt so badly that he wanted to blame daddy and say that he was stupid for letting himself die . . . Then James started to cut up the picture and talk about what he would take with him and what he could leave behind for me — '. . . leave behind the crossness and take the sadness, leave behind the stupid . . . no just cross out the sadness . . .' He buried his head in his arms and said, 'I'm just too sad about the death of daddy . . . I'd like to come here for ever and ever.' Then pulling himself together he said, 'Next week we'll see what we think . . . I'm better but I want to come till I'm fully better; next week we'll talk and talk'.

Next week in fact we did not talk and talk. It was as if he had left already but had come to see if he could maintain it. He arrived with a snakes and ladders board with which he spent most of the session playing, moving a counter for me and one for him, hoping gleefully always that I would come a cropper but seeing to it that I did not lag to far beind . . . He suddenly said towards the end of the session that he really was feeling better — 'It might be all right'.

Before he left he drew a picture of a rocket going up between the sun and moon colouring the sides of the rocket to merge with the colours of the sun and moon saying that the moon was made of cheese and that the sun was dead although it gave warmth to the earth. He tried to divide the picture to leave one half with me and a half to take with him. He tore it and became upset, undecided whether to take the best bit with him or to leave it with me. He then decided that the torn piece wasn't too bad so I could have it because he needed the good one. He left valiantly but wistfully saying he would really like to go in the lift again, but he wouldn't do so as the people on the second floor might need it.

His mother phoned me later to say that he had told her that he wasn't coming to see Mrs Harris again unless something really big happened. By that I assumed he meant unless she too died; he, in a sense, felt that he had two mothers now and would be able to turn to me again if anything happened to his actual mother.

One is left with a great many questions after work of this kind. It was indeed to me a sort of small bereavement not to pursue the work further with a little boy who was struggling so hard to contain and to comprehend the very big tragedy which had turned his life topsy-turvy.

The work of mourning a loved person takes a long time and while part of it has to be done privately, internally, even in a child, part of it can be done with others who have suffered the same loss — when it is a parent with the other parent if that is possible. The dead parent is both mourned as lost and brought to life in spirit each time he is remembered together by the survivors. The pain of loss co-exists with the sweetness of recollection: awareness of the value of the heritage that has been given enriches the present. Guilt from ambivalence related to infantile possessiveness and omnipotence can interfere with this continual process of recollection and internal reinstatement of the lost object and can perpetuate hidden persecution by the dead person and those who by projection are blamed for the tragedy.

It did seem that in these few sessions James obtained enough relief to begin to sort out his muddle, contain his pain and self-blame sufficiently for his former close and trusting relationship with his mother to be resumed, with the likelihood of their working out in time within their cruelly disrupted little family a way of linking past with present and future possibilities and to be able to continue living hopefully.

If one were to ask what were the factors that interfered with this possibility before James came to see me, the material of his sessions provides a number of possible answers. These are inter-related and incomplete in themselves, probably difficult to weigh in relation to each other but certainly illustrate the complexity of the meaning which the event of his father's death had for him, and the immensity of his struggle in trying to grapple with this meaning. In the work which we did together I was all the time trying to follow his lead and to describe and clarify in terms which he could grasp, thoughts which he was driven to grapple with and which he had inadequate means of expressing.

It is important to consider that this was an event for which he had had no preparation; that he had suffered no previous loss of a person in his life. There were a number of indications that it revived previous 'loss of the breast' experiences (as for example in some material about a football which was really a flower), and indeed many of us would say that our analytic experience has led us to find that every experience of later loss, reactivates this primary part-object one. There was nothing to indicate that for

James this early separation and loss had been a catastrophic one, although incompletely accepted in psychic reality as weaning usually is. In his father's death he was faced with a loss both for himself and his brother, and especially for his mother. His whole family, his world was in a muddle; the normal idealisation of the young child loved by his parents, of their power, everlastingness and security was shattered abruptly.

There was the struggle to grapple with the idea who had done it? Someone must have done it. Did he do it with his shouts? This was an intolerable idea, and so Jamie the pig projected his piggishness and made Julian responsible, and as at depth mothers are responsible for everything he projected the blame into his mother.

In adding to his mother's pain by blaming her he became progressively less able to come close to her and blamed her still more — just as a child who has broken a favourite toy might be compelled to stamp on it and say it was no good anyway. Underlying all was the deep suspicion of a devouring primary object, the stegosaurus, one might say the aboriginal bad breast split off in the course of normal favourable development from the ideal object, but in such a catastrophic situation reawakened and overthrowing the trust in the idealised mother which has been strengthened by the child's many experiences of her attempts to love and care for and understand him. When the most trusted person in the world becomes the most suspect and feared the path is open to quite a serious regressive illness in which the child is in the muddle where there is no clear system of values, no safe place or clear direction.

Some analytic containment and sorting out of confusion, re-establishing James's former trust in his mother, seemed to make it possible for him to tolerate better her pain, and to share in identification with her the grief and the loving memory of his father's qualities. I think that this process was set in motion during the first session when I was trying to clarify with him his fear of the dead daddy as linked with the frightening night-time parents; at the point when instead of pushing (projecting) his pamphlet beneath my drawer, he began to push it under his own bottom, to introject, in the feminine position, a good penis, derived from my reception of his outpourings, and from my words which helped him to organise his emotions and thoughts.

In subsequent sessions expression and clarification of persecutory anxieties seemed to facilitate the process of remembering and internalising his lost object, whilst at the same time helping him to recognise the differences between his father and himself; the fact that he, a child, could never 'make-up' to his mother for the loss of his father's place; a process that involved struggling with the conflict between his crossness and his sadness.

This recognition involved a painful struggle with omnipotence, entailing relinquishing possession, accepting a tragedy too big to be blamed on anyone or to be comprehended; entailing a sorrow for both himself and his mother from which neither could protect the other and which could only be mitigated by each bearing his own private grief and sharing some awareness of the other's state of mind. It was recognition that was bound to be intermittent, but once reached then likely to be attained again and again — an achievement of the depressive position.

James was clearly a child of exceptional intelligence and emotional endowment. It seemed that these sessions — by diminishing confusion and persecution — made it possible for him to begin the work of mourning his father together with his mother and brother — a task that was likely to continue for many a long day. If a lost and loved person is to remain as a good and living memory we have to let ourselves be reminded of him continually in our daily life, to remain open to recollection. The closer and more intertwined the relationship the more frequent, the more painful the reminders, until the very pain becomes cherished as part of the precious internalised object.

But each person remembers at his own pace, and has to face again and again the fact that the person once inextricably woven into his daily life — the constant companion in mind if not in body, of his every activity — no longer exists in the external world. The fact that we shall never see him again, when this can finally be accepted and omnipotent possessiveness relinquished, can drive us to turn inward to make better use of the experiences we had with him when he was alive and thus add a dimension to ongoing experiences of living which comes from identification and dialogue with a loved and admired internalised person who lives on in us.

How *fully* James was, with his mother's help, to establish

within himself his lost father as a source of inspiration and renewal of strength I have no means of knowing. I was hopeful at the end of these sessions that with his mother's help the way was open for a process of internalising, of remembering with love.

The following papers and chapters have helped to nurture the background from which I have though about this case.

BICK, E. (1968) 'The Experience of the Skin in Early Object Relations'. *International Journal of Psychoanalysis,* Vol. 49, pp 484-486.

BION, W.R. (1962) *Learning from Experience*, Chapter 27. London: Heinemann.

FREUD, S. (1917) [1915] 'Mourning and Melancholia'. *Standard Edition,* Vol. 14, pp. 243-258. London: Hogarth and Institute of Psychoanalysis, 1957.

KLEIN, M. (1940) 'Mourning and its Relation to Manic-depressive States' in Klein, M., *Contributions to Psychoanalysis 1921-45*. London: Hogarth Press and Institute of Psycho-analysis, 1948.

MELTZER, D. (1973) 'Psychoanalytical Method and its Theories' in Meltzer, D., *Sexual States of Mind*, Chapter 1, pp. 5-12. Perthshire: Clunie Press.

From the *Journal of Child Psychotherapy*, Vol. 3, 1973.

7   Child Analysis Today

ESTHER BICK, PhD

This Symposium is in the nature of an historical event — it is the first symposium on child analysis at an International Congress of Psycho-Analysis. In May 1927, such a symposium was held before the British Psycho-Analytical Society. On that occasion Melanie Klein contrasted the development of child analysis with that of adult analysis, discussing the striking fact that although child analysis had a history of about eighteen years, its fundamental principles had not yet been clearly enunciated, whereas, after a similar period in the history of adult analysis, the basic principles had been laid down, empirically tested, and the fundamental principles of technique firmly established. She went on to discuss why the analysis of children had been so much less fortunate in its development.

I am well aware that progress has been made during the last thirty-four years, both in actual child analysis and in its allied fields, such as in Child Guidance Clinics, progress which has been deeply and variously influenced by the work of Melanie Klein and Anna Freud. To give examples, the range of children who are felt to be suitable for treatment has been extended: play technique is now in general use, though often in a modified form; the importance of interpretations has been widely accepted, and there is a greater recognition of the pyscho-analytic approach in the training of child psychotherapists and child psychiatrists.

However, if we examine the position of child analysis in relation to the whole field of psycho-analysis, we see what a small place it occupies, in terms of practice of child analysis, of training, of scientific discussions and publications. Very few people trained in adult analysis go on to train as child analysts, and very few institutes of psycho-analysis are able to offer systematic training in child analysis, the British Institute being the only one, I believe, to give an actual qualification. Even this training is recognized to be inadequate. Contributions from child analysts to scientific discussions are numerically very low — for example, less than 5% of papers at International Congress are on child cases.

This neglect of child analysis is the more striking when we

consider the vital interest of analysts in the psychology of children as a source of understanding of emotional development and our concern about the prophylactic aspects of child analysis. The position of psycho-analysis in the community must also to a great extent depend on its offering help to children and its understanding of their emotional problems.

There must, therefore, be specific difficulties interfering with the development of child analysis which do not apply to the same extent to adult analysis. In this paper I shall attempt to contribute to the understanding of this problem. In order to do so, I shall discuss some of the differences between analysing adults and analysing children, from the point of view both of the student and of the practising analyst. I shall discuss the stresses and gratifications, both external and internal.

First, to consider some of the external stresses: the student who is embarking on child analysis may be restricted owing to commitments related to his training in adult analysis, both financially and with regard to the times he has available, which may not suit the child's parents. There is also the difficulty for the student that the ordinary parent will only undertake to bring the child five times a week over a period of years if the child is severely ill, and such cases are not suitable for the beginner in child analysis.

An analyst wanting to restrict himself to child analysis would find it unrewarding financially. Certain aspects of child analysis, such as keeping in contact with the parents and caring for the play-room, can be very time consuming. These are real difficulties, but they can be used as rationalizations to cover up the emotional problems of studying and practising child analysis.

Before discussing the emotional stresses, however, it is important to remember the pleasures and gratifications arising out of child analysis, such as the unique opportunity for intimate contact with primitive layers of the child's unconscious mind; the sense of privilege in being entrusted by the parents with their child; the awareness that one is dealing with a human being who has almost all his life ahead of him and who is still in the early stages of developing his potentialities.

I want now to turn to the internal stresses, and shall divide these into two categories: first, those which are in the nature of pre-formed anxieties related to the treatment of children as such,

105

and second, the specific counter-transference problems. In the first category there are the student's general anxieties about his ability to communicate with children, especially if he has had little or no previous experience with young children. There are also the anxieties about taking responsibility. These are much greater with children than with adults, not only because it is a dual responsibility — to the child as well as to his parents — but also because the less mature the patient's ego, the greater is the responsibility resting on the analyst.

The student has to be clear about what his responsibility is in analysing the child, although this may clash with what he feels the parents really want of him. Here belongs, for example the responsibility of analysing such problems as the child's hostility and his sexual wishes towards the parents. This may provoke anxiety in the student concerning his relation with the parents. Closely associated with this is the question of setting independently, on the basis of one's clinical judgement, aims for the analysis, as distinct from aiming to cure the presenting symptoms for which the child was originally brought for treatment. There are also anxieties related to becoming excessively attached to, or hurtful to, the child. The former anxiety may lead to greater strictness, to a type of behaviour which interferes with the unfolding of the positive transference. The latter anxiety may lead to reassurance, to a denial of the child's hostile feelings and persecutory anxiety, or to such behaviour as appealing to the child's reason — suggesting that the analyst has been unable to accept painful analytical responsibility and has assumed the role of parent substitute.

Such anxieties, related to the painful aspects of responsibility, may be kept within bounds and often diminished through the help of a supervisor who shares the responsibility. But if they are too severe, they can impose such grave limitations on therapeutic effectiveness that supervision can be of little or no help and only further analysis can enable the student to overcome the inhibiting unconscious conflicts. Such anxieties approximate to those of the second category, the stresses arising out of counter-transference phenomena.

As Freud stated in 1910: 'We have become aware of the counter-transference, which arises in him (the physician) as a result of the patient's influence on his unconscious feelings . . .

We have noticed that no psycho-analyst goes further than his own complexes and internal resistances permit'. I have suggested that the counter-transference stresses on the child analyst are more severe than those on the analyst of adults, at any rate of non-psychotic adults. This is due, I think, to two specific factors: first, the unconscious conflicts which arise in relation to the child's parents; and second, the nature of the child's material.

With regard to the first factor, the child analyst has the constant problem of his unconscious identifications. He may identify with the child against the parents, or with the parents against the child, or with a protective parental attitude towards the child. These conflicts often lead to a persecutory and guilty attitude towards the parents, making the analyst over-critical of them and over-dependent on their approval. In addition, there is the student's difficulty in understanding the twofold nature of the child's relationship to his parents: his normal and healthy dependence on them, relative to his age, and the infantile elements in the relationship, due to his internal difficulties. The more this is recognized and accepted by the student, the more the infantile parts of the child can come into the transference, with a resulting improvement in his relationship to his parents, even in the early months of analysis. The student can then foresee and be prepared for the risk that the parents will lose sight of the child's illness and want to stop treatment, and for an intensification of difficulties at home during analytic holidays.

I cannot go into the many vicissitudes of the analyst's difficulties in his relationship with the parents. It is an integral part of his work, intricate and delicate to handle, needing flexibility and considerable confidence in child analysis in general and one's own work in particular. If one can take these things for granted, the relationship with many parents can become an added source of gratification.

The second specific factor in child analysis concerns the strain imposed on the mental apparatus of the analyst, both by the content of the child's material and its mode of expression. The intensity of the child's dependence, of his positive and negative transference, the primitive nature of his phantasies, tend to arouse the analyst's own unconscious anxieties. The violent and concrete projections of the child into the analyst may be difficult to contain. Also the child's suffering tends to evoke the analyst's

107

parental feelings, which have to be controlled so that the proper analytic role can be maintained. All these problems tend to obscure the analyst's understanding and to increase in turn his anxiety and guilt about his work.

Moreover, the child's material may be more difficult to understand than the adult's, since it is more primitive in its sources as well as in its mode of expression, and requires a deeper knowledge of the primitive levels of the unconscious. One may have to sit with children for a long time completely in the dark about what is going on, until suddenly something comes up from the depth that illuminates it, and one interprets without always being able to see how one reached that conclusion. It imposes on the child analyst a greater dependence on his unconscious to provide him with clues to the meaning of the child's play and non-verbal communications.

I will bring two clinical examples to illustrate some of the points I have made. The first concerns a case of my own, the second, one of an analyst supervised by me. I am giving an instance from a first session of a nine-year-old boy, referred on account of bed wetting, shyness, and clinging to his mother. He came into the treatment room with me and stood twisting his cap and blushing. I pointed out that he might feel awkward because he might not know what we were going to do here. There was no response. I showed him his box with play material and said that was for his use in the sessions. He made no movement but stood there as if dazed. I said that he had been told that he would be coming to see me five times a week, and that I would try to help him with his worries; but it seemed to me that he expected something quite different which he was not able to tell me or might not even know himself. He continued his silence and immobility, but looked tense and troubled. Then he glanced towards the paper on the table. I said that he indicated he would find it easier to tell me something on paper than to talk. He nodded, sat down, and drew a hut on the mountains, a path, and a tree. When I asked him about this, he told me it was about a young man who lived alone in a log cabin in the mountains. He had a deer who kept him company. One night a man came and stole the deer. When the young man woke in the morning he could not find the deer. He went out of the cabin and saw the tracks of a man and of his deer in the snow. He followed the tracks. He was afraid that the man might kill him, but he went on. He told me this story in a solemn, dull way. I said that there was a Christmas tree in the drawing, and that in this way he was telling me one of the things he expected from me: that I should be like Father Christmas who would make everything wonderful, and that perhaps he had waited for the analysis as he had waited for Father Christmas as a small boy. He smiled, his whole face lit up, and he said: 'Fancy you should say that! This morning a boy at school asked me if a fairy told me I could have three wishes what would I want.'

I interpreted that we could now understand why he could not speak at the beginning of the session. On the one hand he hoped that he would find in me a fairy capable of fulfilling all his wishes in a magic way; at the same time he was afraid that I might be a witch who would cast a spell on him and immobilize him; it seemed that he had felt this when he could neither move nor speak at the beginning of the session. In the story there were two male figures: one was Father Christmas, and the other the man who stole his deer and might kill him. So as with the fairy and the witch he also hoped that I might be a father who, like Father Christmas, would give him what he wanted most — to keep his deer forever. But he was also afraid that I might be like the man who would steal it from him. Such were his hopes and fears before he came, and when he met me, he did not know which of the figures I was. Although he was very frightened, he came with me into the room, perhaps thinking that if he did what I wanted, I would not harm him; and also because he so much wanted help in tracking down his worries and becoming cured.

He said, 'Yes, I didn't tell the boy that my wish would be to be cured from bed wetting, I can't do anything, I can't go camping with the Scouts. I can't stop it.' We then went on to the other important meanings of the deer.

What can be seen in this boy, as in many other young patients, is that, together with the hope of finding a solution to his internal problems, there is also a deep pessimism about being understood by the adult world. This can be seen clearly in the boy's excitement when he exclaimed, 'Fancy you should say that!'.

My second example is taken from the first session of a three-year-old girl. She followed the analyst stiffly but easily into the play-room. He told her that the toys on the table and in the drawer were for her to play with. She looked into the drawer, took out a toy sheep, sat down and began to handle the pencil. The analyst asked whether it was a mummy, a daddy, or a baby sheep; but this made her increasingly withdrawn. She began to rock and suck a sweet she had in her mouth. The analyst interpreted her feeling of being alone and frightened and her wish to be with her Mummy, and linked it with her feeling at night and a wish to snuggle up and have her bottle with Mummy. Her head dropped, there was some play with her fingers of the 'little piggy' type. The analyst indicated to her her wish for Mummy's soft breast to sleep on. Her head dropped and hit the table. The analyst put a pillow there. Her head drooped backwards, and he put the pillow behind her, but she systematically avoided it. He interpreted that the pillow was unable to replace Mummy's breast, and her similar discomfort and dis-satisfaction with the analyst. There was some rubbing of eyes, scratching of the face, and picking of the nose. The analyst interpreted her disappointment in having a man as an analyst and suggested she had hoped to have a woman, like her brother who was also in analysis. He also indicated it was about time to stop. She gave the sheep back to him, looked at him, and seemed in fair contact with him before leaving. In the following session there was a marked change in the nature of the contact with the analyst. She produced rich detailed material in which her anxieties about the transference to him as the brother came to the fore.

We see in the opening session with the little girl how what seemed to be very sparse material became richer and more detailed following interpretations; whereas in the case of the older boy, material rich in detail but impoverished of emotion became flooded with feeling and contact through interpretation. In both cases the interpretations were based initially on the analyst's intuitive response to the situation growing out of the pre-verbal projective process from the child's unconscious into the analyst. In the case of the little girl, the sleeping and the near falling had the effect of projecting into the analyst considerable anxiety for her safety, which he actually dealt with by providing her with a real pillow. Her systematic avoidance of the pillow increased his feeling of hopelessness to protect her. These two projections worked together: 'I cannot help this child; in fact I will damage her because I have not got the right kind of pillow'. It was not until the interpretation of her disappointment in the analyst as a man, without real breasts, that she came into contact with the analyst on leaving and produced the enriched material of the next day, expressing her anxiety of repeating with the analyst her sexual involvement with her brother.

In the case of the boy, he conveyed from the beginning his distress through his non-verbal behaviour. The analyst's anxiety led her to give explanations about the analytic procedure. In this situation, these were tantamount to reassurance and therefore made no contact with the child. Following his glance, the analyst invited him to draw. The picture and the story were produced flatly, lifelessly, although the story in itself seemed vital and filled with anxiety. The analyst felt that the hopelessness which he projected into her, both at the beginning of the session and through his lifeless dull way of telling the story, came from a more primitive level than the oedipal material. She reacted to the Christmas tree as representing a far deeper process of splitting his objects into ideally good and dreadfully persecuting ones, with their magic powers for good or evil. She was able to make contact with his primitive internal world of witches and fairies, and in this way to reach the split-off affects of hope for an omnipotent good object.

Thus with both children, following leads from the depths arising from the taking in of projected distress, the analysts were able to interpret into the deeper strata. In the case of the little girl, with regard to her expectations of a real breast to sleep on and suck; in the case of the boy, the hope for an omnipotent fairy to protect him against persecutors.

In addition to the ability to deal with the kind of material that the child spontaneously produces and to bear his concrete projections, there is the difficulty of allowing the child to experience pain without intruding in a non-analytic way. The strain in bearing the child's suffering is greater than with adults, not only because of the child's weaker ego, but because of his appeal to one's parental feelings. This is painful when the child is persecuted or crying, but particularly so when he is trying to be good and repair, but cannot manage it because of internal conflicts. A little girl broke most of the toy figures following the first holiday in the analysis. After some working through of her holiday feelings, she decided to mend the mother figure of which she had broken the head and an arm. She managed with difficulty to stick

111

the head on with Plasticine, but was very clumsy in fixing the arm. It kept falling off. She was very distressed, but persevered for a long time. Eventually she said, pointing to the figure, 'She is tired', and gave up. In such a situation the child analyst may find great difficulty in resisting the mute appeal of the child for direct help.

My comments on the internal stresses of the child analyst can perhaps be best summarized by a quotation for Gitelson's paper (2) 'The Emotional Position of the Analyst in the Psycho-Analytic Situation'. After quoting Freud's original definition of transference, he goes on to say: 'If the transference is to be a truly irrational recapitulation of childhood relationships subject to psycho-analytic interpretation, then nothing in the current reality must intervene to give it concurrent validity. These are still the guiding principles of classical psycho-analytic technique'. This quotation refers to adult analysis, Klein was guided by the same principle of classical psycho-analytic technique in her work with children. She showed that in order to do this the child analyst has to provide an analytic setting, both external and within himself, to enable the child to re-experience the irrational infantile and childhood relationships. I have tried to show that it is easier to accept the external setting which Klein evolved in her play technique than to accept and tolerate the stress produced by adhering to the fundamental psycho-analytic attitude in work with child patients.

The student of child analysis is thus exposed to great anxieties. It is, therefore, important that he should do the child training while he is himself in analysis; and, indeed, the working over of these anxieties will help to deepen his analysis. I have found that analysis of children brings a greater conviction to the student about the reality of unconscious phantasy than his work with adults. To see this concretely presented in the child's play and in his spontaneous communications, and to see the immediacy of relief from, or change in the nature of, anxiety following prompt interpretations, constitutes in itself an unending source of wonder and delight to many child analysts.

In conclusion, the aim of this paper is to draw attention to the grave neglect of child analysis. I have singled out two factors responsible for its slow development: the external stresses associated with financial and time difficulties, constantly exacerbated by the lack of adequate training, and the manifold internal stresses which are an integral part of the nature of child analysis. I have also indicated the gratifications inherent in analysing children and have stressed the importance of further developing this work, both in terms of its value to psycho-analytic understanding in general and in its contribution to the community.

REFERENCES

1. FREUD, S. (1910). 'The Future Prospects of Psycho-Analytic Therapy'. *Standard Edition* 11.
2. GITELSON, MAXWELL (1949). 'The Emotional Position of the Analyst in the Psycho-Analytic Situation'. *Int. J. Psycho-Anal.,* 33.
3. KLEIN, MELANIE (1927). 'Symposium on Child Analysis'. In: *Contributions to Psycho-Analysis,* 1921-1945. London: Hogarth, 1948.
4. —*The Psycho-Analysis of Children.* London: Hogarth, 1932.

Read at the 22nd International Psycho-Analytical Congress, Edinburgh, July — August, 1961.

8   The Experience of the Skin in Early Object-Relations

ESTHER BICK, PhD

The central theme of this brief communication is concerned with the primal function of the skin of the baby and of its primal objects in relation to the most primitive binding together of parts of the personality not as yet differentiated from parts of the body. It can be most readily studied in psychoanalysis in relation to problems of dependence and separation in the transference.

The thesis is that in its most primitive form the parts of the personality are felt to have no binding force amongst themselves and must therefore be held together in a way that is experienced by them passively, by the skin functioning as a boundary. But this internal function of containing the parts of the self is dependent initially on the introjection of an external object, experienced as capable of fulfilling this function. Later, identification with this function of the object supersedes the unintegrated state and gives rise to the fantasy of internal and external spaces. Only then the stage is set for the operation of primal splitting and idealization of self and object as described by Melanie Klein. Until the containing functions have been introjected, the concept of a space within the self cannot arise. Introjection, i.e. construction of an object in an internal space is therefore impaired. In its absence, the function of projective identification will necessarily continue unabated and all the confusions of identity attending it will be manifest.

The stage of primal splitting and idealization of self and object can now be seen to rest on this earlier process of containment of self and object by their respective 'skins'.

The fluctuations in this primal state will be illustrated in case material, from infant observation, in order to show the difference between unintegration as a passive experience of total helplessness, and disintegration through splitting processes as an active defensive operation in the service of development. We are, therefore, from the economic point of view, dealing with situations conducive to catastrophic anxieties in the unintegrated state as compared with the more limited and specific persecutory and depressive ones.

114

The need for a containing object would seem, in the infantile unintegrated state, to produce a frantic search for an object — a light, a voice, a smell, or other sensual object — which can hold the attention and thereby be experienced, momentarily at least, as holding the parts of the personality together. The optimal object is the nipple in the mouth, together with the holding and talking and familiar smelling mother.

Material will show how this containing object is experienced concretely as a skin. Faulty development of this primal skin function can be seen to result either from defects in the adequacy of the actual object or from fantasy attacks on it, which impair introjection. Disturbance in the primal skin function can lead to a development of a 'second-skin' formation through which dependence on the object is replaced by a pseudo-independence, by the inappropriate use of certain mental functions, or perhaps innate talents, for the purpose of creating a substitute for this skin container function. The material to follow will give some examples of 'second-skin' formation.

Here I can only indicate the types of clinical material upon which these findings are based. My present aim is to open up this topic for a detailed discussion in a later paper.

Infant Observation: Baby Alice

One year of observation of an immature young mother and her first baby showed a gradual improvement in the 'skin-container' function up to twelve weeks. As the mother's tolerance to closeness to the baby increased, so did her need to excite the baby to manifestations of vitality lessen. A consequent diminution of unintegrated states in the baby could be observed. These had been characterized by trembling, sneezing, and disorganised movements. There followed a move to a new house in a still unfinished condition. This disturbed severely the mother's holding capacity and led her to a withdrawal from the baby. She began feeding whilst watching television, or at night in the dark without holding the baby. This brought a flood of somatic disturbance and an increase of unintegrated states in the baby. Father's illness at that time made matters worse and the mother had to plan to return to work. She began to press the baby into a pseudo-independence, forcing her onto a training-cup, introducing a bouncer during the day, whilst harshly refusing to respond to the crying at night. The mother now returned to an earlier tendency to stimulate the child to aggressive displays which she provoked and admired. The result by six-and-a-half months was a hyper-active and aggressive little girl, whom her mother called 'a boxer' from her habit of pummelling people's faces. We see here the formation of a muscular type of self-containment — 'second-skin' in place of a proper skin container.

Analysis of a Schizophrenic Girl: Mary

Some years of analysis, since age 3 ½ , have enabled us to recon-struct the mental states reflected in the history of her infantile disturbance. The facts are as follows: a difficult birth, early clenching of the nipple but lazy feeding, bottle supplement in the third week but on breast until 11 months, infantile eczema at 4 months and scratching until bleeding, extreme clinging to mother, severe intolerance to waiting for feeds, delayed and atypical development in all areas.

In the analysis, severe intolerance to separation was reflected from the start as in the jaw-clenched systematic tearing and breaking of all materials after the first holiday-break. Utter dependence on the immediate contact could be seen and studied in the unintegrated states of posture and motility on the one hand, and thought and communication on the other, which existed at the beginning of each session, improving during the course, to reappear on leaving. She came in hunched, stiff-jointed, grotesque like a 'sack of potatoes' as she later called herself, and emitting an explosive 'SSBICK' for 'Good morn-ing, Mrs Bick'. This 'sack of potatoes' seemed in constant danger of spilling out its contents partly due to the continual picking of holes in her skin representing the 'sack' skin of the object in which parts of herself, the 'potatoes', were contained (projective identification). Improvement from the hunched posture to an erect one was achieved, along with a lessening of her general total dependence, more through a formation of a second skin based on her own muscularity than on identification with a containing object.

Analysis of an Adult Neurotic Patient

The alternation of two types of experience of self — the 'sack of apples' and 'the hippopotamus' — could be studied in regard to quality of contact in the transference and experience of separation, both being related to a disturbed feeding period. In the 'sack of apples' state, the patient was touchy, vain, in need of constant attention and praise, easily bruised and constantly expecting catastrophe, such as a collapse when getting up from the couch. In the 'hippopotamus' state, the patient was aggressive, tyrannical, scathing, and relentless in following his own way. Both states were related to the 'second-skin' type of organization, dominated by projective identification. The 'hippopotamus' skin, like the 'sack' were a reflection of the object's skin inside which he existed, whilst the thin-skinned, easily bruised, apples inside the sack, represented that state of parts of the self which were inside this insensitive object.

Analysis of a Child: Jill

Early in the analysis of a 5-year-old child, whose feeding period had been characterized by anorexia, skin-container problems presented themselves, as in her constant demand from mother during the first analytic holiday, that her clothes should be firmly fastened, her shoes tightly laced. Later material showed her intense anxiety and need to distinguish herself from toys and dolls, about which she said: 'Toys are not like me, they break to pieces and don't get well. They don't have a skin. We have a skin!'

Summary

In all patients with disturbed first-skin formation, severe disturbance of the feeding period is indicated by analytic reconstruction, though not always observed by the parents. This faulty skin-formation produces a general fragility in later integration and organizations. It manifests itself in states of unintegration as distinct from regression involving the most basic types of partial or total, unintegration of body, posture, motility, and corresponding functions of mind, particularly communication. The 'second-skin' phenomenon which replaces first skin

117

integration, manifests itself as either partial or total type of muscular shell or a corresponding verbal muscularity.

Analytic investigation of the second skin phenomenon tends to produce transitory states of unintegration. Only an analysis which perseveres to thorough working-through of the primal dependence on the maternal object can strengthen this underlying fragility. It must be stressed that the containing aspect of the analytic situation resides especially in the setting and is therefore an area where firmness of technique is crucial.

Read at the 25th International Psycho-Analytical Congress, Copenhagen, July 1967.

Section II

PAPERS ON CHILD DEVELOPMENT AND THE FAMILY

1   Infantile Elements and Adult Strivings in Adolescent Sexuality

When I came to write this paper I soon realised that its focus would have to be a much narrower one than the title allows. I also found that I was returning over and over again to analytic material from a fairly wide range of gifted adolescents who, as the world goes, were more than usually fortunate in their external circumstances, young people who from any external point of view might seem to have everything in their favour but who nevertheless seemed quite unable to enjoy their good fortune.

In all of them there existed a deep sense of unworthiness together with the quite opposite conviction of being special. There was evidence to suggest that they were regarded by one or both of their parents as special, and that they expected this treatment from the rest of the world although when it was forthcoming they could not use it to assuage their discontent. One could think of them as young people who were in the painful position of having to learn that their appearance, intelligence, emotional endowment, and social position were not evidence of innate superiority but gifts which had to be earned by carrying them and treating them as a responsibility. Difficulty in learning this showed itself clearly in their sexual attitudes and behaviour.

Defensive structures that had served them well in latency and had allowed them to have a successful and fairly untroubled development at that time, made them particularly vulnerable to the intense sexual drives and frustrations of adolescence. They tended to have difficulty in being one of the adolescent group and in using it to share experiences with peers, thereby working their way towards more adult relationships; they were impatient to leap right into the world of the grown-ups and to that 'happy ever after' which is the young child's idea of marriage.

Theoretical background

It is not possible or useful to try to present anything like a comprehensive summary of the many publications about adolescent sexuality. I shall confine myself to brief references to those which have helped me in my thinking about these cases and in particular to the two to whom I shall then refer.

Freud, as I understand him, saw sexuality in general as dominated by the pleasure principle — the ego seeking a homeostatic solution through gratification and the avoidance of pain (1911). His differentiation between adult and infantile was basically a zonal one, i.e. progression from oral through anal and phallic to genital primacy with eventually the pregenital elements confined to foreplay (1905). This was later amplified by Abraham to include the progress through ambivalence and part-object relations to a non-ambivalent whole object love.

Stemming from her work with children Melanie Klein was able to amplify the economic concepts of pleasure and reality principle to include the shift in values in the progression from narcissism to object relations (from the paranoid-schizoid to the depressive position). This gave body to the concept of the resolution of ambivalence when consideration for the welfare of the beloved object enables the child to struggle with its greed and self-interest in order to spare that object (1939). She regarded development as greatly influenced by the epistemophilic instinct and saw the infant as growing through a process of projection and introjection, through interaction with the object, in the first place the body and personality of the mother. She saw the foundation of the capacity for pleasure as being laid in that first relationship with the world; the origin of satisfactory sexuality in an enjoyable relationship with the breast; the capacity for pleasure between penis and vagina as rooted in prototype pleasure between nipple and mouth.

This led on to Bion's theories of the 'container and contained' (1962 and 1970); of the integral part which maternal reverie plays in the development of the infant and of growth proceeding through mind to mind as well as body to body contact.

Melanie Klein's delineation of splitting processes (1946) gave firmness to Freud's structural theory — of ego, id and superego — and has led to developments such as Esther Bick's investigation of ego strength (of skin and second skin as functions of the personality) (1968) and to Meltzer's delineation of the adult and infantile structures of the personality (1972).

These concepts seem to me to be central to understanding the modal position of adolescence in the transition from life in the family to life in the world. Adolescence may be seen as a period during which the containing function of the family disappears and has to be replaced externally and eventually internally in the personality, when the young person has to proceed through a disintegration to a new integration as an independent adult. During the transition the adolescent group may be seen as performing a second skin holding function. It is a period when all the old infantile conflicts have to be worked over again in the light of new intense genital drives which test the quality of the internalisation of previous object-relations and identifications.

These concepts imply that the development of sexuality is inextricably bound up with character formation and identification processes and that the adult character is different from the infantile structures of the personality. The latter tend to retreat under stress to the paranoid-schizoid position, dominated by self interest and the impulse to avoid pain. The sexuality of those structures is propelled by jealousy, envy, greed and competition for the pleasures which the child believes the parents enjoy and which are denied to him. It tends to be accompanied by a sense of grievance based on lack of recognition of limited capacity.

These infantile elements are markedly obvious in adolescence but do of course persist into grown-up life and are to a greater or lesser degree operative in us all. They are characteristic of what Melanie Klein termed the paranoid-schizoid position: a state of mind in which self-preservation, egocentricity and narcissism take precedence over love and gratitude to good objects. The adult strivings in the personality begin already in infancy, to varying degrees; when the child begins to be able to attain, however fleetingly, the depressive position; a state of mind in which he is able to introject and identify himself with the parental capacity for concern, based upon his gratitude for care that he has received. This implies an attempt to assume some degree of psychic responsibility for his own emotions and attitudes to his objects and to limit the demands that he makes upon them.

In *Sexual States of Mind* (1972) Meltzer spells out the implications of Melanie Klein's theory of the depressive position for understanding the difference between adult and infantile sexuality. He describes how the development of adult sexual attitudes is linked with character development. Infantile sexuality is essentially concerned with getting pleasure and gratification in omnipotent ways, by bodily manipulation or phantasy. It is characterised by the child projecting himself into the phantasied secret relationship of the parents (the primal scene), in various ways, and with varying degrees of illwill and non-acceptance of the fact that he has to wait to be grown-up, and that being grown-up means carrying responsibilities, notably babies, as well as enjoying power and privilege.

He delineates the elements of perversity present to a greater or lesser extent in most infantile sexuality, which derive from a fundamentally narcissistic organisation of parts of the self that are set up against the creative union of the parental couple. This organisation has its inception when the combination of rectum, anus and faeces is set up in competition with the combination of nipple and breast which produce milk for the baby's mouth, and at a later level is set up against the union of penis and vagina which make the baby in parental intercourse. So according to him the core of this perversity is anal negativism.

A central problem in the analysis of adolescents is the teasing out of infantile and perverse elements which hamper the striving towards more adult responsible relationships and which tend to divert development into some cul-de-sac or another. These are usually at the heart of the matter in the case of those gifted adolescents who are not fulfilling their promise or who are unable to enjoy their success.

I shall now present some material from the analyses of two young people in this category.

Rosamund

Rosamund, aged eighteen-and-a-half, came to London to have analysis with me during the year between leaving school and taking up her university place in a town at a distance which would have precluded the possibility of travel. In her last summer holiday from school when travelling abroad with a group of young people she had fallen in love with a young musician a few years older than herself. Not until she had become thoroughly involved with him did she find that he was engaged and that he had no intention of breaking off his engagement. This did not prevent them from having a somewhat idyllic relationship with each other for the rest of the summer.

On her return to school, however, she had drifted away from her former close friends and from her work and had gradually given up eating. She had become imperceptibly thinner until after a term her teachers had realised with a shock the gravity of the situation when she returned home for the holidays. Some consultations with an analyst over a period of time enabled her to work again, to pass her university entrance and to resume eating to a degree that allowed her to keep body and soul together. Anorexia remained an ever-present threat and it was arranged that she have this period of analysis before proceeding to university.

When I first saw Rosamund I was struck by her beauty and an elegance that transformed the usual adolescent uniform of jeans and cotton top into the garb of a young lady of quality. Although extremely thin she did not look emaciated and her facial expression though basically rather depressed in a gentle way could change rapidly and light up responsively. She became eagerly and quickly involved in the analysis propelled by her awareness of the shortness of the time available. Problems of eating occupied her initially, their link with her wonderful summer holiday and her puzzlement at intimations of areas of her personality that were a closed book to her.

By the time she started analysis it was no longer a question of not wanting food or friends but of overcoming something which forbade her to eat and which hindered her in her social approaches. Once she began to eat she was afraid that she might have difficulty in stopping if she did not supervise herself carefully. She would be visited by longing for sweet things like cream buns and stodgy foods and was fascinated by recipes which she would read in the bathroom. She would pick at tempting food in the refrigerator although she could resist it when she was offered it in company at table.

She was puzzled that with her anorexia had arisen an unfamiliar problem of jealousy of the brother rather less than eighteen months younger that herself. She could not remember this as a feature of her childhood at all and could recall only many occasions in which she was enjoying helping her mother to look after him.

In short what she seemed to be indicating in these first sessions was that her love affair had evoked in her an upsurge of baby feelings of greed and possessiveness from which disappointment and wounded pride had made her cut herself off drastically. The analytic consultations she had had, and the eagerness to have more of the same kind of talking when she started work with me were threatening her with a greed that she was now more aware of, but struggling to resist. Interpretations linking her enthusiasm for knowledge and for sexual experience with a fundamentally baby greed for the source of food and knowledge, the breast, were accepted by her instantly. She said she was just beginning to realise how possessive she was; when she baked a cake for the whole family it was still her cake. She wanted them to have it but not until she said so.

This was some indication of how she was controlling her internal family, of how, in apparently supervising her own eating she was supervising her internal objects, her internal family. The cake, the breast, was hers and so she would say who should have it, when, and how much. She had retreated from the adolescent world of competition and struggling relationships to the position of a young matron. That this position of elegant young mistress of the household was achieved by projection into the breast by way of the anus was indicated by the addiction to recipes in the bathroom and the picking of bits of food in the refrigerator.

This became clearer to her when she started to have dreams some three weeks after beginning her analysis. I shall now discuss a few of these dreams, using them to indicate the focus of the work upon which we are engaged during the relatively short period of her analysis.

Following her first week-end back home she came with two dreams. The first was as follows: *There was a white cat in her back garden. It said 'hello' to her which did not surprise her in the slightest but her family and friends were around exclaiming in admiration and saying how clever it was of little Rosie to teach it to talk. They had never heard the like of that before.* This dream was followed by another on the same night: *Rosamund was piloting an aeroplane which was flying to the top of some very high buildings. It was terribly exciting going up and up but she was afraid that it might fall on its tail.*

In the talking cat dream we have the adolescent's craving for admiration, but as in this dream she apparently was also sometimes a little girl and moreover the cat was a pet of early childhood, this dream seems to be about the baby who goes to her own backgarden (her bottom) and fills the pussy cat breast with her clever noises. The intense involvement in this talking analysis, reactivates at depth, as a defence against separation and emotions attendant upon that, an omnipotent anal projective identification into a breast that then becomes her pupil, her baby, while she is the clever one who is teaching it. One could easily see how Rosamund's beauty and quick intelligence were likely in infancy and later to evoke the kind of admiration that would lend credence to this phantasy.

In the second dream the identification seems to be more with father's penis (he had in fact been a pilot during the war), but a precarious identification with a faecal penis. She may flop on to her tail and find that she is just the baby who has been messing its nappy.

Following this dream there emerged further material about her identifications with her father and her brother and the history of the importance of talking to her. Both her father and her brother were apparently talkative,. entertaining, outgoing people. When Rosamund went to boarding school at the age of eleven and had felt homesick she managed to hide this from her companions and then eventually from herself by becoming very chatty and entertaining, a role which she has maintained with great success until in adolescence it had begun to wear a little thin. So this had seemed to be a way of avoiding emotional conflict by slipping into projective identification with her rival object, by becoming it; a way of evading the unresolved infantile conflict about giving up mother and allowing her to be with father or brother, by becoming them.

I shall now report a dream which she had a little later, which is somewhat of a corrective to these two although still a little manic and elated: *Rosamund was going back to school with her two best friends. The younger children were whispering and admiring them while some man was presenting the prizes to those who had left and who had done well. When it was her turn he stopped to make a speech and to give her a specially bound volume of poetry which she had apparently written herself, something like Wordsworth. She then became terribly distressed and tried to say that it was all a mistake and she was not the author. Then when she looked inside the book she recognised some of her words, so the poetry did bear some relation to what she said, had in fact been created out of her statements. She then accepted the prize, trying to persuade herself that she was not a total fraud.*

So here we have the adolescent going back to school hungry for admiration from the younger children, to receive the prize from daddy, praise for her own products, her analytic cookery as it were. There is, however, some truth in it, some recognition of the nature of the analytic work (the 'Words-worth'), the fashioning of some harmony or rhythm, something positive in a relationship that is not merely her production . . . an advance on the talking cat. Hidden in this dream, however, I suspect is the infant's omnipotent phantasy that the beauty and poetry of the breast are created through being filled with its faeces. Hence the lingering doubt that she does not deserve this prize, that she is really a fake, and the fear of being unmasked and humiliated.

So in the talking cat dream she is the bottom that is the breast; in the Wordsworth dream she is just the bottom that fills it. A little later comes a dream in which she is nearer to accepting herself as the greedy baby who empties the breast.

This dream followed upon her moving into a bed-sitting room of her own. She prefaced it by saying that she had introduced an electric fire of her own which had too strong a current so that it blew all the fuses in the house where she was living. She then had a dream about being burned alive. In this dream *Rosamund was with her godmother and her godmother's two little girls waiting to be burned alive taking it all very calmly but thinking it was really rather careless of her godmother to allow the children to see such an unsuitable event. Then it seemed that she had been burned and was reappearing as a ghost to tell the godmother that it was not so bad after all and did not really hurt.* 'My old omnipotence,' she interposed, 'indestructible me'. Later on she recalled that *all she seemed to know about being burned was the flesh flying away from her face.*

She was sure that this dream was connected with her anorexia in some very particular way but could not say how. Then I said that I thought that once again we were dealing with some confusion between top and bottom and that her description of the flesh flying from the face could be referring to something like diarrhoea. She responded immediately, saying that she knew that she had had enteritis very badly as a baby, could not remember whether it followed upon weaning or her brother's birth some nine months later. So this seems to be the connection.

128

One could then see the electric fire that was too powerful for the system, as the passion and greed of the baby for the warmth and life of the breast which it fears it has finally shattered at weaning. Later in the dream as the little ghost that she was after the enteritis, and again became with the anorexia, she is identified with the burnt-out breast, but quite all right and reassuring (god/good) mother with her little children who represent the breast at a part-object level.

This would indicate that she had felt the weaning and the birth of her little brother as a humiliation, the consequence of being too greedy and destructive a baby. To escape from that humiliation she had then slipped into being one of the breasts, into a kind of twin sister relationship with a mother whom she reassured, and with whom she then combined to be another little mummy for the next baby. This dream heralded a period in the analysis of increasingly greedy infantile demands which expressed themselves in longing for food and little girl hunger for attention. Cream buns for instance appeared in her dreams as infinitely desirable but unsafe to eat lest she could not get to the toilet in time. At week-ends she tried whenever she could to make the long journey home and was tiresomely exacting as never before in her life. Then, worryingly, compulsive eating was followed by compulsive vomiting for a period of two or three months: a period when she also consistently forgot her dreams. Her ladylike aplomb wore very thin. She appeared more like an infant alternately gobbling, then spitefully rejecting the food as vomit or diarrhoea. Gradually, however, she began to want to remember her dreams as well as to try to eat more sensibly and to recognise her more envious spiteful impulses . . . in grudging the breast the satisfaction of feeding her if she could not feel that it was totally in her possession. For instance, she would remember a snatch of a dream about going back to school where she was starting to enjoy herself but then at once had to hide this in case the teachers should see and feel pleased. Then followed two dreams that marked the beginning of a period when she started to build up again both physically and in her social relationships. In the first one she simply dreamt *about the forsythia branches in my consulting room but could not remember whether they had bloomed or were dead.* The dream following this was of *a plump orphan with a cross face like Bernadette Devlin whom her father went to fetch back from a*

129

cemetery. He was bringing her back from the dead to go to school and rescuing her from her unfortunate habit of going off to heaven every nine days on her own.

This Bernadette Devlin seems to represent the rebellious anti-government, anti-parent explosive diarrhoea — making part of herself which repeatedly says no (Nein). It idealises being alone in the cemetery as heaven, is confused about death and life and needs in analysis a father to bring her back to learn about it. Interpretations of this dream that were roughly on these lines she did not like at the time. She came back, however, the next day with another dream which she had not been able to forget, although she had tried in her sleep to do so because it had apparently wiped out another very nice dream which she had wanted to continue. The dream she could not forget was as follows: *She was in my family although I was not there, and moreover she seemed to be an intimate friend. My husband was there, tall and fair (like her father) with a lovely cuddly baby. He told her that his wife was not a good wife at all but that she, Rosamund was wonderful with children, the baby was really happy with her. 'Not at all', said Rosamund modestly, 'anyone would love this child' and she thought to herself that the wife must be a hard person not to love a child who was so nice and cuddly.*

Before I was able to say anything at all about this dream she hastily interposed that she knew there was no point in eating because she was just going to vomit it all up again.

In this dream she has come more openly into contact with her competitiveness with the mother/analyst for the baby/patient, as well as with her desire to spoil the parental relationship. The important thing at this point is that she has remembered the dream and has brought it even though she does not like it. From then onwards she began gradually to hold down her food as well as to stomach better these more unpalatable parts of herself. Very gradually she began to resume eating, to return to a more social life and was able to go to university and enjoy her time there.

Gerald

I shall now give some material from the much longer analysis of an adolescent boy, Gerald, who first started with me when he was twelve years old at a time when he was still encased in strongly obsessional latency defences. He had been referred for depression and flatness of affect and a tendency to severe bronchial conditions. He was appreciated by his teachers; in short a 'good' boy of whom any family or school would be proud, but unable to enjoy the appreciation he received.

In the early stages of his analysis he communicated mainly through drawings and paintings that were extremely colourful and beautiful and into them seemed to go all the life and emotion that was missing in his relationship with me, although he helpfully co-operated in my attempt to understand what he was expressing by answering questions and producing associations. We came to realise that his preoccupation with these elaborate productions was holding up the analytic work, that he would withhold thoughts which occurred to him until he had finished the particular part of the picture upon which he was engaged at the time. He then agreed to try the couch and began to speak much more freely, bringing increasing numbers of dreams with many associations.

He continued with the same meticulous co-operation, politely listening and responding to what I said, yet I was often left after a session, with the baffled feeling that it had been much less interesting than it should have been. Dreams and associations that were fascinating and rich in content, full of eminently analysable material somehow failed to lead to development in the sessions. We came to realise that his responses were being carefully edited and were much less spontaneous than they seemed, and were being regarded by him as much more important than anything which I said to him. His productions and most especially his dreams were being regarded as his painting had been, as works of art to satisfy and to keep me happy. The interpretations which I made were not allowed to affect him at the time although he noted them and could make use of them to understand his material in later sessions without remembering where they came from. Gradually he became more aware that he was missing something that he could get from his sessions as from his life generally; that his parents were willing and able to offer more than he was able to accept, and said of himself quoting Edith Sitwell 'I was always a little outside life'.

As in the analysis the latency defences which kept him outside life (i.e. somewhat cut off from his emotions and his internal

131

objects) — were loosened, he began to come into contact with a violent ruthless part of himself which had formerly been split off and projected into his younger brother. A hitherto more distant attitude to this brother one of head-on collision. Then he began to realise in his analysis how this violence was directed towards transference aspects of the father who interrupted his sole possession of mother and that they were experienced more and more strikingly in relation to week-ends and holidays. Also around this time, before his fifteenth birthday, he began to take a closer interest in girls himself instead of being content to watch from a distance with passive voyeurism the vicissitudes of his friends in the sexual field.

The following dream indicated the violent way in which he burst into puberty. He brought it on a Friday following a day upon which, quite unusually, he had had to wait for a few minutes in the waiting room before his session. He had not admitted to feeling annoyed at having to wait but the session was characterised by a subliminal irritation and frustration. On the Friday he arrived preoccupied and filled with foreboding about a party he was giving that week-end; the first to be held at his house. He was wondering how he could deal with possible gatecrashers, recalling the experience of friends who had had their parties invaded, their parents' furniture smashed, crockery broken and carpets stained. In response to interpretations about intrusions into the analytic week-end (the parental intercourse) of destructive unwanted fragments of himself, he said that he had realised the day before on leaving the session that he had been irritable and unhelpful and bent on stopping anything taking place. Following the session he had had a terrible dream as follows: He was at a party in a drawing room sitting on a sofa talking to a pretty fair-haired girl, having a civilized conversation until an older man came up to join them. Immediately he was seized with an ungovernable urge to have sexual intercourse with the girl and rushed out of the room to fetch a contraceptive. When he returned the scene had changed utterly. There was no-one left in the room; it was bare of furnishing and the walls were a dirty cream colour, plaster and paper peeling. He found himself strutting up and down the ruined empty place in jack-boots like a Nazi, but the worst thing of all was that he didn't care a bit. When he woke up he felt shaken to the core.

In the course of working on this dream he gave a wealth of associations which connected it with my consulting room, the session of the day before, and his parents' bedroom in the home of his early childhood. The drawing room of the dream had started off looking like the consulting room but had ended up like the parental bedroom in a dilapidated state with its rose-patterned cream wallpaper hanging down in ribbons. As he had left my room the day before he had noticed some paint falling off by the radiator, and had thought that expressed perfectly the bittiness of the session that he had just had. The man who interrupted him with the pretty girl was connected with someone he had seen coming to my house when he had been looking out of the waiting room window, my husband he presumed. In response to query he confirmed that he had had a nocturnal emission the night of the dream, expressed in the rushing out of the room. Also rummaging in his parents chest of drawers for a handkerchief he had come across a packet of contraceptives which had brought home to him that they still did have intercourse and were not yet past it as he, in his adolescent arrogance, was inclined to assume.

So it seemed that the idealised civilised conversation which he had been having with a girl-friend mother in his analytic sessions had been rudely interrupted when he had had to wait the day before by the thought of the husband/father. This had resulted in an explosive expulsion of destructive sexual feeling which he could not admit or possibly even be aware of during the Thursday session, but which was enacted in the nocturnal emission and communicated in the dream which he remembered and brought to his Friday session.

This violent part of himself is something essentially put down below, as yet unintegrated, awakened by his sexuality and feared as unknown. It has been expressed during the latency period only occasionally — on the rugger field, or in occasional fights with his brother. During the analytic sessions it has been discernible only in very subtle ways: in a certain arrogance in his demeanour, in slightly biting sarcastic remarks. It now began to appear more frequently in dreams, and then burst out in an intensely possessive way a little later in his first steady relationship with a girl which literally devoured most of his time and seriously endangered his studies.

This first relationship with a girl-friend had a passive clinging leech-like quality, infantile in origin, the continuation of the very special exclusive relationship to his mother which was used to protect himself from the violent sexual jealousy that erupted in the Nazi dream. It was a parasitic quality which contributed to his feeling disposed to remain indefinitely in analysis, although from another point of view he did work well and made considerable progress in the work, as in his life outside.

I shall now discuss some dreams which he had had when he was nearly eighteen and preparing to stop analysis and to go to the university . . . looking forward to this but clinging tenaciously to avoid change. Gerald said that in a dream *I was telling him that at last some particular interpretation had got through to him*. The implication was that other kinds did not. He then said that as he was retelling this dream to me he had the impression that he was making me responsible for interpretations working rather than taking that responsibility himself. The interpretation which had affected him was about the way in which he was using his mouth as an anus, and it threw some light on another dream which he had had earlier that same night. *This was a science fiction type in which there was a crisis like the end of the world. The whole family was gathered by the sea watching something that looked like a huge rubber bladder getting bigger and bigger till it exploded. Everyone tried to escape from the dreadful substance that came from it and kept spreading.* He felt that this was some negation of his responsibility for a mad faecal breast, but in the dream *his father appeared to be organising an escape for everyone*.

The dream reminded him of long ago when as a small child with his father before his younger brother was born, he was fishing for tadpoles and found something in a black shiny shell, which was then smashed and soft like a mollusc. He never found out what it was and had often wondered what it was doing there in the pond, just hanging around waiting for something to happen. As he told me about this he said that was making him think uncomfortably of the way in which he still continued to place the onus upon me to get through to him, without making a great effort to understand. He would notice himself just silently waiting and the very silence was being converted into something faecal. It hid an attempt to worm his way in to get benefit from the sessions without being fully committed or feeling at all dependent.

134

This is a preparation-for-weaning dream, a dream about an incipient younger brother whose birth is confused with his own and with his anticipated but resisted birth from the analysis. It is a representation of that aspect of himself that feels it has wormed its way into the mother, into analysis and hangs on waiting for something to happen. One can see how the end of the analysis, birth, weaning, birth of the younger brother, are catastrophic events from which he now looks for help from his father.

In the next dream both parents come to his help. He came to his session saying that he was feeling annoyed with himself for feeling obliged to struggle to think about what he was doing and feeling over the weekend instead of just indulging himself and forgetting all about the analysis: He dreamt about *a girl who was reading Shakespeare and was overcome with a desire to have intercourse with her, but thought that this was a bad thing and so looked over her shoulder at the play she was reading. It was 'A Midsummer Night's Dream'. He recognised the words but they didn't make sense. He wanted to tear it from her and just at the point where he felt he could not control himself any longer his parents came in.* He jumped out of bed immensely relieved.

He associated the impulse to tear the book out of her hands with a phantasy of pulling my electric light switch out of its plug at the end of the Friday session to leave me in darkness. He was aware of a strong and childish desire in his school work to point out to me how clever he was. He knew that he was envious of any-one who might produce better work than he, and was aware of being curious about my daughter's prowess which he had heard about through the adolescent grapevine. He had noticed that people were influenced by their family background, and the implication was that hers was a fairly privileged one like his own and he was wondering how well she managed to use it, in com-parison with the use he was making of his.

The dream and its associations indicate the progress he has made towards a more consistent awareness and a greater degree of responsibility for himself than he had a year ago, resentful though he may be for the need to go on struggling. The girl whom he associates with my daughter may be seen as represent-ing the mother, as a sister at a diminished part object level, and the book at this level as father's penis which is feeding her with information, drama, poetry thereby evoking in him curiosity,

135

greed and desire. He tries to get into this from behind, projecting himself into the intercourse through anal masturbation. But significantly in this way he gets the form of the words only, not the meaning; the equivalent of faeces, not babies; i.e. the masturbatory intrusion does not help him to understand the nature of the parental relationship. He knows theoretically but he cannot experience it as poetry and life. In his frustration and envy that such a relationship should be taking place whose meaning is denied to him he tried to pull this Shakespeare penis out as he was tempted to pull the light plug out to leave me in darkness. The appearance of the two parents rescues him from committing rape (the significance of his masturbation).

When we were working on this dream he asked me irritably why *two* parents as if he were especially infantile or especially dangerous in needing them both. He knew very well by this time that the fundamental struggle in his growing up was about allowing the parents to be together internally, was about appreciating them as whole and separate people. That they have been internalised more as whole objects allowed to be together and therefore coming to his aid to rescue him from his perverse criminal impulses, is evidenced by their appearance in the dream. At that time he was relieved; on his way to the session and in the session he grudged or was humiliated by his dependence on them. It was as if confronted by me externally after the weekend as a parental couple he was thrown back briefly to more primitive part-object relationships again; to the paranoid-schizoid position driven by impulses to plug in and be carried as the leech-like baby, to give up the struggle towards separateness and responsibility although he now has more established internal objects to help him towards this.

I shall give one more selection of material from this final phase of Gerald's analysis in which he was having to continue to struggle with this primitive violence and possessiveness towards his primary object, following the progressive and thorough de-idealisation of his infantile omnipotence.

He began a session by saying that he was feeling bad about his lack of interest in the new car his father was about to buy. He imagined that his father would probably prefer to have a smaller racing car but as he had to consider the needs of the family he would have to compromise on speed in order to get one with a body that would accommodate all the children and their friends. His father's consideration for the family made him feel depressed when he considered his own egocentricity. In some part of himself he remained absolutely convinced that as his analyst I functioned only when he was there. As we elaborated upon this or familiar lines to the effect that he still clung to the idea of a mother who had no room for father's penis or for other babies he burst out that he felt more depressed than ever about plugging in and letting me do all the work. It spoiled the sessions. When I had been talking he had been looking around the room, thinking that my flowers annoyed him, reminding him of the painting of a child, very simple, very bright. They reminded him of hospitals, and his thoughts went to visiting his mother in hospital when she was ill or perhaps after the birth of a baby. All he could remember was his annoyance when he had realised at that time that she was more interested in seeing father than seeing him. It had been a real blow to his feelings of importance and his eagerness to see her.

When we returned to his pity for father at not having mother as a vehicle all to himself he broke in to the effect that he did realise this was a projection, that he didn't need me to go over it all again, and apologised for talking in a boring way saying, 'if I don't grumble a little it'll go bad inside me'. He said he had had a dream, thought that he knew what it meant and that he should not have to tell me, but perhaps should do so, repetitious though it might be. It was about the Germans bombing the island of Crete. He supposed Crete did mean excrete and that this was another defaecating dream. He followed this with an outburst of heartfelt appreciation, 'You can't think how grateful I am to you for listening to this rubbish. No-one else would bother to do so and nobody would realise how important it is to me.'

So what was being worked on in this session was his awareness of his infantile possessiveness and violence of his attempt to project this into father's penis crediting him with an adolescent/ infantile sexuality which would use the woman's body as an exclusive high-speed vehicle to 'get there first'. For some time he has been valuing his dreams more as keys to helping him to understand his internal situation than as works of art to divert or impress. Those simple red tulips which irritated him so, carried undertones of his former childish use of paintings, idealised products at which Mummy's eyes were meant to brighten and her lips to praise the prowess of her little boy, a cherished illusion vanishing.

There is also now a much more genuine spontaneous appreciation of the analyst in the receptive role of the mother, of the maternal reverie (Bion, 1962) that receives the projections which is not choked by the rubbish as he still sometimes feels chocked by his 'inarticulate' rage, but which helps him to articulate, sort out and think about it; which tries to gather together and to hold all the pieces he excretes until they can be evaluated.

Discussion

In the case of Rosamund the disappointment after her first serious love affair plunged her back to conflicts about weaning and the birth of her younger brother evaded at the time. Analysis revealed the central role of projective identification in her pseudo-maturity; a projection via the anus into the breast (Meltzer, 1965) with resultant confusion between breasts and buttocks. This was an attempt to maintain a mutually idealising relationship and to avoid experiencing envy towards a breast with a nipple. At another level this was a defence against envy of the relationship between father's penis and mother's vagina: the creative link between the parental couple.

She had dealt with the mother/father/baby triad by projecting herself into each one, creating a kind of 'holy family'. Later on when she went to school she had dealt with her baby homesickness for mother by identifying with the talkative father or brother and entertaining the family of girls — she became her rival objects. Her charm and genuine kindness and goodness of temperament undoubtedly evoked responses that helped her to maintain the idealisation of herself and to continue to evade grappling with the emotions which she split off by omnipotently taking possession of her objects.

Thus she deeply suspected that she was a fake. The severity of her reaction to disappointment in love was not only due to betrayal of trust — she had a trusting nature and had had every reason to feel trust in her world — but to the evocation of unpleasant unfamiliar feelings of greed and possessiveness which she had little practice in grappling with. Defences that had served her well in infancy due to her parents' love, and at school because of the friends she won by her beauty, intelligence and kindness, were inadequate in adolescence.

The relatively short period of analysis seems to give her the opportunity, which in one sense she deeply welcomed even though it came as a shock, to examine the false grounds on which her self-idealisation was based, and to establish a little better the primary relationship from which her good qualities could be exercised with a stronger belief in their authenticity.

Gerald also illustrates the explosive reactivation of pregenital conflicts by the emergence at puberty of strong sexual drives. As with Rosamund defences that enabled him to be a success in latency, and in his case prolonged latency, crumbled in adolescence. He was a boy of more complicated envious disposition than Rosamund. In latency this had produced a flattening of affect which took some of the life out of his personality. Behind his ambition was a weighty and penetrating intellect which he could use to talk about himself in his analysis with considerable subtlety and a dexterity that would often enable him to pre-empt being taken by surprise and experiencing the feelings he was describing. His analysis proceeded more slowly and less dramatically than Rosamund's because in him the idealisation of his own products was more deeply rooted and linked with a more tenacious negativism and resistance to being helped. He was less easily taken by surprise by his nastiness, less easily repentant, but more deeply introspective and persistent.

So here in brief are some aspects of the analysis of two adolescents who were prevented from enjoying the richness of their endowment because of an element of spuriousness, springing from a self-idealisation which had very likely been colluded in to some extent by parents who were naturally delighted to have children of such quality. The mutual idealisation was used as a bulwark against infantile violence and destructiveness which, uncontained and split off, yet gave intimations of their presence and did not allow the young people to feel that they deserved to enjoy the opportunities and gifts which they had. Not until there was some shift as a result of the analytic work from the idealisation of their own easy products (basically faecal) to some truer recognition of life received from the breast and from the parents in infancy (who could then be allowed internally the freedom to be together and separate), could they proceed more hopefully in the adolescent world towards a more adult attitude to sexuality.

BIBLIOGRAPHY

ABRAHAM, K. (1925) 'A Short Study of the Development of the Libido', *Clinical Papers*, London: Hogarth, 1955.

BICK, E. (1967) 'The Experience of the Skin in Early Object Relations', *International Journal of Psychoanalysis*, Vol. 49, 1968: pp 484-486.

BION, W.R. (1962) *Learning from Experience*. London, Heinemann.

BION, W.R. (1970) *Attention and Interpretation*. London, Tavistock Publications.

FREUD, S. (1905) 'Three Essays on the Theory of Sexuality'. Standard Edition, Vol. 7.

FREUD, S. (1911) '*Formulations on the Two Principles of Mental Functioning*'. Standard Edition, Vol. 12.

FREUD, S. (1923) 'The Ego and the Id.' Standard Edition, Vol. 19.

KLEIN, M. (1939) 'A Contribution to the Metapsychology of Manic Depressive States', in *Contributions to Psychoanalysis*, 1921-1945. London: Hogarth, 1948.

KLEIN, M. (1946) '*Notes on some Schizoid Mechanisms*', in *Developments in Psychoanalysis*. London: Hogarth, 1952.

MELTZER, D. (1965) 'Relation of anal masturbation to projective identification'. *International Journal of Psychoanalysis*, Vol. 47, 1966.

MELTZER, D. (1972) *Sexual States of Mind*. Perthshire, Clunie Press.

Published in the *Journal of Child Psychotherapy*, Vol. 10, 1976. Some of this material appears in 'Discussion of an Adolescent Girl'.

2   Some Notes on Maternal Containment in 'Good Enough' Mothering

In this paper I shall first of all refer to those theories which I have found most useful in thinking about the many details to be observed in the close study of the early weeks of an infant's inter-action with his mother. They are theories which help to bring together configurations seen in the infant observation situation (Bick 1962), with transference phenomena in analytic work with children and adults, in a way that enriches the understanding of both.

I shall then present some sequences from observations of two babies in favourable family circumstances during those early weeks, following them with excerpts from the beginning of the analysis of a young mother referred for treatment because of acute anxieties during pregnancy and severe depression follow-ing the birth of the baby.

The theories are concerned with the pre-requisite for mental growth of a primary maternal object who can be an adequate container for the infant's personality, the 'good enough' mother about whom Winnicott has written (1965). Detailed study of interaction between individual mothers and infants may help us to formulate better the quality that underlies this quantitive differentiation; the constituents that make for that 'good enough'; and lead to a more convincing recognition of the uniqueness of each relationship, and perhaps the importance of 'fit' between the temperament of the mother and the constitution of the baby.

When Freud discovered the phenomenon of narcissism in 1914 his idea was that it was a development from auto-erotism towards object-relations in which the child took his own body as object, in so far as it was identified with, and was indistinguishable from the body of the parent. He considered that this development was an automatic process and called it primary narcissism.

Melanie Klein came to the view that narcissistic identification was brought about by a mental mechanism and was not an auto-matic process. Eventually in 1946 she described this mechanism implemented by the omnipotent phantasy which she named projective identification. In this phantasy the infant splits off temporarily undesired parts of himself into the object. Excessive use of this mechanism she believed to lead to pathological development including impoverishment of the personality and disturbances in sense of identity.

From the earliest time in her work Melanie Klein emphasised the importance of the epistemophilic instinct in children (1921): their innate desire to reach out and learn about the world, expressed first in the infant's curiosity about the mother's body, including the phantasied space inside it occupied by a variety of objects and contents. This is his prototype of the world.

Bion in his paper 'A Theory of Thinking' (1967) and in *Learning from Experience* (1962), links the theory of projective identification with the epistemophilic instinct, in a way that throws more light upon the origins of the capacity to learn from experience. He talks of the infant's need for a mother who will receive the evacuation of his distress, consider it and respond appropriately. If this happens the infant has an experience of being understood as well as of being comforted. He receives back the evacuated part of his personality in an improved condition together with an experience of an object which has been able to tolerate and to think about it. Thus, introjecting what Bion called the mother's capacity for 'reverie', the infant begins to be more able to tolerate himself and to begin to apprehend himself and the world in terms of the *meaning* of things. The mother's failure to respond to his distress results in the introjection of an object that is hostile to understanding, together with that frightened part of himself which is divested of meaning through not eliciting a response. This is then experienced as a 'nameless dread'.

Esther Bick (1968) considers from another point of view the containing function of the mother. She talks of the infant's need in his primary unintegrated state for an object that can hold the parts of the personality together, optimally the nipple in the mouth and the increasingly familiar holding, talking, smelling mother who meets his various sensual needs. Faulty development of this primal containing or 'skin' function may arise from defects in the object, or from phantasy attacks which impair the form in which it is introjected into the infant in an integrated and therefore integrating way.

Disturbance in this primal skin function may result in what she calls 'second skin formation', when reliance and trust in an internal sustaining object is replaced by brittle independence of a muscular kind; some active utilisation of the infant's sensory and mental equipment to hold himself together: a state in which the ordinary processes of introjection and projection are not fulfilling their function. It may lead to a two-dimensional type of personality in which identification is of an adhesive kind, when mimicry and imitation of the surface qualities of people take the place of learning from experience through projection and introjection.

It seems likely that failure to introject a primary object which is able to contain and provide a basis for the integration of the personality may take various forms and be present in varying degrees, from the extremes of autism and functional mental defect, to less obviously pathological or stunted states of shallowness and superficiality, of inability or reluctance to give deep emotional commitment (Meltzer 1975). It also seems likely that areas and states of non-containment, of two-dimensionality and mindlessness exist in the development of every infant and are therefore in us all.

These theories do, I believe, help to throw some light on the meaning of the somewhat arbitrarily selected sequences of infant observations which follow. They were made in both cases by observers who noticed and retained many details and were sensitive to the emotional atmosphere of the relationships which they were observing. Compression and selection may fail to do them justice.

Notes from The Observations of Two Infants

Charles is the fourth child of a professional couple in their early thirties. The other three children are all under five and their mother has not worked at her profession since starting her own family. The father is home earlier in the day than many another might be and is able to help his wife with the older children. The observer found the atmosphere in the home lively warm and welcoming and had the impression that the mother was eager and happy to talk to her.

The observer visited first when the baby was just over a week

143

old but barely saw him because he remained asleep in his cot. She had the impression that in any case the mother was eager to talk to her without interruption, leaving the other children with their father when he returned home. Mrs C. talked of all her children: her difficulties after the birth of the first two who were slightly premature and spent a few days in an incubator which made breast feeding difficult to establish; the easiness of the third child and their hopefulness that Charles too would be an easy baby as so far he had fitted in well. The other children had accepted him although she expected trouble from the next youngest who had wanted to hit 'the lump' in the later stages of her pregnancy.

She was pleased to have the baby to hold immediately after his birth and noted that he turned towards her voice as if he recognised it when she spoke. She thought that he was already beginning to focus because she had noticed his scanning the room in the direction where his brothers and sisters were playing. She had also noticed that sometimes when she was feeding him he would stop apparently listening to the ticking of the clock by the bed.

On his first observation Charles was seen lying froglike on his tummy with his head turned towards the light, fast asleep. His mother said that thus far all he was able to move was his head, which he could turn when lying down.

On the next visit when Charles was two and a half weeks old he was again lying on his front with his head towards the light, fast asleep. His mother was somewhat exhausted because he had been waking up to be fed every three hours and she was hoping to get him on to a four hour schedule. As he began to waken he seemed to be trying to cram his thumb into his mouth but it was still folded. He made some sucking movements at the joint, then gradually the movement became more total-body, pushing with his left leg, thrusting his right shoulder and head into the top righthand corner of the cot, snuffling and giving little cries at the same time. He opened and closed his eyes several times and seemed to be scanning the sides of the cot before he heaved himself into a hump.

When his mother picked him up his hands spread out like a starfish; he seemed startled. She sat on the bed with her legs sticking out in front and laid him facing her on her legs while she took out her left breast. He sucked strongly and steadily with an enormously concentrated expression on his face squinting at the breast immediately in front of him and holding on to the hand that was supporting it. He seemed to be pushing something out, grunting and going red. His mother said that sometimes he concentrates so hard that he falls asleep. After a brief wind his hand relaxed and lay by his side. Five minutes later his mother took him away from the breast, put him against her shoulder, leaned away from him and talked to him gently. He seemed to be trying to concentrate on her face, then to focus on the wall behind his mother. Before he brought up his wind his face, body and hands seemed to open and close, his body bunched and un-bunched, his face screwed up and relaxed. Mother then laid him in her lap again so that his feet were pointing at her stomach. When put down his hands and legs flew out, almost like an astronaut in a gravityless zone. She responded by talking gently to him again and bringing both his hands down to his stomach with her hands. She then laid him on the changing pad saying that he did not usually like to be changed.

This time he was 'good' and did not make a fuss. As his leggings were removed his legs flew out and up in a similar way to his hands a little earlier; as if they were weightless. He remained quite motionless as mother creamed the eczema rash on his genital and navel, saying meanwhile that it didn't seem to be doing much good. As she put his legs back into the leggings he concentrated entirely on the movement and noise of her hands, moving his eyes in what seemed to be three directions following the mother's activities during this operation; hands to popper, hand moving up. He seemed to feel more together once the leggings were on again. His legs began to move again but in a more restricted way as if they were part of him. During this operation he looked at one point towards the observer when he heard her talking.

Mother then gave him to the observer to hold, to 'get a feel of him'. He was fascinated by the stripes on her blouse and started to track them with his eyes in the way she had seen him scan the pattern of the cot when he was laid down. As his mother took him back his tongue went in and out. She put him in his cot with a nappy under his back so that he could look at the source of light, the window. When she left him he wormed his way a little towards the corner of the cot as before but less intensely, and

145

scanned the edge of the cot with rhythmic movements of his eyes as he had done before.

On these first occasions the observer feels welcomed warmly by the mother, who somehow also needs to talk in detail about all the children who are occupying her mind but from whom she wants to have brief respite, to be away from the family hub-bub, reasonably ordered and pleasant though it appears to be. Her relative seclusion with the observer and the baby was to continue throughout the first weeks and months.

On the second visit the most striking features observed are the contrasts between the intense concentration which Charles shows when feeding, and when his attention is held by an external stimulus; and the startled falling-apart re-actions at moments of transition, when he is not firmly held. The concentration returns at points of physical contact with his mother, of visual and aural attention: the pattern of the cot; of the observer's blouse; the sound of voices and of the ticking clock. The rare impression of his being contained without effort and strain on his part, was most marked when he was buttoned into his clothes, and when his mother talked to him bringing his hands closer against his body.

A week later when Charles was 3 ½ weeks old he was observed just after his feed, lying in the cot with his head turned towards the light again and his eyes half open. As his mother lifted him from the cot his bottom lip shuddered markedly and he clenched his hands in front of him, looking at his mother's face. She held him on her lap sideways supporting him front and back with her hands. As she moved her head and the light fell on his face he looked blinded and confused for a moment. With a solemn concentrated expression again he listened intently to the ticking of the clock and looked in that direction, looking more together again.

After a period of still concentration on this sound his lip suddenly juddered and he started grasping into the air, hands moving up and down intently in what seemed to be a sudden feeling of panic. Mother responded by holding him more firmly round the middle by putting her face closer to him. He seemed to be trying to focus on her face once more. Mrs C. said that he could now support his head and shoulders well. Then she put him back to bed on his front, arranging his limbs in a crawling position with his backside in the air. Once covered with blankets he started pushing up in the cot with his whole body, grunting till he found his thumb joint and began to suck on that. His eyes continued to be active, the left one scanning the cot with rhythmic movements, finer than before and more definitely focussed, before they closed gradually. The observer noted that his body seemed more centralised than the week before. He gave more of an impression of moving his limbs himself, than of bits shooting off uncontrollably.

On this visit the mother was tired, strained and a little depressed. She was finding the other children demanding in various ways, and seemed to be wanting some kind of contact with the observer without knowing quite what to say. The latter left feeling that 'politenesses were not enough'!

On this visit the observer notes the same visual and aural holding to external objects, and some progress in his control over his limbs as if he feels more of a piece. Mrs C.'s depression and unformulated longing for some kind of contact herself is more evident.

A week later when Charles was four and a half weeks old he was having more bottle than breast and according to his mother making demands to be carried about to 'look at life' as he became bored with lying in the cot. He was observed having his bath again and once more as his mother took off his baby-grow his arms flew up and out as they had done the week before. The same happened with his legs as his leggings were removed. He strained himself to look round at the observer behind him, squirming as his mother held him in her lap to wash his hair. She commented that he still didn't like his bath at all. When his nappies were taken off and he was held naked on her lap he looked fixedly at her face but his lower jaw was trembling. When lowered into the water his face 'seemed to be collapsing'. For a moment there was hiatus of response, then he worked himself up into a rage, his face went red, his skin turned from white to blotchy red and blue. 'His face took on a look of real rage like the mask for tragedy'; Mother washed him quickly holding him under his head, trying to soothe him, then took him back to his pad but his rage continued. As she dried him his legs were pushing up and down like bicycle pedals. He was not distracted this time when she put the cream on his rash which was still there, but his rage suddenly

147

subsided when his legs were poppered into his leggings. The hands that were grasping at the air in front of him became tensed and crooked as he was being dressed impeding his mother's activities. He then became quite still and looked in front of him. Mother sat down in a chair with him relaxed in the crook of her arm and gave him his bottle.

He resisted the teat at first, then sucked steadily and noisily staring into mother's face, clutching his bib with his left hand. He relaxed both hands gradually as he got something inside. In the course of the feed he belched three times very noisily. The first time his mother held his bib out to catch the burp as if afraid that all the contents of his stomach were about to come up; the second time she felt the wind coming and held him against her shoulder and as it came out his body seemed to collapse against her. After he had belched for the third time he turned his head away from the teat. When mother put him into the cot his eyes at once went to a mobile moving above it. As he fussed and did not settle mother then took him out to put him in his chair. There he sat looking solemn and anxious; first at mother, then at the observer, but moving all his limbs as if he wanted to grasp on to something. When mother took him out of the chair a little later to sit on her lap he seemed to be trying to smile at her face, but as he didn't have quite enough control over his muscles his smile went 'all wobbly'.

On this observation when Charles is having the bottle it seems significant that the observer notes particularly the trembling of the lower jaw, the 'collapsing' of his face when his clothes are removed and he is put into the bath. This is the first time she has seen him totally undressed and having his bath, so this intense reaction may not have been new in that situation. One may wonder nevertheless whether the lower jaw tremble and facial collapse may not be specifically related to the withdrawal from that part of him of the breast-nipple which he was seen to grip with such intense concentration. It is notable that he does reject the teat of the bottle at first, that the expelling of wind during the feed seems quite cataclysmic and that after the third burp he finally rejects the bottle-teat.

The next week when Charles was five and a half weeks he was virtually weaned from the breast but for a token suck of five minutes a day. His mother was sad, but in a relaxed confiding mood with the observer, talking of fruit trees that get exhausted through bearing too much fruit, of the children's questions about birth, sleep and death. Later on she was to confide that the children's grandparents on both sides of the family were all dead. Her feeling of no parental support seemed to be contrasted with the easy life and comforts enjoyed by some relatives in another sunnier climate. On the other hand Charles was progressing for the first time, he had not cried in his bath. 'They hate it when they are falling into space'. He was developing unusually strong back muscles. He liked to sit up and tried to push himself up when put down on his tummy; he cried and became bored if he had nothing to look at. About the breast feeding Mrs C. said that she had been too tense with the other kids to attend to him and had felt too vulnerable, always ready to wrap herself up in case of emergency.

Later on in the hour when Charles was awakened and bathed the observer noted that he did seem to mange the bathing situation better; looking agitated but 'holding himself together with tremendous effort', and becoming perceptibly less jerky and agitated when he was buttoned into his clothes again.

In this observation the mother's underlying sadness is more clearly expressed in her talk of exhausted fruit trees and dead parents, her apologetic attitude at failing to continue the feeding which is connected with her vulnerability and need to wrap herself up. Her regret about the dwindling of her milk seems to make it more important that he should be strong so she emphasises his progress and strength. He does indeed seem to be adapting to his circumstances, to be less overwhelmed by nakedness but continues to have to make strong muscular efforts to keep himself from falling apart.

In the following weeks after being weaned from the breast Charle's strong back-bone continued to be emphasised. The observer noted in the mother a tendency to apartness at feeding-time, a wish to hand him over to someone else to be fed, as if she felt badly about her failure to go on breast feeding and did not want to be reminded of it. The observer saw in Charles a continuation of this tendency to work hard to keep himself together by muscular tension, or by holding on to some external object in moments of stress or change; the sides of his cot, the arms of his chair, the objects which he could see and hear.

Anthea is the first baby of a young couple in their twenties. Mrs A., a slight boyish-looking young woman, has been working until shortly before the birth of the child to which she was looking forward eagerly but with mixed feelings, living as she did far away from her family of origin, near parents-in-law and older members of her husband's family who seemed to be only too ready to proffer advice. As she regarded herself as 'not the maternal type' she was only too prone to feel that things would go wrong, both in the labour and afterwards with the baby, that it would all be very difficult.

The observer first visited some days after the mother returned from the hospital when Anthea was eleven days old. However, she scarcely saw the baby on this occasion. She had the impression that Mrs A. wanted to talk of her recent experiences but was meanwhile assessing her to decide whether she could entrust her with sight of the baby (this mother had not agreed to the observation before the birth).

Mrs A. poured out details about her former anxieties: about the painfulness of the birth but kept returning to her over-riding astonishment at the uniqueness of the experience and the individuality of the baby herself. During the birth she had vowed to herself, 'never again', but the next day had found herself thinking that she must have at least six more, so fascinated was she with this one. She was also astonished that her husband was beginning to take an interest in the baby too. Her absorption was after all understandable as the baby had really been with her for the past nine months, but she was surprised that a baby could interest a man so soon. She had been very doubtful beforehand about managing to breast-feed but it was turning out to be very simple: the baby had started to suck straight away: 'She knew what to do ... she's teaching me, she's teaching *us*. I had no problems, I could relax and now I enjoy the feeding ... but everything seems to go straight through to her and that can be a bit difficult for you can't be alright all of the time'. She then went on to describe how during the fourth day in the hospital, when the elation of the birth had worn off, she had felt 'a bit down', had some tummy trouble and the baby had fussed all day. The nurses had been very supportive, however, and the satisfaction of feeling so close to the baby out-weighed all the worry; they had to learn to settle with each other at close quarters.

She mentioned that she had noticed that the baby not only reacted to her state of mind but amazingly seemed to notice different surroundings; for instance the sounds in the flat that were different from the noises in the hospital.

Throughout that first interview with the observer there were many references to anxieties past and present, but the strongest impression which Mrs A. conveyed was one of being amazed and fascinated by the baby herself and by this new experience which was happening to her.

The next visit took place when Anthea was three weeks old, lying in her pram waiting to be bathed and fed. As her mother approached her she looked up at her, started to kick her legs and move her arms as she was uncovered, and appeared to be trying to reach up and touch her mother with her whole body. Mrs A. then picked her up, chatting both to her and to the observer, including both within her attention, mentioning to the one how the baby was growing and how her eyes were changing colour and commenting indulgently to Anthea that she knew how fond she was of being talked to. Anthea was meantime looking open-eyed and intensely at her mother's face.

After this little exchange the mother put the baby down to go and prepare the bath. Anthea started to kick the air and move her hands as she had been doing before the mother picked her up, at first looking quite contented and as if she felt that she was still touching something. As the minutes passed instead of giving the impression that she was touching something she seemed to be trying to *find* something and then eventually she just kicked and cried anxiously in an unfocused way.

When the mother went over and talked to her she calmed down at once even before she was picked up. Mrs A. then took her and held her on one arm while with the other she undressed her and prepared to dip her into the bath. Anthea looked surprised but confident, her whole body leaning against, and seeming to follow the shape of her mother's arm as she was talking to her, 'Yes, it's always like this. You don't know what is going on at first but once you're in it you like it'. Anthea was stiff, tense and began to make faces, trying to attach herself to the mother's arm as she was being lowered into the water. She relaxed gradually as her mother laughed at her gently telling the observer to come and look at her funny faces. She mimicked the

151

baby's imploring look, translating it as 'Do we *have* to?' As the baby relaxed into her arm again in the water Mrs A. said: 'Oh yes, you see that's what you like', then gradually rolled her over on to her tummy. Anthea started to move her limbs in the water with evident enjoyment. After the bath while being rubbed with warm oil and dressed she looked happy and relaxed. When given the breast she sucked strongly but after a short while fell asleep and remained so in the mother's arms for the rest of the observation.

As she slept the mother talked to the observer reflecting upon the experiences of the past few days. Apparently the day before Anthea had had a pain and kept vomiting after her feeds so mother had carried her about most of the time, contrary to the advice of mother-in-law who threatened that this would spoil the child, who need to be given a regular feeding schedule. Mrs A. reflected on all these women who were now too far away from the experience of having an infant themselves to remember what it was like and again expressed her conviction that the baby could teach her better than anyone else could. She was learning to distinguish between her different cries; when they meant hunger, when they meant pain: and when they were asking for a cuddle. Later on she thought that she might have to discipline her, but not yet. She reflected aloud that something was definitely changing in herself: she had never imagined that she would find motherhood like this. She wondered as the baby slept what she was thinking: did she dream yet? Mrs A. believed that she must be able to tell the difference between her husband and herself because when her husband held her he jiggled her on his knee, but that too seemed to soothe her. There were so many different experiences for a baby to get used to. Mrs A. said that she would not like to remember the time when she herself was born: it couldn't have been a very good experience. But as soon as a baby starts to think it must be interesting. She felt that it was indeed hard to be a mother and did not know how it would have been for her the day before if Anthea had continued to be upset throughout the night, but as it turned out they had both been so tired at the end of the day that they had fallen asleep soundly for seven hours without a break. Again she reflected upon how necessary it was for them to have privacy to learn how to accommodate each other. At the end of the hour she thanked the observer for coming, saying how good it had been to talk.

From this it comes through clearly that Mrs A. is not finding mothering easy: indeed she had not expected it to be so. She feels that her resources are not unlimited, that if the baby were too demanding she could collapse. She is being sustained by her interest in the baby, supported also by her husband's interest and also here by that of the observer: for all of them it is felt to be a learning situation. She is able to identify with Anthea; to wonder about what she is feeling and thinking; to try to see the world through her eyes.

One can see Anthea reaching with all of herself to the mother. The experience of being held in the mother's arms (in a space with boundaries) seems to remain with her for a little when she is put down again: she first seems to be still touching something; then to lose it, but to seek actively to find it again. Then anxiety and disintegration set in when she fails to do so either externally or internally. This would suggest that she has already begun to introject a holding object and that she can maintain it for a little while. One can see how, undressed in the bathing situation she does feel safe on her mother's arm, relaxing into it, and then tensing again as she meets the impact of the water, but relaxing once more in that new environment, into mother's arm in the water and in the sound of the mother's voice.

A week later, when the baby was a month old she was first seen asleep at her usual feeding time. Mrs A. announced that Anthea was now putting herself on a three and a half hour schedule. The clinic had found that she was quite heavy for her age. As her husband was still at home for the first part of the observation the observer found herself waiting while the couple talked about some urgent matters concerning Mr A.'s business. After he left Mrs A. continued to be occupied looking for some papers that he would need shortly. There was a sense of life and work going on with baby and observer for the moment relegated to the background, rather than ignored; for the time being not in need of specific attention.

When the baby began to toss and moan in the pram Mrs A. picked her up and talked to her. They looked into each other's eyes. The mother thought that she might be ready for her feed, took out her breast and gave it to the infant without more ado, but the baby after sucking it vigorously for a brief while, fell soundly asleep again. The mother laughed at the definiteness of

153

this: she was often to say later on that Anthea was a baby who knew her own mind and was good at expressing it. She waited for a while to see if the baby would waken again but when it did not happen Mrs A. put her down in the pram on her tummy and returned to the search which had been interrupted. She chatted to the observer from time to time through the open door, and after a while asked what Anthea was doing. When the observer said that she was still asleep the mother seemed surprised and said that she had thought by that time Anthea would be awake and playing in her pram.

The baby continued to sleep contentedly for a while, her mouth moving from time to time in sucking activity. Then her forehead started to become tense. She turned her head from side to side, her skin growing paler and more taut. Her whole body seemed to shrivel then she stretched and kicked, undergoing some very intense experience. She repeated the shrivelling and stretching, and when stretching seemed to be trying hard to cry. At last she managed to cry which appeared to release something in her. She then kicked and cried more freely, and pushed very strongly with her limbs. After this she calmed down and fell asleep again, with hands and mouth beginning to stir slightly once more in opening and closing, sucking movements. Following this her forehead began to tense and pale again and the whole process was repeated. This happened twice more before the observer left when she seemed finally to be sleeping calmly.

In this observation one can see complicated struggles going on in the baby's sleep. Following the brief holding and suckling by the mother she relaxes into sleep, her sucking movements seeming to indicate a phantasy of still being at the breast. She does not seem to be able to hold this good experience for long however: some nasty 'thought' shrivels her, appears to be eating her up. She has to struggle to expel it and is relieved and freer when she does manage to do so. The process, repeated, suggests considerable capacity to contain and to struggle with persecution; that she is introjecting an internal 'breast' which is strong enough to help her to hold and to get rid of the bad one, the flatus.

And now some notes from a observation some weeks later when Anthea was two and a half months old and had been away with her parents. On returning home she had had tummy pains, wind, and cried a lot.

154

She was seen sleeping, looking red and tense and moving her body especially the head and shoulders. She conveyed an impression of feeling 'caught somewhere', struggling to squeeze out, with the head leading all the movements. She would stop, seemingly exhausted, relax and sleep quietly for a while before starting all over again. This process seemed so significant and intense that the mother and the observer could say nothing but just stood watching her seriously during the time it lasted. After repeating the sequence at least three times she slept quietly for some time.

Later on Anthea started to make an effort to expel flatus, first while still sleeping. She became red, tense, moved her legs and pushed rigidly with them. While doing this she woke up and continued with great concentration, fingers clenched, eyes crossed, pushing with all her energy, all muscles active. Mother commented to her, 'What a struggle: you're working very hard'. Anthea, pre-occupied and concentrating, started to put her left hand on her head before expelling each burst of wind which came out noisily. She would hold her head firmly, press it down and then expel the flatus.

Later when mother was chatting about another baby of the same age whom they had met on holiday, she was commenting on some of the similarities between them, and how this other baby like Anthea would bury her head in the mother's breast before going off to sleep. She sometimes wondered why Anthea did not suffocate. She also went on to comment upon all the different changes during their holiday and thought that it must take her a long time to absorb them all.

Meantime the baby had fallen asleep exhausted, her body quiet, her eyes moving slightly under near-closed lids. Her mother wondered what she was thinking, what kind of images she had in her mind and believed that she must dream.

After a while when Anthea woke up again she started to make searching movements with her mouth, tried to find her right thumb with her mouth, then to find the mouth with her hand. It was difficult. She would introduce her fist into her mouth but find that it was impeded by her cuff, and looked as if she were in any case searching for something more specific. She would lose the fist and start trying again and again. Meantime the left hand stayed aside moving slightly occasionally. Anthea then started to

155

get really distressed, apparently because of the difficulty of finding the right thumb. Her sense of discomfort increased until she started to cry and then instantly the left thumb 'came' to her mouth. She sucked vigorously and happily, quite calmed down. Her mother commented that she had started to suck her thumb a week ago.

Anthea could not hold the thumb in her mouth for long however, and started to look to her mother for attention. Mrs A. changed her nappies and then sat her on her lap, Anthea looked towards the breast, leaning towards it and opening her mouth. When the mother took it out the baby sucked strongly for a while, collapsing completely. During the feeding they looked into each other's eyes, mother speaking warmly to the baby meantime. After she had finished sitting on her mother's lap Anthea became interested in her surroundings, examining objects in the room one at a time with alert eyes, throwing herself forward towards the object of her attention. Between different choices she rested comfortably on her mother's lap.

In this observation if one links the baby's movements in sleep, the impression she conveys of being 'caught somewhere', with the mother's comments on how Anthea buries herself in the breast before sleeping, one may surmise claustrophobic anxieties related to intense projection into the breast. This may have entered into her upset the previous day and could also be connected with the holiday and changes of surroundings and routine. The baby continues to show considerable capacity to find or re-create a good internal object. This has different qualities. First there is the holding, the hand on the head re-creating the function of the mother who keeps the baby's person together, while the bad stuff, the flatus is expelled. Then there is the quality of filling the emptiness, the reminder of the nipple in the thumb which interestingly is perceived as 'coming' to her aid at a moment of acute distress, as if it were the agent of an internalised object in advance of the baby's own conscious control. When eventually the baby turns to the mother as an external object and is given the breast, she sucks heartily. Then, fortified by this experience of taking in mother with mouth, eyes and ears, she turns to take in details of the wider world around her, one at a time in the same wholehearted and intense fashion.

A week later when Anthea was observed sleeping once again

some little while before her feed she had a brief period of a similar kind of disturbance. This time her fist went much more easily to her mouth and while she sucked at the finger of her right hand she brought the left hand quite competently to the right one to help to hold the other one there, until shortly afterwards the sucking stopped, she fell asleep and the hands gradually relaxed so that the thumb fell out slowly.

Notes from The Analysis of a Young Mother

Mrs G., a postgraduate student, was referred for analysis by an obstetrician because of a variety of hypochondriacal symptoms and because of her touchy and persecuted attitude to doctors and nurses at the out-patient clinic during her pregnancy. She began analysis some weeks after the birth of her baby son.

Initially she presented herself in brightly coloured ill assorted 'stagey' clothes that seemed merely to accentuate her air of inner dilapidation. After the first weeks' analysis this somewhat brassy exterior gradually faded in favour of skirts of a sombre hue that were more in keeping with her state of mind.

Initially she had difficulty in talking, then gradually came out with a halting shamefaced account of her crazy behaviour to the doctors in the hospital. She interspersed this with recurrent doubts as to what she was doing embarking upon this treatment because everyone knew analysis was supposed to damage your creativity, that analysts never let you go, and as a promising young writer she could not afford to let anyone monkey around with her mind. How was it possible for any doctor to tell her more than she knew herself about what was going on in her head. Some comments linking more closely her suspicion of the doctors with suspicion of the analyst whom she feared would damage or steal the baby, the contents of her mind, enabled her in the next session to talk more freely about her attitude to two of the doctors: her resentment of the consultant because of his self-confidence, assertiveness and off-hand manner; her bitchiness to the registrar who could easily be plunged into a state of anxiety and indecision, unable to answer her questions. This younger doctor reminded her of her younger brother whom she had bullied as a child so much that now he was unable to study and so surely needed analysis much more than she did.

This was the first delineation of a recurrent transference quandary. If the analyst was experienced as competent, having something useful to say about her state of mind, this immediately evoked competitiveness but also anxiety about the offhandedness of an object that could just go away with its expertise. On the other hand if the analyst couldn't see and give her a point clearly enough she was liable to be experienced as a vacillating wobbly object — a nippleless breast or a soft little brother to be treated like dirt but who could not help her in the need which returned anew after each little spell of flamboyant triumph.

In the first few weeks of her analysis despite her hesitations and feelings of persecution she arrived with punctilious promptitude stating that any lateness would not be her fault but that of her husband; if he dallied at work and did not come home in time to babysit. There gradually emerged different versions of a triumphant male figure always lurking to catch her out: the doctor at the post-natal examination who would not believe she was able to breastfeed the baby and who was just waiting for the two of them to make an exhibition of themselves; her own father from whom she was estranged and who had been unkind to her mother during her last illness a few years before (her mother had died of breast cancer).

In the first weeks there was a notable paucity of references to her baby. The resentful needy infant in herself occupied the couch for the greater part of the time, making sure that she had her due in terms of time and attention, persecuted by any interruptions such as a weekend and grasping avidly but suspiciously at the analyst's comments; scared that she would get 'hooked'. Some work upon the projections into the analyst of an internal object — sometimes overwhelmingly needy (the deprived baby brother), sometimes rapaciously persecutory (the cancerous breast) an object that seemed to stand in the way of her feeling that she was a mother to her own baby . . . resulted after five weeks of analysis in her first brief dream; told with trepidation, but also greeted with relief as a sign of creativity, of inner life.

The dream was of two babies, one healthy and bonny and the other puny, starved, apathetic and about to die. Either or neither belonged to her. The healthy baby did in fact look like her own son but was also like photographs of her little brother in infancy;

sweet-natured, smiling and beloved of all, thereby stimulating in her furious jealousy. In response to queries about the puny starved little one she muttered in low-voiced distress that she feared she would have to give up breastfeeding her child. She had never had enough milk, had been supplementing since the first few weeks, but lately it had been getting less and less. Her husband had told her that she really wanted to wean him on to the bottle in case she might have to stay at home to feed him during one of her sessions. He was demand-fed and not always regular in his demands.

It seemed here that in so far as her baby was experienced as mother's baby, her little brother, and was felt to be a competitor for the breast, for the analysis, she was distressed because her greed would make her place herself at his expense. She had already voiced her conviction that she was the analyst's only patient: an omnipotent way of annihilating the other children. This she justified by presenting her own need as the apathetic infant who started treatment with nothing inside her, no idea about herself. This so easily became the insatiable cancer baby which had to go on and on taking up more and more space in the breast; which taken back into herself containing the incubus threatened to swallow up all the milk needed for her baby, who would then be transformed from a healthy child into a puny dying infant. These comments were digested thoughtfully. To the next session on a Monday she came with pains in her arms which she connected with holding the baby; but also associated with the secondaries that had developed in her mother's neck and arms before she died, and which she had been deceived into believing were merely arthritis. The convincing connection between the dying baby in the dream and the dying mother, the internal breast eaten away by the cancerous insatiable greed, made her burst into a flood of tears. These were tears of despair and love for the baby, and of self reproach that she who had been breast fed for nine months should not be able to do likewise for her own child. This was also taken as grief at not being able to take care of the heritage within her, the goodness given by the breast, so that she could hand it on. She had already made it clear that nothing less than all of the analyst's time was any good to her, and feared that nothing less than all of herself would be demanded by the analyst whom she feared was never going to be

159

able to let her go; a mutually parasitic and debilitating situation. Her grief continued for the rest of the week and the analyst was somehow led to believe that her milk had dried up and that the baby was now completely on the bottle.

The following Monday near the beginning of her session she suddenly noticed for the first time a tall cylindrical vase on the mantlepiece where it usually stood, filled with fresh flowers. This she believed to be a pot made by a friend of hers. This led on to suspicions that the analyst had not bought it from a shop but knew this friend and had been given the pot by him. Then followed a persecuted tirade about the friend learning that she was having analysis and suspicions that she would probably find out that the analyst knew all her friends so that soon she would find there was no-one she could truly call her own. Attempts to connect this emotional outburst with shock at confrontation with evidence of parental intercourse over the week-end, of a father's penis which renews and gives flower babies to mother, elicited details about her intense attachment to her mother and her recurrent resentment of father as a tyrannical intruder. Later on when the analyst was exploring the tirade about the flower vase as an expression of envy towards her as the mother who was able to go on feeding, accentuated more poignantly by the drying up of her own breasts, the patient mentioned casually that unaccountably her milk had begun to return and was now more plentiful than it had even been. She did then in fact continue to breastfeed the baby for eight months.

Discussion

Thinking about Anthea and Charles one could say that these are both babies who are being well cared for, who are having some good experiences with mothers who are pleased with them and very fond of them. Mrs C. is an experienced mother who has good and bad recollections of the time when her older children were babies, and (although the observation sequences selected above did not include evidence of this) the pleasure of seeing these children developing in a lively, interesting way.

For Mrs A. it is all very new but the interest and the sense of discovery are out-weighing previous apprehensions. She seems to have the capacity to respond and to allow herself to learn from a baby who can express her needs clearly and indicate satisfaction when they are met. This enables Mrs A. to gather increasing conviction that she really is a mother — not just a little girl beset by the instructions and criticisms of parents who *really* know. Her pleasure in noting how she is changing is parallelled by her delight in noting the developments in the baby, her wondering about what the baby is feeling and thinking, her maternal 'reverie'. The interaction between the two is close and deep and one may indeed say that Anthea is introjecting an object which is able to learn from experience. One might however speculate on how different Mrs A.'s experience of motherhood might have been with a first child who was essentially more difficult to please, because although she is clearly a young woman of inner resilience and receptivity there were moments when she envisaged that just a little more demanded of her could become too much.

Charles at three weeks comes over as a baby who is much less able to relax and feel contained, less at home in his own skin and liable to 'fly apart', than Anthea at the same age. He tends to look more integrated when attracted and held by the impingement of external sensory stimuli: the light, the sound of the clock ticking, the points of touch, and to disintegrate when these are removed. This is especially noticable when the leggings are taken off. The cycling, the rage, the muscular tension, notably the strong back-bone seem to be 'second-skin' formations which later on help him to hold himself together.

It is significant that he is observed to burrow into his cot but not into his mother. One may surmise that he has some sense of his mother's vulnerability, which later she tells the observer has disturbed the breastfeeding for her. Her need to be wrapped up in her clothes is parallelled by Charles's reliance on his clothing. These clothes, like the general liveliness and activity in the family, seem to be used by Mrs C. as a cover to insulate her from some feeling of sadness and internal loss, hinted at earlier and then expressed obliquely in terms of overburdened apple-trees, dead parents.

In the instance of Mrs G. we have an instance of a pathological interference with maternal containment by hypochondriacal illness and persecutory depression. It emerged that her mothering function was being stunted by her state of projective identification with a dead internal mother — the cancerous breast; her persecution in the face of medical examination, and afterwards of analytic examination was connected with grave doubts about containing a baby at all, rather than this destroyed and destroying internal object.

The bright ill-assorted clothing of the first week of her treatment seemed to be performing the function of holding her together, and of attempting to hide this inner dilapidation. It seemed that she was able to function more fully as a mother after she had transferred to the analyst, and had begun to experience in the containment of the analytic situation, some of the jealousy and greed of the little girl who could not stand mother having another baby who hated her baby brother.

Each mother has her own reawakened infantile feelings to manage after birth of her baby who is somewhere also deeply experienced as mother's baby. Mrs C. exemplifies some of the interferences with pregnancy and mothering which may ensue when these buried grudges against the parents who make babies and the breast that weans the baby are so intense and so unresolved that they infiltrate and paralyse maternal reverie.

Mrs C. to a lesser degree is also preoccupied with something in her internal situation by which she does not feel sustained, so that she has to try to protect herself and is somewhat impeded from being emotionally close to Charles in these early weeks. Mrs A. seems more able to think about and to talk about her anxieties; to shift more easily from her own internal preoccupations to interest in Anthea and her internal world. Charles in these early weeks is a baby who is, and seems to have to be, more preoccupied with survival, with holding himself together. Anthea shows evidence, at the same stage, of her life, of internalising a maternal object upon which she can rely for some containment of her distress, and although alert and interested in her surroundings, she is already less totally dependent upon them.

I acknowledge with thanks contributions from Evanthe Piper and Elisabeth Lemlig.

REFERENCES

BICK, E. (1964) 'Notes on Infant Observation in Psychoanalytic Training', *International Journal of Psychoanalysis*, Vol. 45.

BICK, E. (1968) 'The Experience of the Skin in Early Object Relations', *International Journal of Psychoanalysis*, Vol. 49.

BION, W.R. (1962) *Learning from Experience*, London, Heinemann.

BION, W.R. (1967) 'A Theory of Thinking', in *Second Thoughts*, London, Heinemann.

FREUD, S. (1914) 'On Narcissism: An Introduction'. Standard Edition, Vol. 14.

KLEIN, M. (1921) 'The Development of a Child', in *Contributions to PsychoAnalysis*. London: Hogarth, 1948.

KLEIN, M. (1952) 'Notes on some schizoid mechanisms', in *Developments in PsychoAnalysis*, London, Hogarth.

MELTZER, D. *et al* (1975) *Explorations in Autism*. Perthshire, Clunie Press.

WINNICOTT, D.W. (1965) *The Maturational Processess and the Facilitating Environment*. London, Hogarth.

Published in the *Journal of Child Psychotherapy* Vol. 4, 1970.

Some of this material appears in 'Depressive, Paranoid and Narcissistic Features in the Analysis of a Woman following the Birth of her first Child, and the Death of her own Mother'.

3   Towards Learning from Experience in
Infancy and Childhood
1978

To begin by paraphrasing Hegel: 'We learn from history that we do not learn from history.' This probably applies to the history of psychoanalytic societies and other similar bodies, to the history of the individual personality as much as it does to the history of nations. And yet the psychoanalytic method of observation and of research has given us an impetus and unique tool to study why it is that we find it so difficult to learn from our personal history. It has given us a basis from which to consider ways in which it may be possible or impossible to hand on to others any of the experience we do acquire. Those of us who are in some position of responsibility for the welfare of others — as parents, educators, administrators for example — must of necessity be concerned with thinking about the conditions which enable individuals to develop and to share the fruits of that development with others.

It is of course manifestly untrue from another point of view that we do not learn from the history of man's tussle with his environment. The whole story of our civilisation from the earliest times bears testimony to a utilisation, however sporadically and unevenly, of vast bodies of acquired knowledge about the nature of the world, which has transformed it. It is a truism to say that this progress is essentially lopsided and that man's cleverness in manipulating his external resources so far exceeds his capacity to know and to manage his own nature and internal resources, as an individual and as a member of society, that he is in imminent peril of destroying that world which so far as we know is necessary for his survival. However well adjusted, well appointed and successful we may be, we do live under threat of catastrophe, and in a world where one does not have to look far to see that thousands or millions elsewhere are in catastrophe at this moment, in ways that few of us are able to help significantly. To be constantly aware, or to refrain from ignoring totally, the precarious backdrop against which we all live our lives can help us to be closer to the basic anxieties which infants and young

164

children have inevitably to encounter as a condition of living. We can try to protect ourselves by ignoring these, taking up some collusive self-idealising attitude which claims to banish them; or, through remaining open, sharing and struggling together, we may be able to help children to help themselves a little better, to grow up strengthened by some experience of themselves — of their own emotions as well as of the world around them. Therefore, they would have a better chance of becoming self-determined individuals who are in turn able to contribute a little to the climate of their society.

Freud founded the science of psychoanalysis as a result of studying the hidden psychological origins of various somatic symptoms in his patients. One of the theories he later advanced about the nature of the unconcious was that of the repetition compulsion. This postulated that at the most primitive level of functioning, all experience which impinges upon the personality tends to be re-enacted over and over again regardless of pleasure or pain. This theory replaced an earlier one in his papers on the 'Studies in Hysteria' which postulated that traumatic events remained unassimilated within the personality and became a focus for neurosis. Hence the belief for a time in the detoxifying effect of unearthing buried memories and the attempt to direct psycho-analytic treatment to this end. Freud's work throughout most of his life was directed toward investigating *what went wrong*, in the development of the individual; it was only towards the end of his career when he was concerned with the nature of the ego and splits within the ego, the super ego and ego-ideal, that he began to approach some theory of how the individual does normally develop. But he had evolved no real theory about the development of the inner world.

Following Freud, yet also taking another direction as a result of her observation of children, Melanie Klein brought to pshyco-analysis a more developmental forward-looking perspective. She was struck by the importance of what she termed the 'epistemophilic instinct': the child's urge to know, to investigate the world. She noticed children's interest in spaces and their contents, deriving from their interest in the inside of their mother's body and the inside of their own bodies. She noticed that they had phantasies of mother's inside as peopled by objects from their own infantile experiences — by milk, babies, faeces and urine:

165

that is, that the mother's body is believed to contain objects and desires derived from the infant's experience of himself and of his own body.

Wilfred Bion has carried further the implications of Melanie Klein's observations of the infant's basic desire to know, to reach outwards into the world by spelling out the way in which basic interactions take place and how modification by experience can take place. The infant in distress has a momentary fear of dying and evacuates or projects this distress. A mother who is able to be close to her baby can receive this panicky part of the infant and try to do something to alleviate the distress. If she tries to respond appropriately he feels that he has a place in her mind, as well as in her body, her arms. He has an experience of being understood as well as of being physically relieved. He receives back from the mother that previously intolerable part of himself in an improved form together with some experience of a containing maternal presence which has been able to hold it. He has an experience of finding a place in his mother's mind, in what Bion terms 'maternal reverie'. If he can take into himself, if he can introject that receptive container he begins to develop within himself an internal object which enables him to accept himself, to tolerate the feelings he has about the events which happen to him.

Esther Bick has, through analytic work and through following many detailed sequential studies of infant-mother relationships, investigated the outcome of what would seem to be deficiencies in emotional maternal containment. Deficiency in this respect is of course a general term which may apply to quality as well as quantity and is connected with impairment of fit between a particular mother and baby. There are babies whose responsiveness and capacity to relate to the mother call forth very readily all her latent mothering capacity. There are babies who from birth seem to be so restless and dissatisfied that they evoke in her acutely her own infantile anxieties and insecurities. These babies may become as a result resented, ignored, or attacked. There are on the other hand mothers who have enough strength or enough support (as from husbands) to be able to go on struggling through periods of difficulty towards a happier accommodation.

The work of Donald Meltzer and of others on long-term analytical studies of autistic children has thrown light upon states of unintegration and mindlessness, following the dismantling

166

under stress of sensory equipment and of parts of the personality. This occurs when, for various reasons, a child has been unable to experience and to introject a strong enough internal object to hold him together, to allow the parts of himself and the experiences they have to come together in meaningful and communicable ways. The work of Bick and Meltzer in this field has many implications for understanding areas of shallowness, frailty, clinging and mimicry, probably present within every one of us, but which in some people are major impediments or lacunae in development. These areas are connected with the continuation into late childhoood and grown-up life of undue dependence on external structures and stability. Excessive reliance upon material objects can be a defence against awareness of internal emptiness. This emptiness follows upon the evacuation of painful emotions without which growth cannot take place. It can also be a consequence of the failure of such growth.

We must all, I think, at some moments in our lives be caught unawares by that most primitive infantile fear, of imminently dying as Bion describes it, of endlessly falling as Bick describes it; if only perhaps in the sudden jump of anxiety at the moment of dropping off to sleep, or the dream of falling into space. One can sense that shudder of falling apart in some infants at moments of transition from one physical state or position to another: for instance if picked up from their cot too suddenly. Her empathy with this kind of anxiety leads a mother who is sensitive to the baby's needs, to be gentle in her handing of his body and careful that he should not be subjected without preparation for stimuli which are too abrupt for him to absorb without being rent apart. The work of Le Boyer is aimed at helping those who assist mothers in giving birth to notice the baby as a little person, and to try to minimise the traumatic effect of the transition from the holding milieu of the womb to a world where all too often he is bombarded with a variety of overharsh stimuli which he might be supposed to be too young to notice. We gather evidence in analysis of how shattering events in later life such as the sudden death of a dearly-loved relative can intrude into the personality and may even rupture at a somatic level the internal container which holds its parts together, repeating reactions to earlier catastrophic intrusions.

Traumatic events throughout life, from whatever source, test

167

the capacity of the personality to hold new experience with its inevitable pain and uncertainty, and to grow from it. This capacity must always, to some extent, be influenced by the nature of the identifications with the earliest containing objects and in particular with the primary receptive responsive qualities of the mother. Receptive parents help an infant to have an experience of himself. His identification with them helps him manage later the conflicting emotions and impulses that arise in the ordinary course of living, if he is *being* what he *is*, *feeling* what he *feels*.

Helping a child to be himself does not, of course, mean encouraging him to act upon the impulse of any given moment. Nor, for that matter, does it necessitate immediate response to his demand for attention even in early infancy. In the first days his impulses are expressible almost exclusively in action, but as soon as he has begun to introject, to find within himself a comforting understanding presence, this can help him to hold, however briefly, the urgent demand or pain or need until perhaps the necessary external aid comes to relieve him or to assist him to bear the painful state of mind which is afflicting him.

Introjection remains a mysterious process: how do involvement and reliance upon objects in the external world which are apprehended by the senses (and, as Wilfred Bion has pointed out, described in language which has been evolved to deal with external reality), become assimilated and transformed in the mind into what he calls 'psychoanalytic objects' which can contribute to the growth of the personality? This is a process about which we have almost everything to learn.

It is, therefore, impossible to give any simple guidelines to any particular parent with a child, to tell any mother how she should look after her own baby. One can but try to promote conditions in which she has a chance to think about, to notice and to respect what he is. Respecting the baby, the small child from the earliest weeks of life means giving him a little time to express what he feels, to reach out a little to explore the world as far as he is able, and a chance too to discover his own feelings as they arise.

For the infant to have his mother as a servant who meets or tries to meet his needs before he has a chance to be fully aware of them himself, encourages omnipotence and belief in an omniscient object which can be called into service like a kind of genie from Aladdin's lamp. Encouragement of omnipotence constricts imagination. A hyper-intuitive comforting parental object tends to pre-empt the necessity to turn inwards, to try to recollect, to imagine the presence of the needed object in its absence and to draw from strength upon the experiences shared with it. The capacity for introjection and introjective identifications with admired and loved objects is strengthened by use. So the mother who does what she feels is needed by the baby, giving herself time to think about what that need may be, gives the baby time to experience it and helps him to expand his internal resources: to tolerate some delay between impulse and action, between desire and fulfilment. This allows for thought and for the exploration of different ways of dealing with frustration in imagination.

I would like now to give a series of excerpts from the observation of a little girl of twenty-two months who is learning to struggle with the complicated emotions of the birth of a baby sister: a very ordinary experience in the history of many of us, but nonetheless inevitably traumatic and unsettling to some extent for every child who has enjoyed a close and loving relationship with her mother and father as the sole child in the family. We can perhaps follow in this observation the different positions, the different identifications which this little girl assumes, and the way in which her mother responds and allows her to try out her reactions while at the same time managing to protect the close relationship with the baby from being interfered with.

Observation

Upon her first visit to the family the observer is greeted by the mother carrying her little daughter Nancy while the baby aged one week is still sleeping in her cot. Nancy, who is grizzly with a slight cold, allows herself to be put down while the mother makes a cup of tea for the observer, but she declines to join the grown-ups when a cup is offered to her.

As the women talk the baby begins to stir, apparently responding to the sounds of speech. Nancy notices this and goes off to pick up one of her dolls. The mother wonders whether the baby is waking for her feed and moves towards the cot. As she does this

169

Nancy throws that doll away. Then when she sees her mother pick up the baby she crosses the room to pick up another doll, a rag one, and strokes its hair tenderly. The mother hands the baby to the observer to hold while she gets ready to feed her, settles herself comfortably on the bed, crosslegged, making a comfortable little nest for the baby as she offers her the breast. Nancy watches, looking troubled, hands her rag doll to the observer and clambers close to her mother on the bed, leaning against her as she feeds the baby. The mother smiles and tells the observer that Nancy must like her as she has given her her favourite doll.

As the breastfeed proceeds quietly the mother chats to the observer about the two children and how they differed as babies. Then when the baby has had a fairly leisurely time at one breast, she takes her off and offers her to Nancy to hold for a little while. This means propping Nancy up with cushions on the bed and laying the baby across the cushions. The mother leaves the room for a moment to fetch something.

Nancy beams with pleasure looking proudly at the observer from time to time but struggling momentarily it seems with fleeting impulses of hostility. On the mother's return she says to Nancy, 'Shall we finish the feed now?' to which Nancy replies emphatically 'NO', holding onto the baby mutinously. The mother waits for a few minutes then asks Nancy if she would like to show the observer her little Teddy. Nancy brightens up, lets the mother take the baby, but does not leave the room to get her teddy. As the mother sits on the bed feeding the baby Nancy gets up behind her, begins to jump and bounce until she has pushed mother and baby off the edge of the bed, which all happens fairly smoothly without the baby's feeding being disturbed. The mother continues it from the floor leaning against the bed..

During this the observer feels a little anxious and thinks there are one or two difficult moments for the mother.

Left in possession of the bed now, Nancy bounces up and down, while the mother reflects to the observer that sometimes she wonders whether she is going to be able to control Nancy, saying that fortunately her husband is better at it than she is, and has spent a lot of time with her at the weekend. At one point apparently Nancy had wandered out of the house into the street and was found carrying a screwdriver as if she were daddy going off to work. Reflecting about the baby the mother says that just a week ago she was a lump in her tummy: 'Now she's out and all I have to do is bring her up'; (wryly) 'I feel sad'.

A week later when the observer returns she is greeted by Nancy in a very friendly fashion, accepting immediately the mother's suggestion that she join the grown-ups in having a cup of tea. The baby is asleep again and before she wakes up a neighbour calls in with her little boy, a few months younger than Nancy. Nancy then becomes preoccupied with the little boy to whom she continues to behave with unmingled hostility, smacking him whenever she has a chance to get at him. The observer leaves early, feeling that she might by her presence be complicating an embarrassing situation.

Upon her next visit a week later once again there is a visitor: this time a pregnant friend of the mother with her little daughter almost the same age as Nancy, and to whom at first Nancy seems to be friendly. The baby is fed and again the mother asks Nancy if she'd like to hold her for a few minutes. Again Nancy is delighted, beams with pleasure and bends her face to rub it against the baby's. The pregnant visitor says approvingly (and maybe hopefully, thinking of her own little girl), 'she loves her doesn't she?' Immediately Nancy begins to push the baby away gently but urgently calling in a pleading voice for her mother who comes to relieve her. Nancy then immediately gets down from the bed and goes over to pull the other little girl's hair. The two mothers stop her firmly but tactfully, but have to continue to keep an eye on her for the rest of the time as Nancy clearly remains preoccupied by the presence of this intruder, waiting for a chance to pinch or pull and coming back at one point after leaving the room with a paint brush wielded as a weapon. Her mother takes it from her saying that in the last week she had managed to get one like this up her nose and had to be taken round to the hospital next door. Again she emphasises what a strong determined little girl Nancy is, fearing that she would be too much for her to cope with, without her husband's help. Amid all this she is managing to feed the baby, and to protect her from the disturbances.

From these observations one can get some idea of the complexity of emotions which the little girl feels about her baby sister and about her mother who is occupied with the new baby.

One can see the different positions or identities which she assumes almost from moment to moment to be able to tolerate the painfulness of the situation. One can see how the mother, while able to protect the peacefulness of the baby-breast relationship (details of which for the sake of clarity are omitted here), is empathising with the feelings with which her little daughter is struggling. She is trying to include her in the total situation where possible: in the social situation with the observer, in helping with the baby. But she is not asking her to *feel* what she does not feel and is tolerating unequivocal expressions of hostility when they break through. Her tolerance is clearly on a delicate balance evidently strengthened by the recollection that she can rely on her husband where she fails. Her open friendly attitude to the observer indicates that she is not bothered by being judged and felt to be wanting, by a watcher who has some kind of parental superego function. She seems to be able to reflect upon her experience as she is having it, to share the feelings of being daunted by the long task before her of bringing up the children. And all this is in addition to her manifest pleasure in being with the two children and in talking about them to the observer.

She does not seem to be hampered by preconceptions of how the elder child *ought* to behave to the baby; gives her the chance of being a little mother for a brief while, encourages her to find a little baby substitute of her own when she has to feed the baby, encourages her to share in the actual holding of the baby when that is possible, to join in the tea with the grow-ups, to accept visits from other friends with small children.

One sees how strongly Nancy reacts to the comment of the friend who must be a little anxious about how her little girl will take to the birth of a little sibling. 'She loves her, doesn't she'. The violent negative reaction provoked by this doting comment could be seen as a child's protest at being confined in a role that allows her no leeway to experience unloving impulses, labelled too simply; hence the violent rejection. In none of these observations does her mother seem to be trying to do this. Nancy indeed seems to turn to her mother for help with her hostile feelings towards the baby when she calls quietly and urgently. Her aggression towards the baby is then displaced and violently enacted on her doll in the first instance, and then repeatedly on

172

the little visitor, who perhaps being nearer her own size may be felt to be less vulnerable, as well as a little further away from her family. Her mother stops her from going too far in a matter of fact rather than in a guilt provoking way, as if to say 'You are not allowed to hurt another child', rather than, 'How could you have such nasty feelings about another little child'. The reality of what she feels is being recognised as nothing remarkable or out of the way, but she is getting some help in refraining from translating her feelings into precipitate action. She is being educated in how to manage what *is*, rather than manipulated to twist something into what it *ought* to be and thereby encouraging insincerity.

It is worth noticing that a couple of weeks after this sequence the observer was struck by the marked increase in Nancy's capacity for expressing herself verbally. Her negative feelings for instance about the baby's feeding or the mother who feeds the baby, were expressed in a verbal game with the mother where she continued to insist that milk was NULK.

The matter of fact response to children's nastier feelings is probably worth underlining. Such recognition allows them to feel that they are acceptable for what they are at this point in time and not expected to be good or adult in a way that is impossible. For instance the mother who is unable to notice or to tolerate jealousy of a sibling may be inviting a particular form of what Melanie Klein calls projective identification.

In a situation of this kind a projection, an attempt to get rid of that intolerable unacceptably jealous part of the self may encourage the child to become what mummy wants. She may prematurely step into mummy's shoes and become a little mummy, living in a false identity. To become a good little girl — or good little boy for that matter — living in a prematurely acquired grown-up identity does not help one to grow through learning to live and work with the jealous and envy that in some degree are aspects of human temperament and are evoked to some extent by the inevitable frustrations of childhood. A child who cannot struggle with these emotions is not practising to become an adult. There is a tendency for the good little girl who becomes a better mummy to have to deal with the pain of her unassimilated envy and rivalry by evoking it in other more vulnerable people throughout her life.

Analytic investigation of children and of adults suggests that it

173

is certainly difficult if not impossible to hold, express, and use in the service of development primitive parts of the self that have been unable to find a receptive maternal container in the external world. This may be a necessary step before they can find a place in the personality. And that usually implies some capacity in the maternal person to distinguish between what comes from the infant and what belongs to the infant part of herself.

Clinical Material

Now to give a brief example from analytic work with a young woman to indicate how problems unresolved in infancy recur in later life. Sometimes these may be worked over and dealt with better in the context of the person's life situation and close relationships at some later date; sometimes one suspects that the only way of making headway with them is in an analytic setting where these more infantile aspects of the personality areas can be sequestered, thought about in detail as they emerge, and can be transformed into experiences which enrich the self rather than forces which dislocate the personality.

Mrs A. sought analysis during her first pregnancy because of fits of helpless weeping, fears of collapse, of falling and of inability to hold or look after the baby once it was born.

After some little time a pattern in her analytic week was discernible: hopefulness, easy communication and receptivity on the Monday and Tuesday, then a puzzling cut-off flatness on the Wednesdays. Thurday and Friday tended to be dominated by anxieties about falling apart, about liquifying, and fears of being unable to survive the week-end.

It then emerged through confirmation with her mother that as a baby she had been breast fed for two days but taken off the breast and put on the bottle as her mother could not bear the jealousy and disruptiveness of the elder brother during the feeds. She had been such a good baby that nobody suspected that any strain was imposed on her at this transition, or during her infancy.

In the analytic situation became evident a very genuine friendliness and gratefulness for efforts made on her behalf. She developed a capacity to dream, to make both conscious and unconscious use of interpretive work. With this came a conviction that there was much more to her than she had ever supposed. She had thought she was a pleasant but rather shallow person, designed to be a kind of dogsbody to serve other people — men in particular. When the prizes of life were handed out she was doomed to be last. It became clear that she had delegated to her brother in infancy and childhood much of her strength and force. She had admired him for his looks, attractiveness and vigour, had become his shadow and little brother (rather than sister) imitator, in a way that was hampering the development of her femininity, but which protected her from jealousy, the emotion her mother could not deal with in the brother after her birth.

As references to intrusive exploiting men and greedy colleagues became gathered into the context of the analytic situation, greed, jealousy and envy became associated with some part of herself that she said she felt was whirling around in space. Then one week-end she had a dream, that was almost entirely an undefined emotional experience, *of being rent apart by some violent disintegrating force.* She woke from it terribly shaken but grateful and reassured to be alive, and happy that she had a place to talk about this experience. The next week's work seemed to return to her in a more assimilable form some of the hitherto unexpressed and uncontained violence, jealousy in particular, for which the basic intensity of her nature demanded an outlet. The ability to experience this was related to the growing trust in the analytic situation, enabling her to experience a maternal object able to bear the impact of this violence, and to help her to think about it.

Exploration of her current relationship with her actual mother indicated that the latter was a woman of considerable qualities of warmth and intelligence, but easily roused to feelings of jealousy and envy and liable to behave like a child having a tantrum in situations which evoked these emotions — situations which her daughter from infancy had evidently been too intimidated to evoke. Hence, it seemed, the patient's difficulty in pregnancy in being able to identify with a secure holding mother to support her in her feminine maternal role. There also emerged as a factor hampering her relationships with men, the tendency to project into them, as into the brother and also the father, her own split-off infantile demands. These demanding men she would then reject, or else tend to serve slavishly.

Experiencing those emotions and learning about them within

175

the holding situation of a psychoanalytic session enabled growth and integration of hitherto unassimilated parts of herself.

Observation

And now a brief excerpt from an infant observation to indicate a situation where a mother, with a new baby to whom she has been unable to come close during the first few weeks, is beginning to recover within herself strength which allows her to be more receptive to the needs of the baby, and to give him time to express them and have them met by her.

It is Mrs B.'s first baby, a boy whom she wants to go on breast-feeding. From the beginning she has been very uncertain about providing enough milk, especially as he is such a big baby and she feels herself to be so small. After feeding from one breast he is usually put down in his pram with a bottle propped on a pillow. He always takes a little from this bottle, drops off to sleep afterwards but then usually wakes up and fusses in a muted kind of way which does not exactly demand attention from the mother but gets on her nerves. She can not make up her mind whether to pick him up or not, thinking it better to leave him lying there with the bottle while he is still sucking so that he would be sure to have enough milk. She notices that often after being put down with the bottle he seems to be colicky, drawing his legs up and making explosive noises down below although when she looks he has not usually soiled his nappy.

The comments of the mother about the baby in the early weeks are made, the observer notes, in rather a distant way, as if she is far away from it all. She seems to be much preoccupied with seeing that the house is in order, with worries about having her husband's meal ready in time when he comes home, saying that he is working hard and has evening classes to attend three nights a week. These will enable him to get a qualification which will give him a rise in his job. When eventually the observer meets the father she is surprised to find him easy and friendly, not at all the demanding exacting character described by his wife. Indeed she has the impression that the father would have been very happy to help if the mother were to ask him to do anything for her.

After the first four weeks of the baby's life the observer feels that the mother is becoming a little less agitated and restless, is taking more interest in the baby, beginning to talk more about him than about the demands of the housekeeping and of her husband. On the fifth visit when the baby is just over five weeks old she notes that for the first time the mother does not weigh the baby after the feed at the one breast. She takes him off it, holds him against her shoulder patting him while talking to the observer about him. Then she puts him to the second breast; the first time the observer has seen her give both at one feed.

The observer then notices that his behaviour at this second breast is quite different from his quiet sleepy sucking at the first and different from his attitude to the bottle when lying in the cot. He approaches it with more effort and intensity digging in round the nipple with his fingers, screwing up his face, making panting little sounds. Indeed it seems to the observer that the struggle that had been going on down below in his nappy in the cot with the bottle, is now taking place above, closer to the mother and at the second breast.

The mother seems to be unperturbed, not noticing what is taking place although she is in fact talking much more hopefully to the observer about the way she is now managing the household chores. Then towards the end of the struggling at the second breast the baby's attention seems to be drawn to the mother's voice talking to the observer. He pulls away from the nipple and looks up at the mother's face making a little calling protesting sound which catches her attention. As she looks down at him with a pleased expression he beams widely at her to her great delight. She exclaims that this is his first real smile. The observer thinks that she has never seen the two so close to each other as now.

In brief I would suggest that these little excerpts give some idea of a mother and baby who have been rather far apart emotionally, beginning to approach one another more closely. It seems that the mother's ability to give the baby more time — perhaps helped through feeling supported herself by the ongoing friendly receptive presence of the observer — allows the baby to bring up and to express nearer to her person the complicated sensations he was having down below in his pram with the bottle. Kept closer to her for longer he can then make a bid for her attention and then respond to that with a smile: a moment of meeting of getting to know each other, attended with delight.

Detailed close observations of infants and young children in their developing relationships can complement the observations one is able to make during the development of the transference within the analytic situation, which is one specific setting that aims to provide the opportunity for learning through having an emotional experience. The theories that are formulated about observations are of secondary importance and can never short-cut the necessity for each couple, and maybe also in a different way each small group or family, to go through the uncertainties and delights of new discovery. For learning from experience is based initially on experience shared: the prototype is the mother who does not only love but who is interested in her baby as a developing human being; who through paying attention and thinking about him, provides that holding function which allows a child to have experiences of himself and of the world in a modulating environment. He may therefore internalise an object which enables him to notice and think when the external parental support is absent.

That holding maternal presence is necessary to some degree to enable the infant to feel that he is a personality, that he has an identity to preserve. The infant that is in us all probably requires in stress from time to time throughout life an external manifestation of that presence. But holding is not the same as enclosure — the personality is ossified by identification with closed minds, and can be preserved alive only through developing and risking itself. It needs encouragement to reach forward from some base of security towards further experience.

4   The Family Circle: Brothers and Sisters

A family begins with the parents. Each new individual's relationship with other members of his family is influenced by the relationship that has evolved between him and his parents, not only as he has learnt to manage it in the external world, but as he privately experiences it in his unconscious mind.

When a younger brother or sister appears, the elder child is faced with a new form of the jealousy he first encountered when he realised that he had to give way to his father for possession of his mother — and then later to his mother for pride of place with his father, at times when father was regarded as the most important person in life. Mothers, anticipating and fearful of this jealousy, and eager for the child to share the pleasure of looking forward to the new baby, will often talk to him glowingly about *his* new baby. Then, when it arrives, the child finds that it doesn't notice him, can't do anything, and that his mother is inevitably very much occupied with it; he realises that it's not *his* baby, that he can't feed or bath it or comfort it when it cries, and has to play a very minor role in looking after it. Along with a bitter sense of disappointment he has to struggle with feelings of rejection, anger and depression at no longer being the only child in the family. If the baby is of a different sex, he'll tend to feel that that is what the parents really wanted.

If parents are alive to these feelings as part of normal development, they can give the child time to make acquaintance with them, and to find his way towards an honestly based relationship with the new brother or sister. This can only be founded on some degree of recognition by the child of his own ambivalence.

Each child has his unique fashion of facing or denying or manipulating the situation. Supported by parental recognition of his predicament, his occasional panics, tears, bids for attention and infantile rages, he becomes free to find the positive advantages and pleasures in having the new child. He may identify with mother in her pride at showing off the new baby, or he may seek mutual consolation and conversation with his father when his mother is too busy to have time for them both. He may be warmed and delighted when the baby begins to recognise and

179

to smile at him, when at times it begins to prefer his company, when it wants to play with him, when it learns to speak his name.

In Order of Age

Relationships between brothers and sisters tend, of course, to be influenced by their particular positions in the family. Often, encouraged by the parents, the eldest (whether a boy or a girl) will adopt a maternal attitude towards the younger ones. This caretaker role can satisfy both the eldest child and the others if it is founded on a basically loving, ungrudging attitude, not forced either by parental compulsion or by a too compelling inner need to deny resentment and envy of the mother. It may be carried on long past childhood, and after the parents are dead. The younger children can find in the older brother or sister a figure to admire and to rely on: someone to emulate more hopefully than the parents because more like themselves. They can watch, too, the physical growth and increasing achievements and privileges of the elder and think, for instance, 'Mary has boy friends and goes to dances today, my turn may be tomorrow'.

Sometimes a child's development is founded on a precocious maturity that masks too much unresolved resentment against the parents and the grown-up world. He then tends to flaunt prowess and privileges in order to arouse in his more vulnerable brothers or sisters (often the younger ones) the envy and frustration, evoked by painful feelings of inadequacy and childishness, which he cannot contain and resolve within himself. The younger or weaker child may have his own compensatory fantasies. We are familiar with some of these fairy tales: with Cinderella, who by her meekness and the beauty beneath her rags wins the prince and defeats her elder ugly sisters; with the many stories about the youngest of three brothers who by wit or goodness or magical aid outstrips his elders in some impossible task and so wins the hand of the princess.

Fairness and respect by the parents for the individuality of each child are essential in mediating these grievances, in protecting the more vulnerable from victimisation by the others. Nature is unfair, and children even in the same family are unequally endowed. The dull child among bright siblings, the plain girl with pretty sisters, are obvious examples of those who start at a disadvantage. A less obvious but equally potent inequality concerns the child disposed towards ready but undefended affections who can become the tool or doormat for more omnipotent and managing brothers or sisters.

Parental help

Parents' insight into the transactions between their children depends largely on having come to terms sufficiently with their childhood rivalries towards their own brothers, sisters and parents. They can therefore recognise how similar rivalries are being expressed in their own children and not add fuel to the fire by identifying too strongly and unequally with any particular child because of unrealised and uncontained aspects of their own personalities. So far as their own natures allow, the children can then identify with fair and perspicacious parents; learn to play fair with each other; respect and allow for varying degrees of skill and achievement in different fields according to differences of age, sex and ability. If children are recognised and appreciated by their parents for what they are and for what they have the potential to become, they are freer to recognise the qualities in their brothers and sisters. They are less driven to jealous competition and less of a prey to seeking triumph or being overwhelmed by discouragement. When more than one avenue to fulfilment is open, the competition is not so keen.

Because childishness — dependence on mother — is equated with femininity, the growing boy, struggling for independence, tends for a time to profess to despise his sisters and all girls. Sisters may go through a phase of tomboyish emulation, or react against the physical prowess and privileges of their brothers — and boys in general — in prim-lipped and pseudo-maternal goody-goodyness. If the father has respect for his wife as an individual and as a woman (as more than a housekeeper and a sexual convenience or plaything), and if this also holds good for the mother's attitude to him (as more than the breadwinner and comfort provider), children have a family climate in which they can gradually come to terms with their own sexual identities in adolescence, while respecting that of their brothers or sisters,

Friendships between brothers and sisters, founded on experience of growing up together and surviving the rivalries

181

and betrayals which must at times inevitably temper loyalties, can give that intimate understanding and affection for a contemporary of the opposite sex. This helps people to make a wise choice of husband or wife. For the boys, sexual attractiveness is less likely to be exclusively dependent on looks; and for the girl, less heavily weighted by the man's material prospects. And the brother who gets to know his sister's friends, and who observes his sister's reactions to *his* girl friends, has a better chance of realising what he is marrying than the one who has had a less intimate and extensive aquaintanceship with girls around his own age. Sisters may get a similar advantage.

In adult life the bond between brothers and sisters is tested when one of them marries. This is especially true perhaps if one brother or sister left behind has been especially attached to the newly wed. It may be a test, for instance, of a sister's capacity to cope with her own envy and jealousy at being left out; or of her ability to accept the new in-law, despite reservations, for the sake of the beloved brother.

A further test comes at the death or the incapacity of parents through old age. There may be problems of sharing responsibility for the care of increasingly helpless parents, or of accepting with a good grace the division of property on a parent's death. Whether this death is expected or not — even if it comes in the fullness of time as a relief — it always tends to evoke in the grown-up children buried infantile emotions of dependence, loss and betrayal. It also evokes equally infantile irrational jealousies about their own stake in the affections of the deceased parent, when esteem is measured (as so frequently) by material contributions.

In our society, frequency of contact between brothers and sisters in adult life varies greatly according to the limitations of time and space imposed by their work and family commitments. For many people, however, a family feeling that is rooted in an appreciation of shared parents and shared childhood experiences remains probably a bond that is stronger than most of their friendships, and one on which claims can be made or honoured in times of need.

Where the tie between brothers is *not* the kingpin of the social structure, their early rivalry eventually peters out.

Thus, among Bushmen, one feels, the relation between

brother and sister is very different here, brothers among ourselves: personal, free and carrying no great weight of social
obligation. In such societies the tie between brothers is like that
between sisters the world over. For women always interact in a
much narrower niche of social organisation: their jealousies can
rock the boat, but not so dangerously as the rivalries of men.
Their relations with each other are therefore not so strictly regu-
lated. If a woman's term for sister automatically implies the
seniority of one or the other, it is hardly a ranking device, rather a
reference to which one mothered the other in babyhood.

To return to the second box: the relation between brother and
sister is very different here. No common ranking can possibly
relate them in a single hierarchial order, so there is no point in a
woman distinguishing a brother as older or younger. A brother is
just a brother, united by birth to his sister but separated from her
by the whole weight of the social structure. She is the category of
person of the opposite sex who is not sexually available.

The brother/sister tie is the basis of both 'patrilineal' and
'matrilineal' systems of descent. If succession and inheritance are
traced through males (i.e. patrilineal), then a man begets his heirs
through wedlock, and for this he obtains as wife another man's
sister. He gives away his own sister in like manner. Among the
Lovedu of the Transvaal the sister has high status in her brother's
home, comes back for family rituals and there she lords it over his
wives. The general effect of all this is that the brother is not
allowed to forget that he got his wife in a kind of exchange for his
sister and that he is in debt to her and her children, owing them
protection and help. Thus the role of sister as non-wife is ever
present to the mind, even in the type of society which is built upon
the separation of brother and sister.

It is even more to the fore in a matrilineal society which reckons
descent through females. All over the world there are societies
built up in this way on the permanent, indissoluble unity of
brother/sister. A man's heirs are his sister's children. The
husband mainly gains sexual and domiciliary rights; often he gets
economic cooperation as well. But he is an outsider in the group in
which his wife and his children are permanent full members.

Whatever mode of reckoning descent is adopted in societies in
our second box (where kinship is the intensively elaborated
channel of social obligations) the brother/sister tie is important.

183

No wonder that the prohibition of incest is a dominant cultural theme in such societies. The contrast of savage nature with civilisation is expressed in the incest rule: breach of it is utter bestiality, the symbol of disorder, of witchcraft and sorcery. Royalty is placed clearly above common men when myths and rites of kingly office require brother/sister incest. Whatever happened in ancient Egypt there are numerous African kingdoms — the Bushong, for example — where the king must have sexual intercourse with his sister. He is forced to accept chaos and make it creative for himself however destructive it may be for ordinary men.

Echoes of our own past are found in Mediterranean cultures where the brother is cast essentially as defender of his sister's honour. John Campbell has described how poor Greek shepherds expect their brothers to find pasture for their sheep, fight off encroaching neighbours and maintain the family honour so that any other family of good name will be proud to intermarry with them. Cowardice in men and unchastity in women blot a family's name and it is the brothers who must wipe out a disgrace in blood. Until the last sister in the family is safely married and transferred to the charge of her husband, one of her brothers must also remain unmarried so that his duty of risking his life to avenge her honour does not conflict with his duty as a husband to maintain his family. Roger Vailland, in *La Loi*, describes the south Italian peasants as obsessed by the thought of their sisters; and the tension of a hidden incest theme runs through Latin American literature.

But with us a brother cannot punish his sister for loose living or attack her seducer, still less can he give her away in marriage. Social workers look after the offspring of incestuous unions but there is no public attitude on the subject. As the brother's role is more and more attenuated, the incest theme in Elizabethan drama, even in Cocteau, becomes more alien to us. It would be wrong to interpret the great mythologies of antiquity which depict the horror of brother/sister incest as merely enacting the emotions of childhood. The magnifying and glorifying social dimension gave the relation of brother to sister its special hold on the poetic imagination. For us the brother/sister theme has lost its poignancy as a great literary and dramatic symbol because the social tie has lost its central significance.

From *New Society*, 15th June 1967

5 The Early Basis of Adult Female Sexuality and Motherliness

1975

I must first of all apologise for failing to mention many of the distinguished writers on female sexuality who have made notable contributions to the subject. I shall confine myself in this paper to mentioning those few whose work has had the most direct influence on my own preoccupations. I would like to summarise briefly Freud's position, then to mention some developments proceeding from the researches of Melanie Klein, the light shed by the work of Wilfred Bion, and the help derived from the studies of infant development by Esther Bick, for understanding the early basis of sexuality; and finally, I will mention the clarification which Donald Meltzer has made through spelling out the differences between infantile and adult components of the sexual behaviour and states of mind of adults and children.

Freud, as I understand him, continued to see woman as essentially dominated by organ inferiority (penis envy) and as unaware of the female genital until puberty. To him her sexuality was passive and allied to masochism. Her sexual development was difficult as it was necessary for her to find her way back to an identification with her mother after turning away in disappointment at weaning. He did not see female sexuality as dominated particularly by a desire for babies, although he saw the woman's capacity for love as directed mainly towards her children, and her relationship with man as narcissistic and dependent. Sexuality in general he saw as dominated by the pleasure principle — the ego seeking a homeostatic solution through gratification and the avoidance of mental pain.

Melanie Klein's viewpoint was more developmental. She regarded the infant as propelled by the epistemophilic instinct, and growing by a process of projection and introjection through interaction with the object: in the first instance being the body and the personality of the mother. She saw the origin of satisfactory sexuality in an enjoyable relationship with the breast, the capacity for pleasure between penis and vagina being rooted in prototypic pleasure between nipple and mouth. She viewed the development of sexuality as inextricably bound up with character formation, and recognised that the adult character is different from the infantile structure of the personality. The infantile elements in character tend to be dominated by the pleasure principle, modified by the reality principle — at best, enlightened self-interest. They are propelled by jealousy, envy and competition for the pleasure which the child believes the parents to enjoy in private and which are denied to him.

These infantile elements persist into adult life, to some extent in us all, and are characteristic of what she termed the paranoid-schizoid position, where egocentricity and narcissism take precedence over love and gratitude to good objects. Adult sexuality then, would be based upon a positive identification with both parents, and would have its roots in the perception and benefit derived from their good qualities in infancy. I would also follow Donald Meltzer's interpretation of Mrs Klein's work in *Sexual States of Mind*, in regarding adult sexuality as a meeting of the minds as well as of bodies, from which something new is created. One may distinguish it from infantile sexuality which is essentially concerned with getting pleasure and gratification for the self in omnipotent ways, by bodily manipulation or phantasy. It follows from this that sexual intercourse between grown-up people may have the meaning of masturbation, or be contaminated by the masturbatory elements.

If we assume that adult sexuality in both man and woman is based upon an identification with two internal parents, we imply that each human being is bi-sexual, having both a masculine and a feminine orientation; and this I imagine is generally acknowledged. The nature of that identification will be influenced by the qualities of the external parents as well as by the nature of the child himself. We must also assume that the external parents who are introjected and identified with in infancy, are themselves apprehended as people containing internal objects — their own internal parents.

Before the identification with the parents as whole objects takes place however, there is the infant's relationship and identification with the mother as a part-object: with the parts of her body which receive and hold the parts of his body, and the quality of understanding of his needs which is expressed in the meeting between the two. Bion has used Melanie Klein's theory of projective identification to conceptualise this primary relationship to an object, and has employed the conventional symbols for masculine and feminine (and) to represent the relationship between contained and container: that which is projected, and the object that receives the projection. The infant projects a part of himself, a fear, a troubling sensation, which if it is received, thought about, responded to in some appropriate way, can be taken back by the infant in an improved form, together with an experience of an object that is able to bear and make something of his pain — an understanding object. If the mother derives pleasure from understanding and helping the infant with his distress, he may in due course introject a receptive object which has some quality of joyfulness and resilience. The capacity for enjoyment of all kinds, and for sexual enjoyment in particular, has its origin in the introjection of an appreciative and appreciating object in infancy. Later experience of course will also determine the way in which this develops.

It is not possible here to do more than mention a few of the interferences in the mother-infant relationship which impair the establishment of mutual appreciation, and therefore the introjection of an object that is open to receive and to discriminate between the nature of experiences, whilst being able to value all as part of life: an object that can deal not only with pleasure but also with pain as meaningful, rather than just to be evacuated as soon as possible. (Some of these difficulties in 'fit' between infant and mother are listed rather well and simply by Isca Salzberger Wittenberg: 1970).

First of all let us consider the mother. I am thinking of a mother who is on the whole genuinely well-disposed and wishes to do the best she can for her baby. Experience of infant observations has convinced me that in very many mothers, I would be inclined to say almost all mothers with first babies, the mother's capacity to be close to the baby with all of herself — to allow herself to be deeply receptive to the baby's needs — is interfered with by anxiety and depression. This may be experienced by her as such; it may be fled from in some manic way; or it may manifest itself as a kind of flatness, deadness or inattention. There is enormous variation in the extent to which this depression interferes with maternal 'reverie' (Bion, 1962) and growing closeness of relationship. Mothers can be helped to contain and to work through it very often if the husband is supportive in a parental, protective, undemanding way towards the new mother. The mother may be resilient enough herself to digest the trauma of the birth sufficiently to rediscover in herself internal resources which can support her adequately, and enable her to reorganise herself. When she can find time enough for herself, she can be freer to be more mentally and emotionally available to the baby when he most needs it. In many cases, however, it would seem that the baby himself, by his responsiveness, once his needs are met, is able to educate the mother: to enable her to feel that she really *is* a mother and not just a little girl pretending to be one.

Babies, however, differ in temperament from the very beginning, in their capacity to make their needs felt, in the complexity and intensity of their needs, and in their responsiveness. They thus differ in the qualities they are able to evoke in a mother. *It is probably true to say that no two children in the same family ever have the same mother.* In so far as the infant is unable to bring parts of himself to the mother to be expressed, held and thought about, he is likely to feel that there is something unacceptable about himself. These parts are then likely to become alienated, split off and projected to some distance from his good objects: with the ever-present threat that they will return to endanger these good objects. I say 'likely', but probably not *necessarily* so, as some person other than the mother — notably father or another ongoing parental figure — may be able to provide that acceptance. The child is then able to feel that he is well enough known for what he really is, to develop the kind of internal containing object which can help him to feel at home with himself.

I shall now mention one particular constellation which I have observed in mother-infant relationships, and which I have deduced from observation of the transference-countertransference in analytic work. I believe it leads to some difficulty in establishing adult female sexuality and motherliness, in so far as this needs to be based on introjective identification with an accepting, joyous and thoughtful maternal object. I am thinking here of the kind of infant who seems to be born with an intensely possessive, somewhat greedy, but potentially loving disposition. When the constellation encounters a somewhat vulnerable mother, certain difficulties ensue. She may indeed love her children and spend considerable thought in determining how to

188

do the best for them, but she finds it difficult to come close to and to stay with the primitive demands in the early days of such an infant, and therefore certain depths of violence or intensity in the child remain unknown to her.

One particular child of this kind I have in mind at the moment. She was not a first child, but the first child born to her mother in a strange country, where the mother was far from her family of origin and left alone with her children for much of the time while the husband was away on business trips. Although she had managed to breastfeed the other two children, the mother gave up after the first few weeks with this little girl, feeling that her strength was being drained away by the baby's voraciousness. When she was changed to the bottle, the baby continued to suck heartily and for a while would hang on to the teat as she went to sleep, so that it was squeezed flat in her mouth and needed to be prised out. From the time bottlefeeding began, she gradually became more contented and settled between her feeds; but this was at the expense of an area of non-involvement between mother and infant. As the baby sucked the bottle strongly in her mother's arms, her eyes would fix upon some point in the distance. The mother used to hold the baby and the bottle rather loosely, away from herself, and let the baby get on with it while her own attention was elsewhere, fixed for instance upon the observer, to whom she would talk and talk. When the bottle was empty the baby had usually urinated or defaecated, and began to emit sounds of pleasure as her nappy was being changed. Her smiles and gurgles began to catch the mother's attention, galvanizing her to concentrate upon and respond to the baby — to talk to her, rub noses with her, cuddle her and show her off proudly to the observer.

It seemed that there was something in the intensity of need in this small baby, something powerful which made the mother turn away — 'cringe' as she would say. Possibly she continued to turn away after giving the bottle to the baby because of feeling badly about not managing to breastfeed. That the baby herself felt this shrinking, was evidenced in the way she looked past the mother as she fed, fixed on some point beyond, disengaged from the mother (Bick, 1967).

I would suggest that instead of being able to bring all of herself, all of her senses and her attention towards the mother holding the bottle, instead of being able to accept her mother as a container of her person and the giver of food and comfort, this baby split off part of herself by deploying her attention elsewhere. While her mouth was sucking avidly, her eyes were glued to some far point in the room. When the feed was over and her physical needs satisfied, she could then turn to the mother, not so much in appreciation of what she had just been given, but to hearten and give life to the mother — who seemed to feel this, because she expanded and responded to the baby's overtures.

In the case of this baby, the scene is already set for a character development in which the primary internal object has a certain vulnerability and an area of imperviousness. Consequently there is an impetus to use some of the force of the personality in somewhat manic reparation towards external objects. The observations indicated that there was some confusion in her mind as to what was giving her mother pleasure — the products from her bottom, or the gurgles and smiles from her mouth? The baby's own security seemed to be derived from the teat firmly held in her mouth (later this became the spoon wielded firmly by her own hand), and the surrounding familiar objects to which her eyes clung. Later on, she would become very upset when taken on holiday to unfamiliar surroundings, even though her mother and the rest of the family were with her.

* * *

The main part of my paper will be concerned with some aspects of the analysis of a young woman during which I came to discern many of the features of just such an insufficiently held, passionate infant.

Olivia came to analysis in her late twenties, anorexic and frozen with depression after the death from leukaemia of the man she loved. She was the youngest child in her family, having a sister two years older than herself with whom she had fought in childhood, but loved dearly. Although shy, pretty and feminine in appearance, as a child she had believed that she was really meant to be a boy and she had phantasies of being one. Tomboyish bravado was a cloak for social timidity. When her mother was away in hospital for nearly a year with carcinoma of the bowel, from which she finally made a complete recovery, Olivia — aged

190

seven — and her sister lived with an aunt and uncle in a distant town. At that time, when endlessly riding her bicycle, she remembered slipping and rupturing her hymen when the bicycle seat stuck into her crotch. This memory also expressed her conviction that she had irretrievably damaged her genital through masturbation.

During adolescence she rebelled against her puritanical background, going through a period of relative promiscuity, sometimes with married men, and beginning with one of her university teachers. At that time, like so many adolescents, she appeared to be seeking in bodily contact some assuagement of her emotional isolation. Relationships that were physically satisfactory still did not relieve her hunger to be known, or her sense of fraudulence that the depths of her badness were unplumbed. While her sister did rather badly in her studies and quarrelled intermittently with their mother, but then went on to make a happy marriage with a man of whom the whole family was fond, Olivia studied hard and distinguished herself in a scientific field which her father regarded as unfeminine, but which she believed he would have liked to enter himself had he been given the opportunity in his youth.

Eventually in her mid-twenties, soon after her father's death, she fell seriously in love with a man whom she admired, twenty years older than herself. He was not happily married and appeared to care for her deeply, but after they began to live together he was so tormented by the thought of his adolescent daughters that he returned home again. Numbed and despairing at his desertion, Olivia found that she was pregnant, had an abortion without telling her lover, and left for another university town. Some months later he found that he had leukaemia, and finally left his family to live with her once more, until he died nearly a year later. Soon after that she sought analysis for herself, fearing that she was schizophrenic, or that she had cancer and was about to die, but emotionally too numb to care.

From the beginning she cooperated well, bringing dreams, associations and dutiful responses. She worked hard but there was a flatness of affect which made it difficult to gauge when, or if, she was ever touched by any comment of mine. She was punctual, reliable in her attendance, in payment of bills, and in managing to organise her complicated professional life so that

191

she could find time to travel to her sessions without neglecting her work. This organization tended to break down in acts of clumsiness or violence connected with the week-end break: such as driving through red lights without seeing them or spilling milk off the shelf in a supermarket. These involuntary acts disturbed her unwarrantably, as if they heralded the break-down of the whole framework of her life, and were ushering in the so-called schizophrenia. It seemed as if her hard work, her busyness, was keeping her going, as her bicycle-riding did in childhood when she was away from her mother. Talking and providing interesting interpretable material in her analysis was a way of keeping that going during the early months, rather than a means of revealing herself and her needs to me. Although she was intensely dependent on the analysis and believed it necessary to save her life, she was not able to hope for a real change in her state of mind, or to envisage feeling happy.

She felt, as she said, 'one of the damned', recollecting how her kindly grandmother, just before dying, had opened one eye and stared straight at her to say reprovingly: 'Don't ever do that again'. We spent a little time in the analysis returning to this ever-present memory and trying to figure out just what 'that' was; and also investigating the way in which she transferred to me, the analyst, this sternly prohibitive Presbyterian conscience. It caused her to regard every interpretation of destructive activity (for in the early days of the analysis, destructiveness was expressed in action rather than held as an emotion) as a reproof, a exhortation to 'cut that out'. Or the interpretation would be felt by her as a cruel assault from which she curled into a shell of insentience, or secret manic mockery. The latter was revealed in a terrifying dream which she called 'the nightmare to end all nightmares': *She was in a basement room with a stone floor like a mortuary or an abattoir. Bodies were lying on slabs with missing limbs, with entrails protruding and blood all over the place. But the horror was that she, as a chid of seven or eight years old, was laughing and skipping in the next room using an intestine as a skipping rope.* This referred to her mother's illness with bowel cancer and revealed the horror she felt at the manic and callous way in which she had dealt with her concern and despair about this. She remembered vividly how she had seen traces of her mother's faecal incontinence in the bathroom before she went to hospital, and how she had recoiled in distaste and contempt.

We came to understand gradually in the course of the analysis, how much her way of using her eyes, her way of looking at things, was at the root of her own illness in an extremely subtle way. She recollected as a child standing looking through the open door of her parents' bedroom, feeling that she was doing something naughty. The 'naughty' looking appeared to relate to quietly accurate perceptions of weakness and defects of character. She noticed for instance, her father's tendency to hypochondria — to complain and enlist her mother's sympathy as the most important baby in the family. It enabled her to cling to the infantile belief that the parental intercourse was a pee-ing affair: that mummy liked to be a lavatory, a receptacle for incontinence; and the little boy in her continued to maintain that its pee was better than daddy's. Her childhood masturbation was associated with voyeurism and urination, and her intercourse with men until well on in her analysis was accompanied by phantasies of urinating at the moment of orgasm. The childhood evidence of her mother's incontinence must have underlined her despair about an internal mother who appeared sometimes in dreams as a blocked lavatory. Over and over again in these dreams she figured as a urinating little boy. Father in dreams was also urinating, sometimes to the detriment of plants in the garden. Sometimes Olivia would become so furious at the recurrence of these characters, the perpetuation of this urinary intercourse, that she would become sulky, defiant, or try to laugh it off manically.

She brought dreams in her analysis almost every day, except for a period during which she was struggling to accept the realisation of how strongly this was motivated by a desire to keep me happy so that I could keep going as an analytic mother. In essence she was the baby feeding the breast, or the little boy who believed that with his urinating penis he was mummy's little husband. Until we clarified this gradually, her dreams were undervalued for what they could reveal to *her*. She worked hard to remember them and to bring them to me, but however hard I worked with her to try to analyse them, I always seemed to miss the point. For instance, she would often confirm the content of my interpretation, and would say that my words made sense to her intellectually; but she had no feeling about them and they did not help her. The words that did touch her, she said, were those

193

that spoke to the baby in her. There were indications that a good deal of the analytic work and comprehension were being used by the omnipotent peeing little boy who was doing such good work outside, in a kind of manic reparation with her students, who seemed to represent mother's children and her own aborted baby (regarded fundamentally as mother's murdered child). When she was offered a new post which represented a marked advancement in her career, her first thought was to make a long distance telephone call to her widowed mother, thinking how delighted she would be.

It was difficult to reach the baby in her, which indeed seemed thirsty for understanding and emotional nourishment, and which was so often bruised by my approach. This made me examine my method of interpreting as well as the content of what I said. If, she said, I came to the point too quickly, thrust it at her too suddenly, she felt assaulted, bruised, and retreated; stiffening herself against it. She would behave like an infant that shuts its mouth first or else passively suffers the food to be thrust in while removing its attention elsewhere. If I continued to talk too long or too eagerly sometimes (even when I thought that she must be following me because I was sticking very closely to her material), she could feel choked and flooded. Trying to elucidate and to describe her state of mind in baby/breast terms helped this. About a particular comment she told me it was true but too abrupt, too hard for the baby to swallow: if only I could manage to tell it to her in the form of a story as I did sometimes, she could manage to take it. It seemed that here was a baby who needed some preamble, some holding, comforting, talking, who needed to be thought about, to feel contained and accepted by the mother before it could open its mouth to grasp the nipple and taste the food.

It was not enough of course to spell out her difficulties with the *manner* of my interpretations. We had to get some better grasp of the *content* of the points which she found so hard to swallow: to grapple with the projections whose return was so hurtful. She re-read a fair amount of psychoanalytic literature which she applied to herself, and was only too ready at the slightest provocation to step in to pre-empt my interpretation and flagellate herself with accusations of envy and greed. These seemed to be the factors in the so-called 'schizophrenia' or cancer which she fatalistically assigned to herself as her punishment. They are of course factors in the psychopathology of us all. As aspects of herself, they were *known about*, but largely unknown in terms of emotional experience. They tended to be projected into a hard object, a nipple or a penis which she seized to punish herself with. She would then accuse me of grinding her flat with my rigid mechanical analysis.

These accusations were extraordinarily painful and sometimes left me at a loss as to how to approach her material without hurting her. It was plain, however, that she became distressed and despairing if I seemed to be retreating: if I could not give some evidence of continuing to try to work with her communications and with the pain which she was projecting into me. The picture that emerged for me in the transference was of an intense, passionate infant, avid for the breast and liable to disintegrate if she was not firmly held in mother's arms. It was of an infant tuned to experience a mother who recurrently retreated, who had neither the strength nor the perceptiveness to grasp and manage the baby's violence: a mother who meant well but who could not deal with something that was not in her experience. At other times in the sessions, this infant seemed to be assaulted by that split-off part of herself which appeared in the abattoir dream: which, confused in identity with the mother's insensitivity, functioned as a harsh super-ego, a callous mocking character, standing on the sidelines.

This configuration began to be more contained and workable with in the transference as she gradually came to trust in my ability to trace it, to bring it into the room and hold it there. Acting out in the form of masturbation and of sexual relations without tenderness or love was curtailed. Gradually, as her capacity to internalise a receptive maternal object grew, the hope appeared that she might after all deserve to be loved, that she might become able to carry a baby. She was then able to form a relationship with a man of her own age whom she could respect: a relationship which was sexually and emotionally satisfying and which resulted in marriage.

I shall now relate a series of dreams which Olivia had at the beginning of her pregnancy, which indicate how she was approaching the prospect of being a mother herself. In the first dream, *she was going to an antenatal clinic but found herself in an eye clinic instead, where the woman doctor was telling a young girl that she needed an operation: her eyes were all right but the lids needed to be stitched.* Olivia had a light lesion in the corner of her eye which needed attention. Discussion of the dream referred to the sidelong denigratory judgemental glances with which we were familiar: to the child whose eyes would not close at night when the parents were together, the 'evil eye' cast on the baby inside mother; the abortion and her fear of repeating that involuntarily. The woman doctor was the analyst and was reminding her of this young girl self with the leaking eye.

The next dream was of *two young fair-haired friends whose appearance she admired. They visited her in new spring clothes. She was delighted to see them but had to turn aside immediately to pee. She was then startled to see that she had peed out a small perfect foetus cradled in a little shell.* This dream was accompanied by many associations and complicated meanings, but central to the theme which occupied us at that time was the excitement of the infant in her at the beauty of the breasts (so often represented as young girls); these two particular girls, who are fair like me and like herself appeared as narcissistic objects representing her idealised girlish femininity, which had to be protected from feelings that were too strong. They were not only vulnerable to her infantile excitement but (according to further associations about these young girls) were feared as being envious of her pregnancy.

This was followed by a dream in which *she and her husband were in bed together looking up at the ceiling which was covered with bird droppings. She thought to herself in dismay that this was because she had neglected to clean the floor properly.* Her husband had been talking to her of two tits in the back garden before she went to sleep. This dream referred to the need to clear from her grown-up intercourse the hidden masturbatory quality which still remained and had the meaning of coupling with a narcissistic little boy part of herself evacuating its bad, dirty feelings when the parents were together, by peeing, into the 'tits' on the ceiling (like the baby who looked in the distance). These reminded her then, from above, to clean up her bottom. Following some analysis of this dream, she said that in intercourse with her husband she had feared his penis would damage 'the baby'.

This was followed by a dream in which *she largely relived a film which she had seen, during which she was weeping and weeping. What made her weep was the contrast between the beauty of the countryside as i* was in the film, contrasted with the scenes in which it had formerly been used for trenches in the first world war, during which many of the men in the village had died. In particular the husband of the heroine had died while she was pregnant with his child. There had been so many dead bodies in that area that they could not bury them all completely in the mud. The scene where they squelched as the platoon walked over them filled her with endless grief. She associated this with the abattoir dream with the cut-up bodies, but the horror and mania in that dream was replaced by sorrowful memories of her father's death and her mother's loneliness, of the abortion and her lover's death, of the death of my former husband which she had learned about some years ago. Nostalgic thoughts about the garden of my former house to which she first came for analysis, were mingled with pleasure at noticing that the leaves were budding in the trees outside my present flat, and that the daffodils were about to bloom.

The next day she dreamt that *she and her sister had each been given flower bulbs by a man who said there were two kinds, yellow and striped. They should be out before next Christmas but until they bloomed it wouldn't be possible to know which kind was which.* Her immediate thought when she woke up was that she was definitely pregnant: would it be a boy or a girl? Her sister had two children, two little boys. She wanted a girl, her husband a boy, but hoped for one of each. Again she found herself weeping with sorrow and with happiness: sorrow for her lost baby whose sex she did not know; sorrow and happiness for her mother who would be so pleased for her sake as well as to have another grandchild; and love for her favourite nephew who had said wistfully when she married that when she had a baby she would not love him so much. She loved him for trusting her enough to express his forlorn thought to her, and so believed he was surely going to cope with his jealousy better than she had managed to do with hers.

Following this, she dreamed that *she and her sister were going to an island in a lagoon in an open boat, half submerged under water. There were no oars so she was trying to row with her hands until she realised that it was not necessary; the current was carrying them in to land in any case. She relaxed and the boat finally sank as it brought them to the shore. The sand felt soft and white beneath their feet. For a moment they were afraid of sinking in it till they felt the firm foundation beneath. There was already in the distance another couple, to whom they waved. As they walked up the beach she realised that she had been rowing in the wrong direction and hence*

197

had delayed their arrival. This dream, in which she was in the same boat as her sister and finally gave up rowing in the wrong direction, indicated a further step in the relinquishment of omnipotent masturbation and control, to join her sister in a positive identification with their mother. 'Rowing' of course also means quarrelling; so reconciliation with the mother is implied, and trust in the current of her feelings of her internal objects, to carry her to the shore. Landing on the island could also be seen as birth: the rebirth of herself in identification with the baby, supported by an internal breast that is soft and receptive yet firm, and by another couple already there (the combined object: at part-object level, breast and nipple; or at whole object level, the couple together — the parents who were responsible for her birth).

The last extract of material which I shall present followed upon Olivia seeing me in the street the next day, a Friday afternoon. This was a unique event in the course of her analysis. She said this had been an extraordinary shock. She had felt exposed, vulnerable as if she were losing everything, her blood draining away, her insides falling out. The feeling had continued for the rest of the day, the converse of a feeling she had once had when she shook hands with me, that her touch went on and on forever through my skin. Finally however, she realised that there *was* something left; and ended the day feeling quite separate but complete, with something inside her. She said that she could put it more abstractly, and state that she finally had to give up the idea of being special and essential to me; that I did have an existence of my own. But that would not convey the concreteness of the experience. She had found herself thinking with pleasure of my week-end with my husband. As a result of this experience she had found she was enjoying a dinner party for the first time ever; perhaps because she was realising that it would not go on for ever, that all things come to an end. Moreover she was relieved to find half-way through the evening that one of the people she had thought was a stranger, she eventually remembered meeting some time ago. She was as pleased that she had been able to forget him, as that she had later remembered him.

Following the dinner party she had a dream in which *I was talking to her about a former patient of mine, a young girl who had finished her analysis sooner than expected. The reason was apparently something to do with there being a lavatory*. Her associations to the dream were as follows: first, she had heard that this former patient of mine whom she used to see, was in fact developing well since finishing her analysis. Then, the lavatory in the dream reminded her of dinner table conversation and laughter about an adolescent girl who had thrown a drain cover at her headmistress. She felt guilty that the laughter was inappropriate because the teacher could have been killed. This led on to recollections of a boy at her primary school who would not use the lavatory at home or at school, but wrapped his faeces in newspaper and hid them beneath coats and under cushions.

In this session, Olivia was clearly envisaging the end of her analysis, and relieved to find that eventual separation and loss of the external object could leave her with something innate which she could use to retain experience and to help her go on developing. She did not need to hide her bad parts — her faeces and urine — by idealising them, because there was a lavatory that could deal with them for her (Meltzer's 'toilet breast'). Hopefully she could begin to envisage this as an internal object that could help her to sort out and clarify what she needed: to get rid of what could be forgotten, but recalled again at need. She did not need to feel that unless she was making an effort to remember all the time, vital memories would slip out of her for ever — that the baby would slip out in the urine!

So, to bring together the main points I have tried to make in this paper. The brief account of Olivia's analysis was designed as an example of the progress towards adult female sexuality and motherliness in a young woman who had a defective internal mother with whom to identify. I have tried to link this to a short description of a certain kind of mother-infant relationship, and to give some evidence of how attention to the infantile transference and the counter-transference evolved in me during Olivia's analysis, helped the baby in her to introject a stronger maternal object which could contain a richer and deeper spectrum of feelings. My contention is that adult female sexuality, the readiness to receive emotional as well as physical experience, is ultimately based upon the introjection of a receptive object of this kind.

REFERENCES

BICK, E. (1967) 'The Experience of the Skin in Early Object Relations', *International Journal of Psycho-analysis*, Vol. 49, 1968, pp 484-486.

BION, W.R. (1962) *Learning from Experience*. London, Heinemann.

FREUD, S. (1905) 'Three Essays on the Theory of Sexuality'. Standard Edition, Vol. 7.

KLEIN, M. (1945) 'The Oedipus Complex in the Light of Early Anxieties', in *Contributions to Psycho-analysis* 1921-1945. London: Hogarth Press and Institute of Psycho-analysis, 1948, pp. 339-390.

MELTZER, D. (1967) *The Psychoanalytic Process*. Perthshire, Clunie Press.

MELTZER, D. (1973) *Sexual States of Mind*. Perthshire, Clunie Press.

SALZBERGER-WITTENBERG, I. (1970) *Psycho-analysis and Casework: A Kleinian Approach*. London, Routledge and Kegan Paul.

6 Discussion of an Adolescent Girl
1975

I would like to explore further, using material from a particular adolescent girl, some of the problems of adolescents in general as introduced by my husband yesterday. It may be worthwhile first of all to rehearse briefly some of the general points that he made, and which she seems to illustrate.

1) First of all there is the adolescent's disappointment about the latency child's fantasy of knowledge as something concrete which he would be able to achieve, to have when he is grown up.

2) Then there is the fading, in adolescence, of the young one's belief in omniscience and omnipotence, as attributed to his parents and to grown-ups in general; and in particular the omniscience and omnipotence that is attributed to sexual relationships — which almost always contain elements of disappointment for the adolescent when he first embarks on one.

3) Then there is the task which the adolescent has of getting in touch with the experiences that he has internalized from the past; the task of trying to get in touch with what we would call his good internal objects, and to become receptive as to what they have to teach him and the means they have to help him. I think my husband suggested yesterday some of the ways in which the adolescent is able to do this: in analysis in dreams, and in ordinary life through literature, music, the arts.

4) And then there is the adolescent's problem of dealing with the enormous confusion in his feelings about himself and about his objects, the people in his life; the confusion about what is good and what is bad, and how to know more of what he feels about the distinction between good and bad. This of course in later adolescence becomes very much linked with sexual experiences. In the girl we are going to talk about, a disappointing sexual experience is a very important factor in her uncertainty and confusion about her own feelings: associated with confusion in her idea of what is going on inside — what is her internal world — and what is happening in the world outside.

5) Then there is the confusion about the adolescent's own

identity: in either male or female, what are the masculine and what are the feminine characteristics?

6) There is confusion between adult and infantile.

7) There is confusion about the different zones and parts of the body and their functions. This difference is the basis for the difficult concepts that I hope will be illustrated in some of the dreams I am going to present, which my husband will discuss, and I would like people here to give their ideas as well.

8) Then there is the adolescent's problem that comes out very forcefully in this girl, of tolerating the pain of depressive states: the depressive states that are precipitated through awareness of violence, ruthlessness, greed or envy towards loved objects both in the external world and internally.

9) And I think there is in particular something one finds in very intelligent adolescents, as this girl is: namely the damage that is thought to be done to one's loved object through a greed for knowledge or the hunger for knowledge in the service of ambition.

10) And then there is the point of fluctuation in the adolescent between the four groups: between being the child in the family, being one of the adolescents, being a member of the adult world, or being isolated.

I think that Rosamund, the girl I am going to talk about, illustrates this fluctuation particularly. She came to analysis after a period of seven years in which she was one of the most successful members of a group of adolescents at boarding school, where she was very much liked by the other girls and very much a member of their group; but in a sense it was not a very typical adolescent group because it was not particularly rebellious against authority. The girls were intelligent, gifted, good at work, and actually hadn't quite come across the need to have to be rebellious to get what they wanted. From this, her venture into the adult world through a sexual relationship with a man a few years older than herself, during a long holiday, brought about a very severe disappointment which resulted in her cutting herself off and becoming isolated. Then, getting in better touch with some of her feelings resulting from the analytic work and from the consultation she had before this, seemed to bring up some of her infantile childish dependent feelings, and longing to go back as a little child toward her family.

202

My patient was eighteen and a half years old when I first saw her. She is a quite exceptionally beautiful girl in a very delicate refined way, both sophisticated and graceful in her manners; she talks very perfectly and very musically. A particular symptom that precipitated her seeking analysis was anorexia. She was indeed very thin; though she was anyway fundamentally a very slim, willowy, graceful girl. The effect this beauty had on me was striking; it did not make me feel inferior as a very beautiful girl might make one feel, because there was in it something vulnerable and somehow affectionate. She aroused in me the immediate feeling of liking her very much and wanting to help her; and this is the feeling she evokes in people generally. She is also extremely intelligent and responsive, always listening courteously to what one says to her.

In order to be able to have an analysis she had to defer going to University one year, and the idea was that she would come to London from the north of England where her parents were at that time staying. As her father is a rather high ranked officer in the Air Force, Rosamund had lived from birth onwards in a number of different countries and the family was always moving; and that of course was why she was at boarding school. The idea was that she would come to London, find a job and keep herself from her own earnings, while her family would pay for her analysis. She was with me only nine months. For the first seven weeks she stayed with friends and with her godmother. She found herself a job very easily in a fashionable beauty salon in Bond Street. I think she expected almost as easily to be able to find a flat; but that of course was much more difficult than she had anticipated, and after some time looking for one together with another girl, she gave up this idea and ended up in a rather shabby bedsit. There, after the initial elation of being grown up, managing her own room and so on, she became really very lonely and very miserable at times. And then she took to going home to the north of England, a long journey, nearly every week-end.

The parents, as far as I could see, seemed to be still very much in love with each other. The child next to Rosamund in age was a brother, David, who was rather less than two years younger than herself, and then there were two other daughters, six and seven years younger. They are a 'county' family — well-bred, provincial, country people, but not intellectual in any way.

203

Rosamund had been to a girl's boarding school since she was ten years old — a 'good' school but not very academic. She is a very intelligent girl and her intelligence was as yet pretty well untouched. She attained her University entrance to study fine art, but I had the impression from her that art was associated more with being a rather beautiful 'Elizabeth Arden' girl, than with appreciating the great painters of the past.

I have a very definite picture from her analysis of how she coped with having a younger brother. She very quickly became a sister to her mother, joining her in looking after the baby and later the other children. From the material I got the impression that she was hardly ever a troublesome child, owing to this very close, mutually idealized relationship with her mother, then her father and later her grandparents. Her boarding-school is in the town where her grandfather practises as a doctor; and these grandparents, from the age of ten onwards, became second parents to her. When she first went to boarding school she felt desperately miserable, although she did not remember this until feelings of intense depression came up later on in her analysis. But it seems she managed to shake off this misery by becoming witty, amusing, a good story-teller, and the centre of a group of girls who admired her.

Her first boyfriend at school was the brother of one of her best friends. This was when she was seventeen and half, and she had intercourse with him on one or two occasions that seem to have left her quite untouched. Then in the summer holidays before her last year at school, she went to Germany, where she met a beautiful young actor with whom she had an intense love affair for about one month. She seems to have been extremely happy with him but absolutely devastated when, about a week before the end of the holidays, he told her that he was engaged and intended to marry his fiancée. Until that moment it had apparently never crossed her mind that they would do other than get married and live happily ever after.

When she went back to school for her last year, she broke off with her former boyfriend entirely. But as she had been used to going out with him every week-end for the past year, she found herself completely at a loose end during the week-ends at school. She dealt with this misery by cutting herself off from her former school friends, withdrawing, hardly even chatting with them.

She also stopped eating and, as she described it later in analysis, wanted to feel that she could do without food: that she was special, did not need it, and would go on not eating for as long as possible. Her teachers and friends were worried about it; then when she went home for Christmas her family were absolutely devastated by the change in her appearance. At this point she was referred for analysis through the grandfather. She had three consultations with a man psycho-analyst at Christmas, and began analysis with me about six months after the last consultation, on a three times weekly basis. She had wanted to come twice a week, but I suggested to her I thought it would be better to come three times — which was all I could offer at the time.

Initially she concentrated on talking about her problem with eating, but said she was much better; she had in fact been eating and putting on weight and feeling well for some months. But it was necessary that she constantly think about every morsel that she ate, and supervise extremely strictly all the food she took in. It wasn't a question of not wanting or of not liking to eat, but of feeling very greedy, so that when she began to eat she was afraid she was never going to stop. It is as if she was really trying to canalize all her greedy feelings into the actual eating of food, and to supervise and control them in this way. When I said something of this kind to her she at once agreed, and said: 'I like to bake cakes, I like to bake cakes and to feed all my family, but even when I bake for all the family I still like to feel that it is mine and, although everybody should eat it, I always feel possessive about it'. She went on to say that almost as much as the eating she liked to study recipes, which she would often read in the bathroom.

I took up initially this possessiveness towards the cakes that she baked, and linked it with the way in which she listened with great interest to everything I said, as if she was reading it as a recipe that she was going to be able to feed herself later. This material came just before the first week-end; so I said that I thought she was telling me here, though she might not know it, that she was going to resent very strongly feeling that I was to determine when she could eat this analytic cake. I had said several times that very soon she was going to be annoyed about the coming week-end. She listened with tolerance and interest when I said this, but it didn't touch her. Then I went a little further to say I thought here too she was telling me about some baby part of herself that wanted to pretend that she was the mummy, that pretended when feeding from the breast that it was really making the food that came out. Here again she listened with interest and agreed, but I didn't find until after the first week-end that it had gripped her and made a link with her internal object.

Rosamund had gone home to her parents; her brother happened to be at home, and she suddenly found herself at one point, when David was talking to her mother, going into the kitchen, on her own, ready to burst into tears. But instead of doing so, she had an inexplicable crisis of rage and wanted to smash all the crockery in the kitchen. From then onwards, we had very great problems every week-end and at any unexpected or unusual break in the analysis. For a long time she was unable to feel that these phenomena had anything to do with her infantile transference to me in the analysis. She told me that she was very surprised at such a reaction in herself — she who did not remember being jealous of her younger brother at all, as a child, and had in fact always felt quite motherly towards him, friendly and protective. Clearly the separation situation, lived strongly in the analysis, had stirred in her a violence which till then had been hidden from herself as well as others: a violence, jealousy and possessiveness in a part of herself with which she was very unfamiliar.

DONALD MELTZER: I have an anorexic patient whose anorexia is very close to an anti-intellectual aspect of herself (although she comes from a very intellectul family — her father and husband being professors and she herself a university graduate). This anti-intellectual quality in her seems to be connected also with a great inhibition towards work — work of any kind — and with choosing social races instead as a path to success. And I think that Rosamund also, evinces this same quality of expecting that her beauty, her grace, will simply open the whole world to her. Now in today's material, in particular, I think you will see how in Rosamund the desire for knowledge, and oral greediness, are absolutely melted together.

MARTHA HARRIS: I was also thinking of a period in Rosamund's analysis when the anorexia returned in the form of vomiting and being unable to stomach food. It seemed to me as if she were rejecting physical food and at the same time rejecting thinking and feeling about some very unfamiliar, ancient part of herself with which she was being put in touch; and vomiting gradually ceased as she became able to tolerate thinking again, and able to have feelings again.

*   *   *

I would now like to describe in some detail the first dream that Rosamund had in her analysis. I had told her at the beginning that it would be helpful if she tried to remember her dreams, but it was nearly three weeks before she managed to do so. This first dream, she said, was about a girl called Virginia, and she prefaced the dream by telling me about Virginia. Virginia had been one of her friends at school over a number of years, who at about fifteen years of age began to become anorexic, and over the course of one whole year became progressively more anorexic and more withdrawn until she was finally removed from the school. Rosamund had felt very guilty about this in some obscure way; she felt that she was the cause of Virginia's anorexia, because it was connected with her own growing up, being attractive and being able to have boyfriends; whereas Virginia had remained less attractive, rather childish, in the background. As she herself had grown more beautiful (she didn't quite say that, but she implied it), she moved into a rather more exciting social circle in the school. So Virginia was her abandoned best girl friend.

She then said she had in fact dreamt of Virginia more than three months before this, some time following her last consultation with the referring psycho-analyst. In that first dream, before starting analysis, *she had been telling Virginia that she herself was much better, and thought that Virginia should come with her to see the analyst; then she too would be cured. But Virginia had refused to enter the door when Rosamund had tried to take her into the analyst's office.* She said then that her present dream about Virginia, from the previous night, was quite different. In this dream, *Virginia was looking very well and plump and happy and seemed to be quite cured, and Rosamund felt very pleased about it.* In fact she did not know what had happened to Virginia since she had been taken away from school at the age of sixteen she had neither seen her nor heard anything about her.

This was the first appearance of Virginia, who from then

onwards figured very prominently in the analysis in Rosamund's dreams. At a later date she actually made contact with this girl again. At this period I was not quite clear how to take Virginia; I assumed she represented some part of Rosamund herself. From the first dream after seeing the consultant, a man, this part of Rosamund seemed not to want to be cured, did not want to come through the door to see the doctor. I suspected at that time this might be connected with a resentment about the consultant not continuing with her, because it was after her last session with him that she had this dream. I think in the second dream, where Virginia is plump and smiling and quite cured, she seemed to represent both some part of herself that was confused with the object — a virgin mother or a virgin breast —, and also Rosamund herself as doing the curing. I felt there were elements of projective identification with the mother, with the breast, and in the analytic situation, with me. Some tentative interpretations along those lines seemed to produce the following dream, associated with her being about to move into the bed-sitting room which she had discovered. It occured at the point when she was feeling very elated at having her first room with her first little gas-cooker in it, and at being able to do her own cooking for the first time. This dream I called the 'talking cat' dream. In it, *Rosamund went into her back-garden at home and in it there was a large white cat that said to her: 'Hello, Rosamund!' She seemed to take it quite for granted that cats should talk to her; but her family and friends were around her, and they exclaimed in admiration, saying to Rosamund; 'How clever of you! How did you manage to teach it to talk?' She felt a little modest and confused and was trying to say it was nothing really.* After relating this dream, she said that the same night she had had another one, that she called 'the aeroplane': *She was in an aeroplane flying high up at the top of a very tall building and it was very exciting; she was going up and up and up and going to go over the top; and then she became afraid that it would fall on its tail.* Rosamund said she thought she had many other dreams that same night, because there seemed to be a lot of talking, talking, talking going on; but these were the only two she could remember.

I should say the aeroplane is clearly related to her father, who flew aeroplanes and was in the Air Force. This aeroplane going right up and up, represented some identification with father and father's penis. It seemed to be related to the elation about being grown up and moving into the room of her own, as if entering and taking possession of the mother's inside space. It also seemed that this aeroplane was somehow linked and a bit confused with the cat in her back-garden, because the aeroplane was going to fall on its tail. There seems to be some confusion here between the breast and the bottom, anus: the large white cat that is in the back-garden and doing the talking there. The confusion is about possessing a talking cat or a talking breast or a talking penis that is somehow linked with her tail, her bottom. Some sort of infantile mobilization is brought about, idealising her own back-garden, her own bottom doing the talking. The tail of the plane (anus) and the white cat (father's penis) and her own tongue, are confused with each other and also with the analyst's admired tongue (nipple).

DONALD MELTZER: The situation at this moment in the analysis is one in which all of the confusions are about to break out, and it is quite typical that they are about to do this at a point when she is also somewhat manically elated owing to moving into her own room. You can see that in the background is the dream about herself and Virginia (the virgin mother) in which she was about to invite the mother to have intercourse with this analyst-daddy and be cured by it the way she has been cured. Now in the analysis, also, there is an intercourse taking place, and Rosamund is about to move into that too — both as the mother represented by the talking cat (really a part-object, the mother's breast) and as father's penis, represented by the aeroplane. That is the manic situation; but behind it is the proliferation of confusions about to break out: she cannot tell whether it is the breast or the bottom she is in; she cannot tell who is doing the talking — the mouth or the anus; she can't tell whether it's a good or a bad thing that's going on; she can't tell whether it is herself or her object that is having this intercourse; she can't tell whether it is a good penis or a bad faeces engaged in it, and she can't tell whether it is moving in the direction of happiness or of catastrophe.

MARTHA HARRIS: Rosamund was living with her god-mother before she moved into the flat, and she was clearly cutting off some feeling of uncertainty about moving out of her family into the flat on her own. What was also being cut out at that moment was anxiety about a forthcoming long week-end in the analysis. It would appear she was denying the sadness about separation in the same way as she had done when she went to school at the age of ten, when she overcame it by talking and talking, to the admiration of everybody at school. I think this is also linked with liking to bake cakes to feed others, as if she were the mother and they the children.

Another dream she had shortly afterwards was a bit of a corrective to the manic element. This dream was associated with actually going back to her school to the prize-giving, where she was to receive the art prize. In the dream *she was going back to school with Virginia* (who had in fact left the school two years before) *and with Jean, to receive a prize.* (Now Jean was her best friend in the last year or two of school, the sister of the boy with whom she first had intercourse. Jean was an attractive, intelligent girl whom Rosamund in fact admired greatly and who got a very good university place). In the dream, *she goes back to school with Virginia and Jean and all three of them are feeling very excited and important in relation to all the younger girls who are still at school, and felt to be whispering about and admiring the three. When Rosamund's turn came to receive her prize, it seemed to be a man who was giving out the prizes and she was astonished when he stopped to make some special speech about her. He was going to present her with a book of poetry which apparently she had written herself. It was something like Wordsworth's. She became terribly distressed about this and wanted to say this was all a mistake, she hadn't written this at all. Then when she looked inside the book, at the poetry, she realised it did bear some kind of relation to things that she had said: that in fact the poetry was really made around some of her words or statements. So she then accepted the book, thinking perhaps she wasn't a total fraud to accept this prize.*

In this dream one can see the adolescent going back to school, hungry for admiration from all the younger children, wanting them to see how marvellously she has got on in the outside world. She is hungry also to get the special prize given by the man, who seems to represent daddy but is also linked with the consultant who referred her, judging from her associations. But most importantly, one gets some feeling of the essential truthfulness in Rosamund. When she looks at this Wordsworth-like book it isn't all her words, although the poetry has been made from some of her words. I think there was some recognition here of the value of the words of the analyst, of what is in a sense my 'words' worth' in relation to what she said to me: some recognition that poetry of a kind was being written from her material through our co-operation. So this dream is a more truthful version of her 'talking cat'.

The next dream I wish to cite was again connected with the new bed-sitting room into which she had moved. She arrived in distress one morning, having proudly fixed the plug on a new electric fire and then, apparently, plugged it into a lighting point not a power point, so that it fused all the lights. So she had to go to bed in darkness and had the following dream: *She was with her godmother and her godmother's two children and was waiting to be burnt alive. It seemed quite inevitable that she had to be burnt and both she and her godmother accepted this as an inescapable fact. But she was wondering with a little surprise why her godmother was allowing her two children to witness this, since surely such an event would not be good for children.* Then it seemed in the dream that *she had been burnt alive, and she was reappearing as a ghost to tell her godmother that it had not been so bad after all, that it hadn't hurt.* She then said to me with a smile: 'I suppose that's my old omnipotence again — as if I were indestructible'.

I was puzzled by this dream to begin with. I could see that it had something to do with the electric fire. Rosamund then said she thought it had something to do with her anorexia and the wish to do everything by herself; but she couldn't explain or add more. Then she said that in the dream, when she was being burnt, it was not at all clear what was happening, except that she noticed at one point the flesh seemed to fly away from her face. I said that something about the way she described it made it sound like diarrhoea, as if there were again some kind of confusion. She immediately fastened on this, connecting it with the enteritis she had had as a baby. She couldn't remember whether it was after she was weaned or after her brother was born, but she had been told that at that point she became very thin. So that seemed to confirm the unconscious connection which she couldn't explain, with her anorexia. I thought perhaps there was a link with the electric fire that was too strong for the electrical system, that broke the system because it took too much from it; and this might then link with her passion and greed towards the breast — the warmth of the breast engendering some feeling that her greed broke up the breast, sucking out all the milk current and destroying it. The dream would therefore illustrate an immediate

211

identification with the destroyed breast, the burnt-out breast, in that she herself becomes the one who has to be immediately burnt up.

I deduced a little later on in her analysis that this dream came at a period when she was being extremely demanding and infantile towards her mother when she went home to her parents; she seems to have been very offended if mother wasn't always on hand to speak to her alone, instead of in the presence of her brother or father. It is quite characteristic of the analysis of adolescents that the strong infantile feelings evoked in the analytic situation, can very often not be felt in relation to the analyst, but are taken and worked out in the home towards the family, as a small child will do. I have the impression that this was the first period in Rosamund's life when she was actively trouble-some to her parents: spiteful, possessive, demanding, and in fact a real burden to them. It can be a very difficult problem for the analyst to help the parents of adolescents in analysis in such situations; although in Rosamund's case, the grandfather helped the parents very capably.

A few weeks later, there was a valuable dream following the Christmas holidays. Rosamund had missed the last couple of sessions before the holiday owing to contracting flu so that she was taken home by her parents. With this complete justification, she allowed herself to be an infant, put to bed and looked after. Then after the holiday, appeared the first signs of any avowed reluctance to come to analysis. Those two sessions had been missed for a very good reason, as it were; but now, she began to become aware of not wanting to come, of feeling persecuted, very angry with me and wanting to shout at me. These nasty emotions ruffled her lady-like exterior and idea of herself. She was still having dreams at this point, but was more reluctant to tell them. When she did tell them they were long and complicated. In the first part of a double dream, *she was given a dog that was supposed to be a corgi, like the Queen's; but somehow she was disappointed with this dog. The dog seemed actually to be a Dalmatian; but this was not quite what disappointed her. Then her grandfather took her to the opera and this dog seemed to be the star of the show; it was singing, and her parents, aunt and uncle were all coming to hear it. She was rather late in getting ready for the opera and seemed to be hanging back in the background; her grandfather started to tease her as he used to do when she was ten or eleven and first went to boarding-school*, when she would answer him back with short clever retorts. In the dream *she was also answering back, but with rather more biting and sharp replies* than she remembered them to have been in actuality.

The scene of the dream now changed, and *she found herself in Germany with the family, looking at an album of photographs that had been taken of her parents before she was born; but the scenes in the pictures didn't actually look like Germany as she remembered it, but like a garden in Cambridge in the summer-time at a place where she had stayed with her parents when she~was seven years old. And when she looked at the photographs she seemed to be back in this idyllic scene in the summer garden at Cambridge. Then she was looking at a photo of her mother, who looked indescribably beautiful in a very floating, romantic, idyllic fashion, and Rosamund said as she looked at it: 'Where was I when that photograph was taken? I wasn't born'. Then she thought: 'Of course I'm inside mother; mother was pregnant with me at the time this photograph was taken'. Then it seemed in the dream to become the summer garden in Cambridge again, but this very beautiful mother in the photograph was now much more like a particular young aunt who had just married her mother's brother.* Rosamund remembered this very romantic couple in the Cambridge garden: being her young aunt who looked like a German fairy-tale princess with long golden hair and was only eighteen or nineteen years old at the time, and her mother's younger brother — of whom Rosamund was particularly fond, for he was very handsome and she remembered him turning somersaults on the lawns of Cambridge, to the delight of the children and the applause of the grown ups. She also remembered how he helped her to shake the cherry trees to get the cherries.

This was a rather long dream, which took most of the session to tell. Although it was quite clearly shaking her emotionally, it was not at all clear what the emotion was, apart from nostalgia. Rosamund said the second part of the dream about the garden in Cambridge was really a lovely dream and she wanted it to go on and on and never stop, so she was very disappointed when she awakened. The one thing she felt sad about was that this German fairy-tale princess aunt, whom she had admired and loved so as a young child, no longer makes her feel the same way, because she feels that this aunt does not like her now. She had no evidence to justify this; it might just be a feeling, not a reality. She also said that the reason she wanted the second part of the dream to go on

213

and on, was that it seemed to cancel out the first part about the dog, which was somehow very unpleasant. I asked her what it was about the dog that was so unpleasant; she replied that it was very peculiar looking: it was white with black spots but it also had a long neck and very staring pink eyes that were bleeding. In the dream she very much wanted the dog, but she had the feeling that she was being palmed off with something second-rate. Then she added that she hadn't told me before she is actually very afraid of dogs, dating from the time she tried to make her grandparents' dog, Oscar, (also a Dalmatian) dance on his hind legs; it had bitten her, though not badly. It was not the actual physical pain that hurt so badly but the sense of being horribly let down.

Immediately after telling me that, although it didn't seem to follow in any logical way, she said: 'I never feel ... funny ... I never feel resentful or hate my mother; I always feel warm and protective towards her; in the dream I felt warm and protective as I do too in reality'. It is a long and difficult dream, and very difficult to convey how Rosamund and I worked it over together. Clearly she had wanted a dog-penis-nipple like the Queen (the male consultant), but felt fobbed off with a Dalmatian breast with black-spot or bleeding-eye nipples (the female analyst), who interferes through being the poet-singer-star of the analytic show and does not allow Rosamund to step into projective identification as the princess who marries mother's brother (the daddy). Instead she feels ridiculed by the grandfather-daddy and bites him back, in order to divert her hostility from the mother, the breast, the nipple, the bleeding eyes. This is a new experience in the analysis, because 'of course' she has always been 'in mother' previously, being mummy's mummy, protective, nurturing, never resentful.

This in fact turned out to be a vĕry important point in the analysis, because this was the last real dream that I had for quite some time. What set in instead from this point, was a gradual onset of compulsive vomiting. The anorexia in a sense returned, but in the form of being unable to hold down what she was eating. The compulsive vomiting, linked with the inability to remember dreams and her great difficulty in producing material, clearly declared that the analysis had become something that was extremely unpalatable and difficult for her to swallow.

For nearly two months this vomiting difficulty continued. She was staying at home because she felt too ill. She was trying very hard to remember dreams, but they would be gone by the morning. At this time she was aware of feeling extremely jealous of her father, possessive of her mother, and of continually wanting to take her mother's part in any little argument that happened between the two parents. She came back after one week-end, having had a dream *about some forscythia, but she couldn't remember whether it had been that this forscythia had burst into bloom, or that all the buds were dead and had not managed to bloom at all*. She then went on to say she had had a much longer, very strange dream which seemed to her very significant. This dream was *about her father, who went to fetch an orphan from the cemetery and was bringing the orphan back from the dead. Her father told her that this orphan went to heaven every nine days on her own, but never with a friend*. Rosamund said the orphan was small and plump with a very cross expression and was just like Bernadette Devlin (the Irish militant who was unmarried and pregnant at that time). It seemed to me that this small, plump Bernadette Devlin-orphan was a somewhat new introduction into analysis of a very rebellious, anti-government, antiparental part of herself that wanted to have a baby without a husband, that was very negativistic and whose idea of heaven — perhaps — was 'nine', = 'nein', 'No!' Rosamund had spent quite a bit of her youth in Germany and spoke German. The idea was heaven on her own, very egocentric. It would represent the typical adolescent rebellious part of herself of which she had hitherto been totally unaware, managing to keep it quite split off.

I think Rosamund did not like my interpretations on that day, pointing out the cross orphan and Bernadette Devlin within herself. The next day she came saying she had had a dream in the night from which she woke up feeling very satisfied and pleased with herself; then she went back to sleep again and had another dream that chased the first one away; she didn't like the second dream at all, but it was all she could remember. This dream was about my family (the first time she had really dreamt about them): *She seemed to be a friend of my family. I was not there but my husband was, and he was tall and fair, in his late twenties with long curly hair. He had a lovely child with him, also with long, curly and very bubbly hair, a beautiful baby. He said to her that his wife wasn't a good wife at all. Rosamund said she longed to have this child as her own, and my husband told her how wonderful she was with children, to which Rosamund replied*

215

very modestly: 'Oh no, not at all. It's not me, it's the child; anyone would love this child'. And then she said the wife must be a hard person not to adore this lovely cuddly child. Rosamund awoke feeling very annoyed about this dream, and tried hard to remember the other one she'd had. And before I could say anything about it, she said to me: 'I'm feeling there's no point in eating anything, because I only vomit; it's completely hopeless'. I think that she was anticipating the sort of interpretation I would make about such a clear dream, and pre-empting me by saying: there's no point in telling me that, I'm only going to spit it out, I'm not going to hear it.

This dream was very important in Rosamund's analysis; for although she did not like it, she nevertheless brought it to me and recounted it to me.

Some of this material appears in 'Infantile Elements and Adult Strivings in Adolescent Sexuality'.

Section III

PAPERS ON INFANT OBSERVATION

1   A Baby Observation: The Absent Object
1980

From quite early on, even a few weeks — as soon as a baby becomes aware of there being a difference between himself and the breast, his mouth and the nipple, himself and the mother — the problem of separation becomes observable. How does the baby let the object go; and how does he deal with this in his mind? Long before a baby is actually weaned from the breast, some sort of weaning process is taking place or failing to place, with every separation from the mother. In the first baby I have in mind, it is the use of the eyes which is revealing of aspects of this problem. The observer who had been watching him develop for over a year, had been struck by the different uses that he made of his eyes. This baby was born to a Japanese mother and an Australian father, both of whom were temporary immigrants to London. The observer saw the mother before the baby was born, and found her a very charming, pretty little woman, greatly looking forward to having the baby. But in fact she had a terrible time during her labour, because she was very small and this was a very big baby.

When the observer went to see the mother in hospital, a day or two after the baby's birth, she found her still in a state of shock and very withdrawn with difficulty in talking to her. The baby had been in an incubator for two days after birth. They discovered later that he had various minor things wrong with him, which all mended during the course of his first year: it was a renewed shock for the mother each time she heard about one of these things. He was suspected to have a fractured collar bone, a hip that was slightly dislocated, and a hole in the heart that closed by the time he was twelve months. The mother was not aware of all this initially, but said in a rather listless way on the first visit: 'I couldn't hold my baby'. This seemed to set the theme for the next few months. When the baby came home, the father took a fortnight's holiday, and was very caring and supportive towards the wife; the baby was being breastfed. Then her mother came over from Japan and stayed for a few weeks. The observer noticed that when the baby was being breastfed, he had a habit of pushing his shoulder backwards, as if he was straining away: she didn't know whether towards or away from something, possibly related to discomfort in the collar bone.

At about six weeks, the grandmother went back to Japan, and the baby was very quietly and rather unnoticeably weaned on to a bottle, without seeming to show any reaction. The mother clearly felt very badly about it, but didn't want to talk about it, and simply said: 'You know, my milk dried up'. And he took the bottle quite happily, according to the mother; the observer noticed very little crying. He was a baby who seemed to be very placid, well fed, didn't cry, and generally quite accommodating. The mother didn't hold him for very long once he was put on the bottle, so he had a fairly short feed. But the observer noticed how in some of these bottle feeds the baby was again markedly turning around; and this time he wasn't just pushing himself backwards with his shoulder, but would turn and look round. She felt that this time, when he was turning and looking round, it was as if he was really putting some sort of experience behind him, with his eyes. Yet he wasn't crying, or making a fuss, or openly showing the mother that there was anything disturbing him. At this period, the mother seemed to recover the former cheerfulness that was characteristic of her before the baby was born. She talked of him being quite an easy baby, who fitted into the household routine. She was apparently a very artistic little woman, who took a lot of care about the baby's clothes and surroundings. For instance, the family were living in furnished lodgings to begin with, and she changed the curtains that the baby looked at because she felt that the imprint of these un-aesthetic curtains would probably spoil his aesthetic taste for the rest of his life. She was also quite careful to put on good classical music for the baby to listen to from the early months onwards so that he should develop his taste in this. The mother thought a lot about the baby; but the observer noticed that she didn't spend much time holding or cuddling him. She talked a lot to him; he would cry, and she would go up and say something like: 'What's the matter, matter ...' in a little sing-song repetition, in a soothing, musical way that seemed to comfort the baby and make him feel all right.

Now, around the age of six months, when the baby as well as

having the bottle was being fed from the spoon, different things came to the observer's notice. She saw that the mother made very nice little meals for the baby, and fed him very neatly and skilfully from the spoon. He always took what he was given without any protest. The observer wondered whether he had a chance to protest, because the mother was somehow quick and deft and she would talk to him while she was doing it, slightly distracting him. The observer noticed about this time that he was very preoccupied in following his mother with his eyes when she moved about the room or went out of the door. It seemed that he was placed in such a way that he could always see what the mother was doing in the room; and when she went out of the door into the kitchen, his eyes would remain fixed on that door, looking somewhat blank, until she came back again. Then he would make a little sign of notice, but his responses were fairly muted.

At about this time, one of the most upsetting events for the observer took place. One day, when the baby was about six months old, the mother had asked her if she'd like to see the baby being bathed. The baby burst into quite frantic tears during the bath, and cried and cried. It was a very upsetting experience for both the observer and the mother, who didn't seem to know what to do. The father also came in about the same time, and both parents seemed very distressed about it. Afterwards, they said to the observer that they thought the baby was upset because she didn't smile and talk encouragingly to the baby; that he might have been frightened of her because she was a stranger and she wasn't being friendly enough to him. They further suggested to her that she should engage with him more, talk to him and play with him. It was a very difficult moment, because the observer felt that this really wasn't so at all. They were so upset about the baby being upset, that they were almost colluding with him to make her into the 'bad object'. In fact she was told not to come any more; but she then had quite a little talk with the parents and they seemed to get over this.

This event did not happen again. But the observer said that at that time, before the baby burst into tears, there was a moment when he looked at her, and she had felt that if looks could kill, she would have been dead. At that moment, looking at her as a stranger and intruder, he may have projected onto her everything that was wrong, so that she became the 'bad mother'. The observer had been there regularly every week, and had seen baths several times before, though not for some weeks before this. The mother had invited her particularly because she said the baby so much enjoyed his bath. Although the baby saw the observer each week, he had never actually come out to her or smiled and become friendly. He would lie and look at her with a sort of interest, but he was not forthcoming. She had also begun to feel that in certain ways he was remarkably expressionless; he would quite often look rather blankly, and at times when you might have expected him to be upset, this look of blankness appeared instead.

It seemed as if the baby had some sense of the mother's frailty, and of the depression that did continue to crush her cheerfulness. The business of attending to the baby kept her going, and kept away feelings of nostalgia about home and her mother having gone away; and the mechanics of bodily care of the baby kept her from worrying about those various physical problems that were gradually disclosed, such as the hole in the heart. The mother would tell the observer about them, but usually not immediately, only after a little while, after she had somehow managed to encapsulate the knowledge. Perhaps the blank looking was a means the baby used of putting emotions away, because they could not be dealt with. This phase of watching the mother go out of the room and fixing the spot where she had left until she came back, developed into something else; he would watch her go out of the room, and then he would look up at the ceiling, and sometimes he would point. It was as if he had some picture of his mother in his mind which he put up there, on the ceiling. This great interest in the ceiling continued for many weeks, sometimes when the mother was in the room and sometimes when she was out of it. It may be that he was hallucinating at these times.

By the time the baby was nearly a year old, and beginning to crawl and move about the room, the observer and the parents, particularly the mother, were very friendly with each other. The mother very much looked forward to her visits, and was trying to get the baby to engage more with the observer. She would talk about him to the observer, and talked a great deal to the baby himself in the observer's presence. She still didn't hold him much, or pick him up on her knee when he was crawling; if she did so it was only for a moment before putting him down again.

The observer felt there was much closeness and fondness between the mother and the baby, but it had a cool edge to it — well mannered, and under control. They were still living in the same place, but by this time had replaced more or less all the furniture with their own.

Around this time, when the baby was beginning to move about quite a lot, the mother used to employ his favourite toys, which were little picture books. She would spend quite a few minutes every observation pointing out the names of things, animals and so on, in these little books. Then the baby would pick the book up, come and open it and hold it out to mother. He began to be able to make some sounds rather like the names that the mother was pronouncing. This was absolutely his favourite game. The observer began to feel that he was extremely interested in her when she came, would often look at her in a wondering way, although he wouldn't make any move to talk to her. When she left, the mother would carry the baby with her and say to him: 'Say bye bye' — but he would never say 'bye bye' nor raise his hand to wave goodbye. He would turn his face away, or look a bit sad.

And so I have come to the observation which took place when he was nearly a year old, during which for the first time he did say 'bye bye' to her. In this observation he was definitely much more friendly in his attitude. When the observer came into the room and he was sitting in his crib, he looked up at her in quite a friendly way. He was holding a little brick in his hand and he reached out to offer it to her — the first time he had done anything of the kind. When she put her hand out to take it, however, he immediately took his hand back, and wouldn't give it to her. But later on in the observation, after the mother had come in and had been talking to him and feeding him, he took up this little toy and gave it to the mother. She took it and she handed it back to him; then this time, he looked at the observer and then gave it to her. He let the observer have it, and when she gave it back to him he took it back from her; and she felt that this was almost the first real interaction that she had ever had with him. He seemed terribly pleased to be having a game with those two, the mother and the observer. He looked at the one, then he looked at the other, and started making lots of talking noises, while continuing to look from one to the other. Then he looked

223

up at the ceiling and pointed up in the way that he'd done sometimes before when he'd been on his own and not paying attention to anyone. He was pointing up and was talking to the ceiling as if he were seeing things there, and then he turned very eagerly to the mother and to the observer. Clearly he was trying to tell them both something about what he saw up there.

The observer felt that this performance had something to do with his feelings about the mother going away, and the sort of picture that he had in his mind. I think that in some way he was trying also to bring the mother and the observer together, as if they'd been mother and father. That he was saying something about the absent object, she felt was confirmed at the very end of the observation: because, for the very first time, when she went away, he looked a little bit sad, but he waved his hand and said 'bye bye'. He seemed reconciled to her coming and going; connected in his mind with the attempt to allow the mother to come and go, and to feel that he had some kind of picture of the mother inside him, that could enable him to do this. He was about a year old before he did this. One can see this happen sometimes with babies much earlier.

2

The Contribution of Observation of Mother-infant Interaction and Development to the Equipment of a Psychoanalyst or Psychoanalytic Psychotherapist

1976

Esther Bick's paper in the *International Journal of Psychoanalysis* (1962) described the history of infant observation as initiated by her at the Tavistock Clinic, and as adopted later at the British Institute of Psychoanalysis. It continues to be a valued part of the training of analysts at this Institute, and plays an even more central role in the training of psychoanalytical psychotherapists in the Department of Children and Parents at the Tavistock Clinic. Mrs Bick's paper described the method of observation and the aims in setting up this exercise. She gave indications and examples of what could be observed together with some discussion of the relevance of both the method and the observations made accessible by it, to the work of the psychoanalyst.

One must consider that weekly observation of an infant with his mother in a family throughout the first year or two years, the detailed recording of these observations and the necessary discussion in a small seminar group, take a great deal of time in the training of an analyst or of a therapist. The importance and relevance for a student who may not even be planning to work with children afterwards may be difficult to see, and yet in my experience those students who have undertaken this exercise while being able to discuss their observations in a seminar led by someone who has already undergone this rather rigorous and persevering study, have almost invariably felt it to be a central if not *the* central item in their analytic training. Many have followed it up later by making another series of observations or by participating in discussions of those made by others.

One may ask: is it not possible for a candidate to learn in the course of his personal analysis and from supervision of his cases, everything that he needs to know about the child within the adult, and about the infant within the child? In view of the

distinguished analysts, theoreticians and imaginative practitioners who have made their contributions without the benefit of
structured infant observation or even of child analysis, one can
hardly say that experience of these is essential in the formation of
the analyst who intends to work with adults.

However, one can make a case for the view that the development of psychoanalysis is in danger of being choked by too many
theories, and that too much time is spent in societies and in
groups, debating these theories from a background of insufficient common experience founded on detailed observation. All too
often adherence to theories is dictated by personal loyalty or
adherence to analytic pedigrees. In no area are these theories
debated more hotly than in that of child development and infant-
rearing: in psychoanalysis, as in paediatrics and pedagogy. All
the experts know about it and how it should be done; but few are
willing to take the trouble to stay long enough with the infant to
see how their advice and prescriptions work in practice.

If one approaches psychoanalysis as a science-art concerned
with the study and description of phenomena, rather than as an
explanatory science which seeks to find the *cause* of mental illness
and to offer prescriptions which will teach people how to avoid it,
one must regard the enlargement of the capacity for observation
as essential to the development of an analyst. Lacking, as he
does, a clear map charting the route and a definite goal to focus
and funnel attention, the analyst is exposed to uncertainty, confusion, anxiety when bombarded at close quarters by the
emotional experience of another person, as a mother is
bombarded by the emotional state of the infant.

The essential intimacy and nakedness of the analyst-patient
relationship, if an analytic process is taking place (the 'whitehot
experience of the consulting-room' as Winnicott once called it),
is probably more analogous to the mother-baby relationship
than to any other. This can be more easily lost sight of in training
analyses or in the debates of psycho-analytical societies, than in
child analysis or in work with patients outside the analytic
community who have come because they feel ill and are in need
of help.

As in psychoanalytic debates with colleagues, so also in the
consulting-room; all too often the child is talked *about*, maybe
eventually trained to behave in the way that the adults — the

226

psychoanalytic establishment — think is appropiate. This tends to produce the well-adjusted child, the 'well-analysed' candidate; allowing unexperienced, uncomprehended and therefore unintegrated parts of the self to be split off and projected elsewhere (the other family, the other group), taking with them some of the potential strength and richness of the personality.

If we look at the role of the observer in infant observation we can consider how learning to become an observer, may help in learning to become a psychoanalyst (a process that continues long after qualification). Close observation of a mother and young baby is an emotional experience which requires mental work if it is to be thought about rather than reacted to. The tendency to project one's own unconscious infantile desires and dreads into the situation between the mother and baby is ubiquitous. If one does not come close enough for the relationship to have an impact, many details will be missed and the quality of the learning impaired. On the other hand, in order not to be drawn into action — into acting out the anxieties evoked instead of containing them by reflection — one must find a sufficiently distanced position to create a mental space for observing what is happening in oneself, as well as in the mother and baby. If one takes up the detached stance of an experimenter looking through a microscope in a laboratory one is likely to disquiet the mother and to impose an extra burden upon her, as of course many an observer fears to do when first beginning his visits.

One must find one's way to a position with the mother from which one can be friendly, receptive, and willing to forgo judgemental attitudes, explicit or implicit; taking an uncritical interest in whatever she wants to confide about the baby or about her own feelings in dealing with him. This may involve learning to bear the projection of a good deal of anxiety, and to restrain the impulse to rush in and relieve with advice or support in action. One has in fact to restrain therapeutic zeal, while making a human response which indicates to the mother that one can appreciate her feelings without criticising or colluding. The state of inward suspension of judgement, of 'negative capability' (so aptly quoted by Bion from Keats), is indeed a precondition for learning from experience. It is also achieved more easily through experience which teaches one humility by revealing the fallibility of one's omniscient preconceptions.

227

By exchanging experiences in a seminar discussion group one learns that one has to respond to each mother as an individual and also to notice the effect which one's own presence, conversation and acts may be having upon her; also to recognise the transference of infantile expectations and fears from her to the observer. Those observers who are in analysis have the opportunity of sorting out their own countertransference feelings there; much as candidates, while learning to work with patients, may also get help in clarifying their states of mind in this way. Nevertheless each observer's particular problems in finding a useful stance that potentiates a friendly non-intrusive relationship is usefully discussed and shared in the seminar where the observations are being discussed. The private psycho-pathology of each individual observer is a matter for his analysis or self analysis, but the problems of understanding the projections and provocations to action through countertransference reactions to the baby's or the mother's distress are to some extent common to all, and can be shared learning experiences.

Invariably the observer discovers that he approaches the observation with certain preconceptions and implicit, if not explicit, theories of how babies should be treated, accompanied by a tendency to criticise the mother. These may be defended against by an idealisation of the particular mother-baby relationship, especially as presented to the seminar group in an atmosphere of competition with other observers' couples: 'How well my mother and baby are getting along'. One has heard the same sounds frequently from analysands in a state of idealised projective identification with 'their' analyst. Again these tendencies are usually discussed in a general way in the seminar as phenomena that are evoked by closeness to the most primitive infantile emotions. Attention to the details of the observation presented, and discussion of their possible implications, is also then likely to bring out hitherto unapprehended aspects of the situation which may assist the observer towards recalling further details which he did not realise he had noticed at the time.

Discussion of the observations in a seminar can have much the same function as a clinical discussion or supervision of a patient, if one is encouraging the candidate to recall all the details he did not understand. By trying to reconstruct the muddle he was in at different periods in the session he is reporting, the candidate or observer is helped to reconstruct with hindsight some possible meaningful patterns in this muddle. A candidate who is able to tolerate his muddle and to share it with the supervisor is much more likely to derive benefit from the superivision than one who presents a polished performance that leaves no room for further questions. An observer who has really come to learn how a baby grows and who becomes increasingly interested in the complexity of its development, is likely to reinforce the mother's interest in her baby and to encourage her to value her capacity to understand him as well as to perform services for him. The presentation of observations in a seminar and the sharing of unique yet similar experiences of emotional involvement can greatly help each observer in his own weekly visits to the family of the infant of his particular study, to participate in a more unself-conscious way in its atmosphere and to learn from his own countertransference. In order to make the best of the situation he must allow himself to *feel*, but needs to *think* about his feelings in order to restrain himself from acting them,

These points have an obvious immediate relevance to the student who is learning to become a psychoanalyst. In the consulting-room he will be in a sequestered observational situation where, if he can learn to bring this attitude of emotional receptivity, he will receive not only the confidences of the patients but also increasingly the projections of the more primitive infantile parts of the patient's personality. In work with adults one can so much more easily be misled by the *apparent* meaning of the words than in work with children. This applies particularly to the training analysis. And as an adult, especially as one aspiring to treat disorders in other people, one tends to become rather clever at learning *about* more vulnerable or nastier parts of one's personality: to develop a facility to talk about them in oneself as well as in others in a way that keeps them at arm's length.

The infant-observer attitude helps the aspiring analyst to take not only the words, but also the details of the patient's total demeanour and behaviour into account: to read between the words and to discern the nature of the experience which is being conveyed or avoided. It can help him to wait until he gathers from his own response to the patient some intuition of what may be happening. If he cannot bear this period of uncertainty and confusion he is likely to pre-empt the emergence of the emotional experience in the patient by explaining it first. As many an infant/mother observer has noted, books on child development can be a comfort to an inexperienced mother but one which can also come between her and a direct experience of pondering about the child. Maybe there are times when, as an analyst or a candidate, one does need the comfort and protection of well-tried theories and learned interpretations, or simply to rely upon the rules; but it is useful to be able to notice when one is doing this too mechanically.

The observer may learn from his own experience and from watching the mother's reactions to the first few weeks of the baby's life, how painful it is to stay with the recognition that something as helpless as a young infant — helpless in the way that a young animal is not — does experience intense anxiety and does have a mental life. Unlike small animals, babies can do little about their bodily needs and discomforts; they have to suffer the pain of waiting until help comes. Their pain is relieved not only by their bodily needs being met, but through understanding, social contact, love.

If we understand the analytic transference as a process of externalising infantile relationships and desires, then the opportunity of following historically from week to week the growth of the infant's relationships — the way in which he utilises his developing capacities within the context of those relationships to make sense of his world, the phantasies he weaves about the stimuli which impinge upon him from within and from without — undoubtedly adds to the analyst's sensitivity to the quality and movement of that transference. Observation during the first six months for instance affords an opportunity to study how the infant's object relationships begin, by the baby relating unintegrated parts of himself to parts of the mother. It brings home what we all know and talk about fairly glibly: the reality that emotions at the most primitive level are rooted in bodily states and sensations located in particular parts of the body, sensations that are educated and achieve meaning through the mother's emotional responses.

This has an obvious relevance to the understanding of psychosomatic symptoms in patients. It may also help one to understand how, hidden in the presentation of narratives about people

230

in patients' material, is concealed another layer of meaning concerned with the earliest part object relationships, centrally the combination of nipple and breast: the giving – withholding – organising, receptive – comforting – indulgent qualities of the primary object. For although obviously it has been possible to help and for that matter 'cure' many patients without reference explicitly to the first year of life, we are dealing with people whose psychopathology, whatever its later intensification or crystallisation, almost certainly has its origins to a greater or lesser extent in that early period. The richer the opportunities we have to observe and think about this period, the more likely are we to be able to talk to a patient about these unconscious areas in evocative metaphorical terms which help him to link with them in a meaningful way; the more likely are we to perceive the operation of infantile phantasies in patients as phenomena to be described, rather than to try to work from some abstract idea of their existence.

Let us, for instance, consider the education of one's capacity to utilise the countertransference to perceive the quality of the emotion or lack of emotion in a patient's verbal communications; the meaning or lack of meaning. The work of Esther Bick, influenced by following many infant observations, and of Donald Meltzer and others who have followed the development of autistic children, has alerted us to the phenomena of two-dimensional relationships and modes of learning: to imitation of behaviour and copying, as methods of avoiding mental pain which do not lead to the development of the personality. One can see that this two-dimensional way of clinging to external objects and of imitating more grown-up behaviour has its place in the growing up of every infant, and in the life of every adult. One can also see the impoverishment or stunting of development which occurs when this becomes a pervasive defence against emotional experience, more detectable in gross pathology than it is in personalities who behave in an apparently normal way. It is seen in the consulting-room as patients who are behaving as if they were having an analysis, but cleverly avoiding a really distressful experience. One may think of these patients as having a defective internal container or internal breast which would enable them to hold and make use of painful emotions, and therefore of all new experience.

231

The study of ways in which the infant's experience on a sensual level, with objects in the external world, does or does not become internalised, can throw light on such patients, or upon such states of mind that at times probably present in every patient. The questions about the conditions that favour or impede introjection in infancy, are applicable to the study of the analytic process — in the course of which one hopes that a patient will be able to internalise a more receptive and a stronger object which will enable him to enlarge his acquaintance with himself, to add to and to think better about the experiences he is having.

In order to be able to utilise meaningfully potential qualities and parts of oneself, these probably do need to be expressed and worked with at an infantile level with someone else. This is certainly so with aggressive and painful emotions. Observation of how the infant needs to be able to express his pain and aggression can help one when analysing both children and adults to take that aggression less personally. For instance, apparent aggression or hostility in words or in behaviour may express on the part of the patient a need to make the analyst *feel* something which he cannot as yet tolerate feeling himself, because he has not developed the equipment for thinking about it. It may be better understood as an evacuation of pain than as a negative act. The 'toilet breast' in analysis, as Meltzer has termed it, appears in the transference as a need for one of the primary functions of the mother, first apprehended by the infant at a part-object level.

Relieving the infant of intolerable discomfort — basically the fear of dying — decontaminating that fear and returning it to the infant in a more assimilable form, can be seen together with nourishing as recurrent primary functions of the mother in the infant's first weeks and months. One can study the outcome in situations where the mother cannot sufficiently tolerate the impact of the projection of primitive anxiety to allow herself to *feel* it, but instead quickly gives a part of herself (the breast), or a substitute — the bottle, a dummy, or later a sweet — to stop the protest. Interpretations, reassurances, can be given in analysis in much the same way: to stop the gradual unfolding or expressing of hitherto unapprehended emotions, which bring with them pain but also the possibility of greater strength and enrichment. Anxious over-activity is one way whereby dependence on external tangible objects is perpetuated, reinforcing the infantile belief that there should always be somewhere a good enough *external* object to take care of one.

The central truth one can learn through one's own experience as an observer, and through observing the development of a mother who is learning to be a mother, is directly applicable to the relationship of the analytic couple. It is more painful to wait, to remain receptive and not cut off, to bear the pain that is being projected, including the pain of one's own uncertainty, than it is to have recourse to precipitate action designed to evacuate that pain and to gain the relief of feeling that one is doing something.

The observer so often feels initially and maybe for a long time that to be present, attentive and interested in situations of distress is not enough; that he must justify his presence by doing something to help. He may be observing a mother who, over-whelmed by anxiety about the baby's helplessness, feels too in those early days that she must always be doing something: giving the breast, giving the dummy, lifting the baby in a way that is consciously designed to stop the pain he is feeling. But what is likely to be conveyed to the infant in this over-busy attention to his bodily needs, is a projection of unassimilated anxiety which confuses and does not help him to distinguish his own emotions from those of the mother. If the anxiety projected by the infant can be thought about by the mother she may not necessarily manage to respond with the degree of understanding required, just as an analyst who tries to understand a patient's communications may indeed manage to achieve but a limited comprehension; but the capacity to continue to try to understand is in itself an encouragement to develop and to identification with a thinking object.

The observer may often find that as the baby grows and thrives the mother's anxiety is lessened so that she may be able to learn from the baby how to meet his requirements and may understand him better, as she can give herself more time and space for reflection. But the observer will see that it does take time, and that the process of finding each other cannot be hastened by active intervention or teaching by others. The same kind of process may also take place in the establishing of an analytic relationship. Supervisors of anxious candidates could sometimes learn from the persecutions of overactive mothers-in-law (frequent visitors in infant observations) how not to intrude too helpfully between the untried pair, and how to find a stance that supports and does not undermine the budding analyst.

Through discussion of different mothers and babies one can see how greatly not only mothers, but also babies do differ in temperament; how much in fact certain babies are able to do for themselves in the way of containing anxiety; how well others may be able to convey their needs and to respond rewardingly when these are met, thereby bringing out the latent mothering qualities in the mother. On the other hand, there are those who seem to have a difficult temperament from birth and tend to be discontented, exacting and tyrannical in ways that require infinite thought and tolerance from a mother who may or may not learn to develop these qualities in herself.

These considerations also apply to the patient-analyst relationship. There are some patients whose desire to develop and to become more acquainted with the truth of themselves is so strong that they are able to do a good deal of the work from early on in the analysis; there are others who continually sabotage the work that is done for them and are infinitely more exacting in their requirements.

I shall now give two examples: the first from observation of a baby over a period of fourteen months, the second from the material of a young man who has been in analysis for almost fifteen months. These excerpts are given in the hope of conveying how a background of infant observation can be of assistance in helping one to form a picture of the infantile configuration in the transference.

William is a first baby aged fourteen months, born to a young couple who have taken a great interest in his development. He has been breastfed, sucking eagerly from the start. There was a brief disturbance when he was three to four weeks old, when his mother's milk supply dwindled owing to antibiotics she was given for some delayed postnatal infection. At that time William wanted to feed continually, waking up frequently and searching frantically for the breast. This persisted when the milk supply was evidently quite restored, until the parents decided they must have some sleep and that constant feeding didn't help. His father just held him soothingly and let him continue to cry until he went to sleep. Thereafter he began to sleep again through the night.

For some weeks after this crisis, however, following his feed he would push his tongue forward between his lips as if to fill up the hole that had been occupied by the nipple.

His relationship to the breast, and to his mother as she came to be perceived as a more whole object, was characterised by a passionate intensity and involvement, evident also with his father to a lesser extent. Towards other people he tended to show a friendly but cooler interest. From about four months of age he began from time to time to have periods of intense distress during his breast feeding, usually towards the end when he seemed to be overwhelmed by the realisation that it would finish. Also occasionally after the start of a feed he would pull away and seem to scold the breast as if he resented its having been away. Despite these periods the breastfeeding continued for another four months, very enjoyably in the main both for him and for his mother.

During these second four months Williams began to extend greatly his range of other food, sampling almost everything he saw his parents eating. To begin with these other foods were tackled with great and indiscriminate avidity, shovelled in with his thumb as if he were too ambitious for their possession to really enjoy them. He approached solid foods as if he were determined to master a task. 'He thinks it all comes from his thumb', said his mother.

By the time he was finally weaned from the breast he seemed less avid and more discriminating, able to enjoy the taste of different foods. The importance of his thumb had receded, and instead came a great spurt in his mobility and increased impetus to explore his surroundings. Thumb-sucking began to be replaced by efforts at talking sounds. As a comforter in moments of distress and before going to bed he turned to a small eiderdown which he had had in his cot since birth. He would bury his mouth and his face in this in much the same way that he used to bury his face in the breast. After a period of being intensely addicted to this, he then gradually seemed to be giving it up in favour of expanding relationships with people, but also intense explorations of objects around him, most especially of handles ad light switches. From the early months he had been fascinated by lights going on and off. Now he became obsessed with trying to work them.

Shortly after his first birthday there was a period of minor illnesses in the family, colds and 'flu. At the same time his mother was more deeply occupied than usual in trying to finish a piece of writing she had started before his birth. William resented this, regarded the typewriter as an enemy, and suffered from a prolonged cold himself. He became increasingly re-addicted to his eiderdown, demanding it at all times, even in the bath. He became dilatory and fussy about his food for the first time in his life, unusually fitful in his sleeping and noticeably less friendly and responsive to people. He tended to cling to his mother but was less affectionate and appreciative. He would cling to her clothing in much the same way that he buried his face in the eiderdown, but often he would prefer the eiderdown to either mummy or daddy. The important things about it seemed to be its softness and the fact that it could be picked up, put down, stood on, lain upon, or thrown away, but was always there to hand in the explorations he was making of his environment. He also began to resent at times his nappy being changed and his bottom cleaned, 'yelled as if he were being robbed', his mother said.

His parents began to worry that the eiderdown (a real 'transitional object'), was taking something away from his relationship with people and decided to confine it to its proper place, the cot. The first day that it was removed William became most upset, threw tantrums, behaved piteously, throwing himself on the floor and kissing the carpet and the velvet chair-cover. After a couple of days, with extra attention from his mother he did not seem to expect it any more and was quite happy to have it only in his cot. His sleeping improved and he became noticeably more friendly to people again, treating them less like mere articles of furniture among the other things in the world which he was so intent upon exploring. In short what was quite a marked regression to a part-object relationship, centred round the expendable controllable eiderdown, was arrested.

Dr P. is a young registrar in his late twenties who began analysis some fifteen months ago, initially rather cautiously to see whether it would help him with his patients. He has become increasingly involved and appreciative of the analytic method. He is a particularly intelligent, conscientious young man of a basically open and friendly personality, but with marked obsessional traits. He has had a privileged but very moral up-bringing, admires his very successful father and consciously wishes to work well and honestly himself, but is suspicious of his tendency to be over-clever and pretentious, to rely on his connections rather than his work for advancement. This goes with feelings of regret at never quite making the top grade at sports at which he is very good but not outstanding.

The material of his session at present centres around the impending Christmas holiday which is hitting him quite hard this year. He fluctuates between fear of being depressed, apathetic or disabused of his faith in analysis, and fears that something might happen to the analyst — she has a cold, might have a road accident.

He has five sessions a week. On the Thursday he came with a dream about three international rugger players, one of whom he knows personally, the others more distantly. They are all good scorers and he is not in their class. He becomes annoyed upon realising that his car is due to have an M.O.T. in the Christmas holdays before it can be re-licensed. He is also rather depressed about the condition of his room in the hospital which is used as a dumping ground for his belongings because he spends most of his spare time in a flat which his girlfriend shares with another girl. This material seemed to have the transference significance of rueful comparison between the infant's incontinent penis and bottom and daddy's potent (goal-scoring) baby-making, mummy-servicing one. Interpretations on these lines seemed acceptable to him.

The next day, Friday, he arrived saying that he could describe a dream he had just had but that it seemed rather foolish to do this without introducing it and going thoroughly into his present state of mind. In the past he has always been pleased and eager to bring dreams and has tended to feel that those sessions to which he brought them have been the most fruitful, those in which he came closest to having illuminating experiences about himself, so this approach was an unusual one. He managed to spend most of the session talking about this dream as if he were about to give it but could hardly bear to let it go, talking continually yet managing to say practically nothing — pseudo-analysing his motivation for not mentioning it at once.

The withholding of the dream seemed to be connected with the

237

material of the day before: little boy humiliation at not having daddy's first class status (the penis and testicles that could keep mummy going), trying to avoid this experience again by evoking curiosity in the analyst in order to convince himself that he has something of value that is not just faeces.

As he continued talking in a desultory frustrating fashion the picture formed in my mind of an infant threatened with weaning from the breast, still struggling and unreconciled to the recognition that he is not it and has not exclusive possession of it; an infant who has recently learned to walk but who is ruefully and recurrently meeting with evidence of his limitations in skill; not yet a walker like daddy, or a talker like his daddy who can entertain and renew mummy, give her babies and perform services that he cannot. This is an infant who is so preoccupied with trying to possess and control his object that he is unable to accept what it has to offer: seated as it were in his high chair playing with his food, while innerly preoccupied with sitting upon the stool in his bottom; provoking his mother to say, 'Let's change your nappy and get rid of your stool and then maybe you can get down to eating your dinner'.

Description of his behaviour in metaphorical terms something like this brought an amused reaction and finally the withheld dream.

The dream was as follows:- *There was a sick child with some unspecified illness. After a conference the doctors decided she needed special treatment and sent for a consultant from Melbourne. When he arrived this consultant seemed to become the analysand himself. But before he could prescribe treatment for the child, it seemed that he had to go into another room, a seminar room in which a group of doctors and nurses were seated round a table presided over by an American woman who was addressing the conference.*

The sick child was associated with a child about whom the analysand had been asked to send a long overdue report which was needed for the next step in her treatment. He had delayed writing the report to a consultant whom he resented for his arrogant ways. The American woman seemed to be the analyst, who he knows is married to an American. Presiding over the table she seemed to represent a combined figure of nipple and breast. The *Melbourne* is probably also similar in significance — *born of Meltzer*, whose books he is currently reading — a combination of parents from whom he has to learn how to consult about the child in him that is in need of treatment.

So, like baby William in the face of his anxiety about being unable to switch on the light (the analysis, the breast), to cure both himself and his primary object (the motor car mummy), in the face of his competitiveness with daddy's penis and greater powers, Dr P. was retreating to a part-object relationship and substituting a ruminating control over what was essentially a meaningless faecal object for an experience at the breast.

The experience of listening to observations of baby William — almost as old as Dr P.'s analytic age — was helpful in approaching this analytic material. As already stated these two examples have been chosen, almost randomly, to suggest how one may find that infant observation can aid one to discern and form a vivid picture of infantile behaviour in the consulting-room.

3 Notes on Infant Observation in Psycho-Analytic Training

ESTHER BICK, PhD.

Infant observation was introduced into the curriculum of the Institute of Psycho-Analysis in London in 1960 as part of the course for first year students. The detailed observational material that I am quoting in this paper is mainly drawn from the work of these students. Infant observation had, in fact, been part of the training course for child psychotherapists at the Tavistock Clinic since 1948 when the course began. We then decided to include in the first non-clinical year some practical experience of infants.

I thought this important for many reasons but perhaps, mostly because it would help the students to conceive vividly the infantile experience of their child patients, so that when, for example, they started the treatment of a two-and-a-half-years old child they would get the feel of the baby that he was and from which he is not so far removed. It should also increase the student's understanding of the child's non-verbal behaviour and his play, as well as the behaviour of the child who neither speaks nor plays. Further, it should help the student when he interviews the mother and enable him to understand better her account of the child's history. It would also give each student a unique opportunity to observe the development of an infant more or less from birth, in his home setting and in his relation to his immediate family, and thus to find out for himself how these relations emerge and develop. In addition he would be able to compare and contrast his observations with those of his fellow students in the weekly seminars.

I want to turn now to the method of observation which has evolved over the years and has been constantly discussed in seminars. The child psychotherapy students visit the family once a week up to about the end of the second year of the child's life, each observation normally lasting about an hour. The observations of the candidates at the Institute usually stop at about the end of the first year. Contrary to our expectations, there was no difficulty in finding mothers willing to have an observer — either through acquaintances or through other channels. Mothers have frequently indicated explicitly or implicitly how much they welcomed the fact of having someone come regularly into their home with whom they could talk about their baby and its development and their feelings about it. We found that it was best to give a simple explanation to the parents — namely, that the observer wished to have some direct experience of babies as part of his professional development. Note-taking during the observation was soon recognized as unsuitable and disturbing as it interfered with free-floating attention and prevented the student from responding easily to the emotional demands of the mother.

Much thought had to be given to the central problem of the role of the observer in the whole situation. This problem seemed to be twofold, as it involved the conceptualization of the observer's role, and also the conscious and unconscious attitudes of the observer. First the question of role; as infant observation was planned as an adjunct to the teaching of psycho-analysis and child therapy, rather than as a research instrument, it was felt to be important that the observer should feel himself sufficiently inside the family to experience the emotional impact, but not committed to act out any roles thrust upon him, such as giving advice or registering approval or disapproval. This would not seem to exclude him being helpful as a particular situation arose — by holding the baby, or bringing it an occasional gift. In other words, he would be a privileged and therefore grateful participant observer.

The second problem, that of attitudes, is, however, more difficult. Here, in the house of parents with a new born baby, the observer, however experienced with babies or in psycho-analysis or in scientific methods of observation, is confronted with a situation of intense emotional impact. In order to be able to observe at all he must attain detachment from what is going on. Yet he must, as in the basic method of psycho-analysis, find a position from which to make his observations, a position that will introduce as little distortion as possible into what is going on in the family. He has to allow some things to happen and to resist others. Rather than actively establishing his own personality as a new addition to the family organization he has to allow the parents, particularly the mother, to fit him into her household in

241

her own way. But he must resist being drawn into roles involving intense infantile transference and therefore countertransference.

To give an example, an older child in the family may try to monopolize him as an ally against the mother-baby couple. The mother may attempt to build up a strong dependence relation. He may find himself being influenced by the baby to become a substitute mother. In other words, if he becomes involved in the family organization as do other members of the family — grandparents, father, relatives, friends, who all 'observe' after all — his observations would then be as little objective as those of a father or mother student wanting to bring observations of their own. Further the tensions of the situation would invade him; particularly, the inadequacies in the care of the infant would upset him and the whole mystery of the situation intrigue him too much. He must not allow his behaviour to be dominated by these feelings which, on close scrutiny, will often be found to have been intensified by projections from members of the family. Whilst much of this must be dealt with in the student's analysis, the seminar can at least uncover some of the projections into him that are operating and which intensify his own internal conflicts.

To illustrate this function of the seminar I have chosen for discussion a problem which has appeared the most ubiquitous and difficult, namely the operation of the mother's post-partum depressive trends. While we have known for some time that these trends are almost universal, I was not prepared for the intensity with which they impinged on the observer. What one was struck by was the exclusive preoccupation of the students in the seminar with the mother's handling of the baby. Their attitude was highly critical and emotional. At first I tried to mitigate the problem by encouraging them to give more attention to the baby and less to the mother. This did not help. I realized it was necessary to give more consideration to this factor — the depression in the mother and its impact on the observer as well as on the baby and other members of the family. It is, of course, not the purpose of this paper to attempt to give a systematic account of depression in the mothers of newborn babies, but before giving the observational reports I want to clarify how I am using the word 'depressive' here. I am not using it primarily descriptively, but rather metapsychologically, to describe those aspects of the mother's relation to the baby in which a clear-cut regression to part-object relationship is evident. The mother can be clearly seen to be experiencing emotional detachment from the baby, helplessness in understanding and meeting its needs, relying on the baby to make use of her breasts, hands, voice, as part-objects.

Naturally depressive trends tend strongly to disturb the observer's detachment, both because of the mother's needs which pull the observer, and counter-transference anxieties which push him. He is pulled towards augmenting the mother's vitality and pushed to identify with the disturbed and resentful aspects of the baby. To illustrate this problem of the way in which the mother's post-partum depressive trends tend to draw the observer into roles unsuitable to his function and to place him under greater emotional stress, I will bring two different types of material: one, a summary of two months' observational work, and the second, more detailed observational notes. I think in both examples one can feel the observer's struggle to tolerate the situation. In the first example it will be seen how the crumbling of the manic trends in the mother tends to draw the observer into the role of a dependent figure.

K., a male baby, was the first child of young parents (about 25 years old) who worked together as office caretakers. The baby was unplanned and came after two years of marriage. Some months later, when the mother was much more secure about herself as a mother, she confessed to the observer that when other girls at school had talked of getting married and having children she thought privately to herself: 'Married may be, but I'll never have a baby; I am sure I should let it die.' This mother was specially selected by a health visitor as one who was normal, capable, and unlikely to be disturbed by being observed. The mother continued work up to term despite diarrhorea and backache, as part of her dependent and grateful relationship to her devoted husband. She described the rather precipitous delivery which had caused her some lacerations as a delivery in which, once his head was through, 'he shot out'. Thus she expressed an attitude emphasizing the baby's strength and independence which she maintained later.

At the first observation, when the baby was two days old, mother and baby were enthroned amid flowers, presents, and new furnishings; the mother, radiant, talked incessantly in an excited way about her pride in the baby, her delight that he was a boy and so strong, the presents she had received, and her gratitude to her husband who helped her so much in the last weeks. At the same time she was planning to fit the baby into a routine which would enable her to go on with her work and to help her husband. She reiterated her intention to breast-feed, driven by the conviction that it produced less flabby babies, but she was plainly very uncertain about her ability to do so.

Five days later all was changed. The mother was up, tired and harassed-looking, feeling burdened by the observer's visit but impelled to incessant talk. She said she had never thought that feeding a baby and keeping him clean would take up so much time, or that it would take so much to satisfy him. She had a blister on her nipple and pains under her arm, and talked in terms of trying to continue breast-feeding for six weeks.

When the baby who had been asleep in the pram, began to cry, the mother seemed at a loss to comfort him, talking rapidly to the observer of his strength, the beauty of the pram, and of her over-worked state. Finally, she turned the baby over, saying, 'Mustn't spoil you, young man', and told the observer that though they had not specially wanted a baby she and her husband were quite delighted, but since she had never much liked other people's babies she did not know what to do with him, and ended, 'I've really let myself in for something now . . .'

Further observations in the early weeks were similar, as the mother struggled to satisfy this 'wild, hungry baby', as she called him, who strained so hard both to get at and get away from the breast, who wanted but seemed unable to get all 'the dark part of the nipple into his mouth', who wriggled and struggled when being changed, quite unlike the doll they practised on in the ante-natal clinic. She continued to try to comfort him in the pram, to dress and undress him on the table. When the baby was scream-ing with hunger and impatience after the bath she would go on talking while dressing him in an apparently unconcerned way. At other times, when the baby was distressed, she pressed him on the observer while she got on with other tasks or even while she chatted. The breast-feeding ended at six weeks.

The father seemed to give the mother a great deal of support; he sometimes impersonated the baby to express gentle criticism of the mother or to indicate the baby's feelings to her. He did not

→ could itself be seen as a criticism.

compete with her in her role as mother, he regarded her unquestioningly, despite all her uncertainties, as the expert as far as the baby was concerned, and was at hand whenever possible. This supportive behaviour of the father seemed to be an important factor in the gradual improvement in the mother's closeness and tolerance towards the baby. In this material the manic defences of an immature and dependent mother can be seen to collapse, revealing her great anxiety about being able to take care of the baby and her distrust in her ability to do so.

The observer's anxiety about the inadequacy of this baby's mothering comes through in her difficulty in tolerating such points as the mother's incessant talking when the baby was in distress and the mother's lack of warmth and concern for her baby, as well as in her own relief at the father's support and its effect on the family. The seminar also felt that as the relationship between mother and observer went on there were indications of a helpful improvement, evidenced, for example, in the mother's being able to tell the observer of her adolescent anxieties about ever being able to be a mother at all.

In the second example I will give an account of a first observation, both to show the observer at work, indicating, as I said earlier on, the impact of the mother's depression on him, and also to show the richness of observational data — a point to which I shall come back later.

Charles, a baby of ten days at the first observation, was the second child of a professional couple. I shall quote now from the report.

'I rang mother and explained who I was in terms of the line of contact and we arranged that I should come the next day so that we could meet and see how we liked each other and whether we could make an arrangement for observations. In fixing the time of this meeting mother asked whether I would like to see the baby awake or didn't it matter. When I said I would prefer to see the baby awake, she suggested a feed, which I took up very readily. She showed some eagerness to accommodate me, being prepared to move the time of the feed up to half an hour. I said I could come when he was usually fed.

'Mother is aged about 25, has glasses, short thick light-brown hair, a square masculine sort of head and face, rather quiet and

Negotiation to meet needs of observer.

245

serious in looks and voice, but smiles readily with a warm smile. She was wearing a Swedish-Liberty striped blouse and a large black skirt; rather shabby-looking was the general impression, but somehow not in an unattractive way. She had quite a dignified manner, although visibly anxious about how to deal with me.

'I was first taken out to the garden behind the house where the mother's mother sat holding Charles wrapped in a blanket. The mother muttered something about it being feeding-time and would I care to see the feed. I followed her and Charles back into the living-room. The mother sat first on a divan and invited me to pull up an armchair opposite, then changed places because there was a draught on to the divan from the door to the garden (and grandma). By changing places the door could be left open without any draught on her. It also meant that the mother could be seen by her mother from the garden. While the divan where I sat could not.

'When I first saw Charles he was wrapped very voluminously in the blanket on his grandmother's lap. When the blanket was drawn back he was lying with his left hand on his ear, his right hand over the whole front of his face, kneading his cheeks and mouth and nose. His right thumb was in his mouth. He had several scratches on his cheeks and upper cheekbone and his right eye looked faintly discoloured, as though he had poked it too hard. When the mother and Charles settled in the armchair for the feed I could see very little of him indeed. I asked his name and how old he was. The mother asked me about my work. I explained that I hoped to work with children ultimately. We discussed possible times for me to come, and the mother seemed to prefer me to come to see the bath rather than a feed. This, however, was a misunderstanding. We found a suitable time and agreed that arrangements would be flexible because Charles's time-table would change and we could see how things went. Mother apologized for the unfinished state of the house, pointing out the packing-case legs of the dining table. I said that the food probably tasted just as good, to which — 'It's O.K. now that Mother's here!' There was a long pause in the conversation and she remarked that she ought to have my telephone number.

'Mother was timing the feed with her watch off her wrist. When she took the nipple out of Charles's mouth and put him over her left shoulder the watch dropped off her lap and I picked it up for her. She patted his back firmly but not too hard, and he brought up wind almost at once. He straightway began to shout and roar in ever-increasing tones of anger, was not quietened by his mother's talking to him, and when she gave him the right breast he made several attempts to take the nipple, making a kissing sound as he did so. The mother finally put the nipple right into his mouth and he began to suck. This time I could see a bit better and he seemed to be sucking very gently and slowly. There was the same motionless quality to his whole body as he sucked.

'As he began to suck he gave the breast a pat with his right hand just above the nipple. His hand seemed to interfere with his mouth (as it were, falling on to the nipple), so that the mother twice moved his hand away. He finally arranged it in a trumpet shape around his mouth. His feet were motionless, except that I noticed he once made a small stroking action against the chair with one foot. Mother said: 'Come on, work', very gently, and in a somewhat resigned sort of way.

'After a certain time mother took Charles off the breast, very sleepy, and first held him sitting up facing her, saying that Spock advised winding this way before trying the shoulder method, but that she had never had any luck with this nor heard of anyone who had. I agreed, and mentioned my own son and our experiences in winding him. She asked how old he was and remarked that Jack, Charles's brother, was 19 months old.

'The mother then put Charles over her shoulder, very sleepy and lolling and with a replete air. I don't recall that he brought up wind.

'She then put him back to the right breast, where he sucked even more slowly for a while. She then carried Charles against her shoulder upstairs to change him. I walked behind, and at this point Charles's face was quite calm but rather bloated and expressionless really. He was more in a stupor than asleep, it seemed, and made no sound.

'We went into the little room where the mother slept with Charles. The bed was unmade, and there was an empty chocolate wrapper beside it. The mother arranged the blanket on the bed and laid Charles on his back, at which he woke up quickly and began to scream. She left the room to fetch clean napkins. He continued to scream, both hands constantly round his face with pushing and scraping-off movements, his feet doing the same; pushing the left against and down the right.

'The screaming stopped when the mother called from another room, and was replaced for a moment by a happy low cooing sound. Then screams till the mother came back and talked sympathetically while she changed him. During the changing he cried miserably, but without drowning the sound of his mother's voice. His hands were constantly around his face, his left hand moving in front of him with a stroking action which reminded me of a blind man.

'The mother powdered his genitals, and stomach generously, drew attention to his rash, and remarked that lots of babies around had such a rash. When he was changed, she laid him on his left side in the cot, leaving his hands free of the blanket which wrapped him. She then left to get Jack up from his sleep, as they were going for a walk.

'Charles lay with his left thumb in his mouth, the fingers of his left hand over his face, especially over the right eye (the left eye was turned somewhat into the sheet); his right hand was curling over his temple. He breathed fast and noisily, and irregularly from time to time. Then his left hand assumed the trumpet shape that his right hand had done during the feed. His face showed scarcely any movement. All at once there was a sudden, heavy, heaving sigh and he seemed to relax altogether. His breathing became inaudible, his hands moved slightly away from his face. Over the next few minutes he gave several jerks forward, his arms out-stretched as though he was falling and clutching at someone. This seemed to happen sometimes to external stimuli. (The mother's voice talking to Jack in the next room, a door banging, and sometimes without any external stimulus that I noted.)

'Finally he lay quietly asleep. Two or three times he half woke at some loud noises from Jack's room, began to pucker and cry, but then fell asleep again. He began to cry when his mother came and put a cardigan and bonnet on him, treating him sympathetically and talking to him. He fell asleep again and was carried downstairs on the cot mattress which was going in the pram. As he lay on the mattress while the mother and grandmother gathered together things for the walk, I was struck by his expression, which had quite altered in the meantime and was

248

now fixed in a look of great pain of an intense kind, and not a muscle moved for the two or three minutes between when I first saw it and when I said goodbye to them outside the house'.

I have given this material in considerable detail to show the observer at work and the impact that this experience makes on him. Further, I want this baby to become familiar because I shall discuss other material from him later in this paper.

If we consider this material from the point of view of how it affected the observer, we naturally take into account that this was his first meeting with the family. The observer noted the mother's anxiety about how to deal with him. Between the lines the observer's tension can be discerned. He notes that the mother changes places with him so that grandmother in the garden can see the feed while he cannot. His sensitivity is registered in the record by calling the mother's invitation 'muttered', and perhaps by misunderstanding her remark about times in the sense that she did not want him to see the feed. When, to the mother's apologies for the state of the house, particularly the dining table, he remarks that the food probably tastes just as good, the mother says it's O.K. now that her own mother is here. Here we can see the first glimpse of the mother's depression and dependence on her own mother and the observer's attempt at comforting her. 'There was a long pause in the conversation and the mother remarked could she have my telephone number'. That two relationships are going on — baby-breast, mother-observer — in relative isolation is evident. The observer's sympathy for the mother's depression comes through again when, after prolonged attempts at the second breast, the mother said to Charles, 'Come on, work', and the observer notes she said it 'gently, in a somewhat resigned sort of way'.

Identification with the baby's misery (the scratched face) and later feeling of desertion in favour of the older brother whom the mother now went to awaken is written in each subsequent line. The mystery of the face scratches begins to be solved as both hands constantly move round his face with pushing and scraping-off movements, his feet doing the same, while the mother is out of the room.

After being changed the baby is seen to fall asleep, an event described by the observer vividly with great attention to detail, but on parting he was struck by Charles's expression, which had quite altered into a look of great pain of an intense kind although the baby was alseep. That the observer could have noted and reported in great detail with these tensions going on and in his first baby observation is striking.

The problem in such a paper as this is to convey the use that the seminar makes of such observations, and this I can do only to a very limited extent. To convey it correctly one would need to report the discussion in the seminar in as much detail as the observational material itself. And even this could give a fallacious impression, since the deductions drawn necessarily depend upon previous observations and discussions, from which, slowly, series of observations can be linked and patterns of behaviour seen to emerge. The point that I am stressing here is the importance of consecutive observation of the individual couple. The experience of the seminar is that one may see an apparent pattern emerging in one observation, but one can only accept it as significant if it is repeated in the same, or a similar, situation in many subsequent observations. Paying attention to such observable details over a long period gives the student the opportunity to see not only patterns but also changes in the patterns. He can see changes in the couple's mutual adaptation and the impressive capacity for growth and development in their relationship, i.e. the flexibility and capacity for using each other and developing which goes on in a satisfactory mother-baby relationship. The excitement in the seminar has been just as much in searching backward as in looking forward.

I will give two examples of such patterns of behaviour from the same baby, Charles.

In the first observation the observer described the baby's difficulties when feeding at the second breast; how the feeding was slow, long drawn out, and how the mother remarked that he did not work hard — but went on with the feed. In later observations we began to see that this was part of a pattern in which he related himself differently to the two breasts. At the first breast he sucked vigorously, sometimes gulping whilst at the second breast he sucked very gently, his mouth barely moving. The mother remarked on one occasion that he usually takes his meal at the first breast and 'fiddles around', as she puts it, on the second. However, she persevered, taking him off and putting him back, saying that he would not sleep the right length of time if he did not get enough. At the second breast Charles also made many movements with his hands, patting, making the trumpet shape, holding to his mother's jersey, stroking.

Thus after some weeks we had noted the pattern in the way Charles related himself to the two breasts, but it was only later with additional material about the hand movements that certain links suggested themselves — and these I am going to discuss later.

Another pattern emerged from the second observation when the bathing was watched. Charles began to cry as soon as his napkins were taken off, but his crying became much more intense when his nightdress came off. It became fainter when his mother handled him, washed, soaped him and spoke to him softly. When put down on a sheet his crying became louder. Once back in his nightdress the crying stopped immediately; he relaxed and began to look around. This pattern of crying intensely when his body was exposed during the bath or when put down was repeated in every observation until the end of the second month. He was soothed by his mother's voice and her handling, but quietened immediately when wrapped up, i.e. in his nightdress, or covered with a blanket in the cot.

While the foregoing patterns seem to suggest the working of intrapsychic defensive operations, patterns of communication between mother and child can also be observed, in which the mother's fundamental role of 'holding' in Winnicott's sense or containing projections in Bion's sense can be observed.

It becomes apparent that between a particular mother and child certain preferred modes of communication become central in their relation to one another. It is difficult to tell whether this choice originates in the mother's or the baby's preference. I would like to give two examples.

One of the mothers, whom I will call Mrs A. was uneasy in the feeding situation. She held the baby very awkwardly, and seemed tense and anxious at having the baby so close to her body. This is similar to the mother on whom I reported at the beginning of this paper, who also could not stand the close physical contact with the infant. Mrs A. showed that she was happiest when, after the feed was over, she would either put the baby comfortably on the floor or hold it with both arms away from her body. She would look at it, make movements with her lips (open and shut her mouth), to which the baby responded in the same way, or she would talk to the baby and the baby make various sounds back. One day, when the baby was in his fifth month, the mother had to go out shopping and left him with the observer to whom she gave various instructions. The observer sat down with the baby, and as long as he held it on his knee with its back to him, the baby was quiet. As soon as he started talking to the baby, or turned it round so that it could see him, it began to cry. This happened several times. In the discussion in the seminar it was felt that to this baby the association to a happy relation with mother was predominantly visual and vocal. The voice and sight of the observer was different from that of the mother, and awareness of this made the baby cry. It occurred to the observer that while the baby was sitting quietly on his knee it looked fixedly at the part of the room where the mother had been just before she left, as if it found comfort in looking at the area which was connected with the mother, while the voice and sight of the observer was proof that the mother was not there, and the baby cried.

Here is a contrasting example in which the kinaesthetic pattern is the key to the nature of the relationship. The observation began when baby James was four and a half weeks old. His mother had been undressing him in preparation for the bath. As she first put him on his back he tried to reach for the breast and made some protesting noises. The mother talked to him continually, saying, 'It's horrible, isn't it?' . . . 'Poor old fellow, never mind, you will soon be in the water'. She told the observer that he loved actually being in the water, unlike her other children who disliked it when they were babies. When in the water he lay quietly bringing his knees up to his stomach, making no sound and looking quite contented. In later observations he splashed, kicked, and played in the bath and often protested when taken out, as at this first observation when he was four and a half weeks old. Then when mother put him on to the breast he attached himself to the nipple at once and sucked vigorously. He had his eyes open and with the right hand he touched the breast and the button on the mother's dress alternately. This touching of the mother's body was observed as a regular pattern of behaviour whenever the baby came close to her. At thirteen weeks, the mother gave the observer the baby to hold while she went out to prepare the bath and said, 'Go to your auntie, she's got to study you'. James lay on the observer's lap looking at her, but did not touch her. When the mother returned he looked at her and followed her with his eyes until she took him. On her lap he felt for the breast with mouth and hand and later held her arm with his hand. After the bath, at the breast, he clutched at the breast; his mother removed his hand. He then put his hand on top of the mother's hand and moved it rhythmically while he sucked. At twenty-two weeks he was stroking the breast with wide movements. 'At twenty-four weeks' (I am quoting from the student's notes) 'James took the breast eagerly. His mother said he would not be having it much longer, the milk was giving out. With his left hand James played with the mother's breast and then with her hand. His movements remained lively all through the taking of the breast. As I watched him I wondered if his movements might be a conscious caressing of the mother; he appeared to me to be aware of what his hand was doing. The mother put James to the second breast and he took this eagerly, stroking her breast and neck and touching her mouth, although usually I have only noticed him do this during the first breast. He was weaned to the bottle at twenty-seven weeks. There followed a week of distress when he refused food, falling asleep between mouthfuls, whilst sleeping badly at night. The mother remarked that he behaved as though he was a little baby. In the following week he started touching the bottle, later reaching out for it, stroking it lovingly, as he had done with the breast and eventually settled down to keeping one hand on the bottle and touching, stroking, and caressing the mother with the other hand'.

I have, of course, described the overall patterns — the gross trends — and have had to omit the many finer details of the ups and downs, as time would not permit of recounting them. The material convinced us in the seminar that the relation of this baby to the breast and mother was close and intimate, and he expressed his love as well as anger towards her, predominantly by handling her body. We noted that although the mother was very vocal herself, the baby remained relatively silent, with a preference for tactile and kinaesthetic modes of relationship and communication.

Before closing I would like to mention some aspects of the baby observation as training for scientific data collection and thought. In the seminars it comes out very clearly from the beginning how difficult it is to 'observe', i.e. collect facts free from interpretation. As soon as these facts have to be described in language we find that every word in loaded with a penumbra of implication. Should the student say the nipple 'dropped' from the baby's mouth, 'fell' was 'pushed', 'released', 'escaped', etc.? In fact, he find that he chooses a particular word because observing and thinking are almost inseparable. This is an important lesson, for it teaches caution and reliance on consecutive observations for confirmation.

What we also find is that the students learn to watch and feel before jumping in with theories, and learn to tolerate and appreciate how mothers care for their babies, and find their own solutions. In this way the students are slowly able to discard rather fixed notions about right and wrong handling and become more flexible about accepted principles of infant care. What is borne in upon them is the uniqueness of each couple, how each baby develops at its own pace and relates itself to its mother in its own way.

Probably the most exciting aspect of the seminars, as they develop during the year, is the opportunity for teasing out of the material certain threads of behaviour which seem particularly significant for a particular child's experience of his own object relations. An item may strike the group as having a meaningful configuration. Its earlier history can then be traced in the notes, hypotheses made and predictions evolved for validation in further observations. For instance, it will be remembered that in the first observation with baby Charles, at ten days, it was noted that he patted the second, right breast and formed a trumpet shape with his hand around his mouth as he sucked away very gently and slowly. When left alone on the bed later his right hand was exploring around his eye and temple whilst his left thumb was in his mouth. Then gradually his left hand assumed the trumpet shape and all at once he went to sleep.

The fact that hand activity was an important mode of contact with his object and his body seemed clear in a general way, but of no special interest until the observations at 9 and 10 weeks. The observer reports: 9 weeks — after a disturbed feed because of a change in routine, Charles played with his hands in a complex way. First one hand seemed to be plucking and squeezing the other, twisting the fingers and thumb quite hard. Occasionally one hand described a small circle in front of his mouth while his face had a disagreeable, discontented expression, rather screwed up. After this a change came about. He became very much calmer and played with his hands in a much more playful way bringing them together, rubbing them and poking his fingers through each other. Put to the right breast he sucked regularly. His hands were on each side of the breast well away from the nipple. The mother remarked that he often touched the breast while feeding with a pat and a poke, quite hard.

'10 weeks — his mother had her hand on his chest and he began to play with her fingers, curling his own round hers and gently drawing his forefinger along her wrist and hand. He also looked at her face and made friendly sounds in response to her talk. Prior to this, at the left (first) breast where he sucked powerfully and regularly, his right hand was lying high up in the centre of the mother's chest. Then he began to stop and resume sucking. During the stopping his right hand began to clutch and clench markedly. Later at the right breast he sucked less regularly. He had both hands on the breast close to the nipple on each side and gently moved his fingers on the breast, occasionally bringing his hands momentarily together.

'From now onwards a definite pattern could be observed. When he was at the right (second) breast he would stroke and caress the breast in a variety of gentle movements, but when he was at the left breast his hand was either on the mother's chest, his fingers sometimes clenching, or both hands were on either side of the breast, motionless.

'We were struck by the way in which the hands related to each other, at first twisting, plucking, squeezing rather hard, later rubbing and poking the fingers through each other playfully. At the next observation Charles was seen to play in this second way with the mother's hand after the feed at the first breast, at which he had alternated between powerful sucking and stopping, while his right hand clenched and unclenched when his mouth was inactive. We could see in the seminar a strong suggestion here of his hand being mouthlike in its activities and mother's hand being breastlike in its significance, thus suggesting that his two hands might at times also be relating to each other as mouth to breast.

255

'When put to the second breast Charles sucked gently, having both his hands on the breast near the nipple, gently caressing and occasionally bringing his hands together. In contrast, at the first breast powerful sucking alternated with hand clenching, the hand being held far away from the nipple'.

As I have indicated earlier in this paper, this split in his relation to the two breasts and the accompanying pattern of hand activity subsequently became quite firmly established. Whichever way we may attempt to explain it, the vital significance of these minute activities is undeniable. Charles clearly relates himself to the two breasts in a very different way. His hand tends to behave like a mouth. He brings his hands close to the second breast but away from the first. He treats his mother's hand with his hand as his mouth treats the breast. His hands relate to each other at times as mouth to breast just as his mouth relates to his hand as a breast. Is this evidence that the relationship to the breast as part-object is the basic unit of relationship from which more complex relationships are built? Is the poking through and the poking in of fingers evidence of a projective mode of achieving identification? Are the hands held away and the clenching alternating with powerful sucking to be seen as a primitive attempt to spare the breast? Innumerable exciting questions arise, showing the students the vast area of the unconscious still to be explored by psycho-analysis.

My impression is that the students find the observational evidence for the early working of the splitting processes and identification of body parts with objects fascinating, regardless of the theoretical framework within which they may choose to express the recognition of infant mental functioning. I think that the infant observation experience, linked later with clinical experience with adults and children, will add to their conviction of the importance of observing patients' overall behaviour as a part of the data of the analytic situation as well as strengthen their belief in the validity of analytic reconstruction of early development.

A paper read to the British Psycho-Analytical Society, July 1963.

Section IV

PAPERS ON TRAINING IN CHILD PYSCHOTHERAPY AND PSYCHO-ANALYSIS

1   The Tavistock Training and Philosophy

Introduction

The following is an account of one of the three trainings in child psychotherapy which currently exist — that of the Tavistock Clinic. The two alternative trainings are undertaken at the Hampstead Child Therapy Clinic and the Society of Analytical Psychology.

The Hampstead course has its theoretical orientation briefly described in the previous chapter by Sara Rosenfeld.[1] The newly inaugurated training at the Society of Analytical Psychology is not described in detail here. It is a Jungian course, and the writings of Michael Fordham form a very relevant introduction to that training.

To describe and compare all three of these trainings in detail would go beyond the scope of this book. We have therefore included one full account only. This is of the Tavistock training. In it we are shown vividly the process of self-discovery that the child psychotherapy student there undergoes. It is believed that something of this process is also experienced in the other available trainings. Anyone seriously attracted to this work will of course wish to investigate the alternative approaches to discover the one most suitable for them personally.

One of the points made by the author of this chapter is worth emphasizing: many child psychotherapists, while feeling they owe their training schools the gift of the basic equipment of their profession and the beginnings of their own self-development, feel that their individual style of working has in time diverged from the strict letter of their original training. This is a sign, perhaps, of an ability to work freely and creatively. It means that child psychotherapists cannot be narrowly labelled — and that in the practical day-to-day work of child therapy some of the various individual approaches may come much closer together in their common aim of understanding children.

M. Boston and D. Dawes

The Training

This chapter begins with a brief note on the history of the Tavistock course and its present position in a rapidly changing social framework. I shall try also to describe some of the thinking which has shaped and continues to shape this training, although the responsibility for the views expressed must remain my own. There is some description and discussion of aspects of the content of the course·and of our teaching methods. However, no attempt is made to give a detailed account of the syllabus. An up-to-date prospectus can, of course, always be obtained from the Tavistock Clinic itself.

The History of the Course

The Tavistock training in child psychotherapy began life in 1948 in the Department for Children and Parents, under the direction of John Bowlby. He saw the need for an analytical training for non-medical personnel practising psychotherapy in clinics. The organizing tutor during the first eleven years was Esther Bick, who set a high standard of learning from precise and detailed observation. This has continued to influence both students and tutors long after Mrs Bick's retirement.

For a number of years applications for this training were relatively few. This was no doubt due to the infancy of the profession, the degree of commitment required and the expense entailed. The current position is very different: despite the expense and commitment, which have not decreased, applications are many and our resources for training are strained. Although the Tavistock Clinic and Institute have expanded greatly and the teaching staff increased, we are able to meet only in a small way the demand for trained therapists.

The Place of the Course

The Tavistock is an amalgam of organizations and disciplines accountable to different governing bodies. The Clinic itself is within the National Health Service, which supports the bulk of the training of child psychotherapists, as well as the post-graduate training of psychiatrists, psychologists and the advanced training of social workers. Nevertheless it is at present necessary to ask students to pay fees in addition to their personal analysis, as part of the training is supported by the Tavistock School of Family Psychiatry and Community Mental Health.

Although the Tavistock is multi-disciplinary, various in its aims and speaks with many voices, there is nonetheless a certain consensus of ultimate goals and beliefs. These give it coherence as an institution. People who study and work there have over a period of time the opportunity to gather a rather wide experience of the way in which different disciplines and departments set about trying to implement their aims.

I think all would agree that we are concerned with the promotion of healthy growth in the individual, the family and society. In this aim we pay attention not only to illness but also to the conditions which seem to permit developmental change. We are averse to fostering privilege, although oriented to allowing individual growth and eccentricity. We are aware of the responsibility we have to share with the community at large the knowledge and insights, which we as privileged individuals acquire in pursuing our work. We believe that change is initiated by the enthusiasm of individuals and small groups, enabled by the very process of close observation of inter and intra personal relationships. We recognize that the possible quality and range of that observation has been radically affected by psycho-analysis, which obliges the observer to scrutinize himself, his feelings and motivation, the counter-transference which may be used to enrich or to distort what he sees.

Organization

The training is organized in two parts. Minimally it comprises a four-year full-time period. Circumstances may arise, however, which make it desirable or necessary for a student to take some aspects on a part-time basis, and in this case the total course exceeds four years. Students have to complete both parts of the training in order to be recommended for membership of the Association of Child Psychotherapists. The teaching is geared throughout to on-going professional work; in the first two years that work takes place in an institution outside the Tavistock.

Students are employed in a variety of roles with children, families or young people. Teaching during the first two years

261

takes place in the evenings, so that it is possible for students to work full-time if necessary, but this would ordinarily be undesirable — preparation and writing of observations together with the necessary reading and attendance at seminars themselves should occupy around twenty hours a week during this section of the course.

Students are responsible for finding their own jobs during this two-year period. They are accountable to their employers for the work they do. Nevertheless, we are often approached with a request for someone in training to undertake certain work, and are therefore often able to make suggestions to students about suitable employment. The kind of tasks which students are able to undertake during the first part of the course tends increasingly to be determined by their previous training or qualifications. It is likely that in the future the Tavistock will be required to evolve a more official relationship with the employing bodies, but it is unlikely that any tutorial or supervisory role which it has with students could extend to taking responsibility for the work they do with these employers.

Of several essential seminars which run throughout the first section of the course, two are now described.

The Work-Study Seminar

Seminar members, who are working in varied settings with children, adolescents and families, take turns to present detailed accounts of some aspect of their work. This presentation almost always includes aspects of the interaction between themselves and their 'clients'. The presentation is discussed by the rest of the group, led by a psychotherapist experienced in analytic work with children and adolescents, although not necessarily in the particular work-roles of the group members.

No particular technique is taught in these seminars. The members are encouraged to consider and discuss appropriate ways of dealing with the situations and material described after the possible 'meanings' have been explored. The aim of the seminar is to sharpen perceptions and to enlarge imagination, to understand more fully the underlying dynamics of the personality interactions described. Our belief is that education in sensitivity and awareness is a gradual process which takes

262

place through working and discussing work with a more experienced colleague, through a close study of individuals and groups, and of one's own role and responsibility.

As a leader of one such seminar my task would be to elicit as fully as possible the details of the case, the problem, the situation concerned. It takes a little time to do this. Time is also required to allow the other seminar members to feel their way into the situation and to ask questions. The questions can sometimes cause the presenter to remember details he had not registered as important. It then takes further time to consider and to try to link together apparently disparate elements in the presentation, in ways that can make it more immediate and meaningful to the participants.

I consider it important to pay attention to the emotions evoked by the case presented, both in the actual work and in the seminar group. Further, to consider these as relevant to the understanding of the material — and whether, in fact, the emotion evoked in us is the one we are meant to feel. In this way one tries to encourage the worker to make use of his own feelings, recognizing that these are a valuable part of imaginative perception without which any relationship and any attitude to work is two-dimensional.

It is vital, conversely, to recognise when some of the feeling evoked is not a true response to something actually communicated by the child, but an arousal of inappropriate emotions connected with unresolved infantile conflicts in the worker himself. These may be projected in ways that distort the perception of the child's real message and individuality. When projection is taking place it seems to me inappropriate to comment upon it in any *personal* way. It is appropriate, however, to try to make the members of the seminar aware as we go along that such distortions of perception happen at times with us all. It is a possibility that has to be kept constantly under review. Projections may be examined and understood by renewed scrutiny of the situation in question, by discussion with colleagues, or by self-questioning. The personal analysis is of course the place in which the student has the possibility of fuller examination of personal motivation, and of disturbances and blocks in the capacity to see and feel for the object.

The exchange of experiences in different work settings helps students to feel for the problems which other students encounter and to respect the work which they do. I shall single out for mention here the task which a number of students have undertaken in the past five or six years, that of working with small groups of children in primary schools.

This work arose initially out of the request of various head teachers for someone willing to take charge of small groups of children unable to benefit from ordinary class teaching. These were children with behaviour and learning difficulties. Licence was given to the group worker to engage the children in any kind of activity which seemed profitable. This would at least give the class teacher some respite from coping with one or more children whom she found a source of trouble or despair. With these fairly free terms of reference, and despite great difficulties with chaotic and unmanageable children, as with others who began as inert 'lumps' and only then went through periods of volcanic and destructive behaviour, many students found this an invaluable learning experience. It was for them, and I think for many of the teachers, both surprising and illuminating to watch the emotional and intellectual development of such a group of children, usually from chaotic and deprived homes. These were often thirsty for the interest and attention shown, relieved at the acceptance of their more unacceptable behaviour and at the opportunity to translate them into more constructive means of communication.

In some of these small groups the children achieved a stage of deep intimacy and trust. This made it possible for a rich spectrum of the most intense emotions of infantile dependence, sadness and loss, jealousy and rage, to be talked about and lived through with the worker. Children who were formerly drawn together only in collusive, thug-like alliances learned to show interest, friendliness and attentiveness to each other. Such behaviour would have seemed unthinkable in the chaotic early days of a group. Beneficial developments within the group invaribly carried over to some extent, sometimes dramatically, into the child's relationships in the wider areas of school life.

There is much to learn from these small groups concerning interpersonal relationships. The parts and roles played by members of the group can be seen to be operating within the individual personality. The experience of taking a group has often helped the therapist of the individual child to describe and talk to these different parts of the child's personality.

Since the work study seminar runs parallel to the infant observation seminar, which I shall describe next, there is some cross-fertilization between the two. It may in the future be possible for seminar leaders to initiate more formal and organized ways of making links between relationships and patterns discerned in the work experience and those seen in the baby-mother-family observations. At present we do this where we can and hope that students will be encouraged to integrate the variety of their own experience in a manner which may lead on to further fields of enquiry.

The Mother-Infant Observation Seminar

This seminar was initiated by Esther Bick at the outset of the course in 1948. All the current seminar leaders at the Tavistock have at some time or another taken part in one of her seminars and have made observations themselves. I mention this not only to acknowledge the debt of those of us who have found this a unique method of learning about the fundamentals of personality development, but also to emphasize that this kind of observation does require the help of trained and experienced people if it is to become meaningful.

For most people other than the mother concerned the movements of a small baby are chaotic and fairly meaningless, except in generalized behaviour terms. One has to allow oneself to come close to the baby in order to see and retain details, and to cope with the emotional impact and struggle with a great deal of uncertainty in oneself before understandable patterns begin to emerge. At a distance one baby (or one person) is much like any other.

This particular seminar more than any other is valuable in helping students to discover the value of being, and themselves becoming, a receptive observer. In this exercise there is no obligation to *do* anything beyond observing — indeed, one has to learn to refrain from action. The mothers are asked if they are willing to have an observer who, although he may be a professional worker with children and may even be a parent himself, would like the opportunity to learn by observing for one hour each week how an infant grows and develops within a family. The mother is also told that it will be helpful and interesting for the student to be informed of any changes and developments which she has noticed in the baby during the intervening week. Her thoughts and feelings about the baby are welcomed, and one often finds that the interest of the observer seems to encourage the mother to take more notice of the baby as a developing individual.

In some cases of course — where for instance there is another child below school age, or where the father is at home when the observer visits — the process also becomes a family observation. If it is possible to learn to retain and record complicated details of interactions and conversations, the observation affords a very rich experience to study and ponder over. Tentative interpretations and hypotheses about current family interactions may be checked when ensuing weeks offer further data.

Most people who undertake this exercise find that the closeness to the infant and mother arouses in them extremely intense feelings deriving from their own infancy. These are not always readily recognizable as such, but even when recognized, not to be explained away. Clearly, it is important for the seminar leader to recognize when such feelings are aroused, in herself as well as in other seminar members. She must encourage them to feel both for the mother and for the baby, not to over-identify with one or the other. By allowing himself to feel his own counter-transference, by trying to contain it and refrain from action or interference, the observer may learn to comprehend the impact on the mother of the responsibility of the baby. He may feel the change and vulnerability evoked in her by her own aroused infantile feelings. He may learn how her sensitivity to the baby and his needs does indeed spring from her capacity to be open to reverberations of his gropings and disturbances, to learn to differentiate among messages by feeling and responding appropriately to them. This, rather than to do what she has learned or been told she ought to do by precept, hearsay or academic psychology.

Not every mother is able to respond in this way. In some the necessary learning comes only slowly. There is every possible variation in degree and in areas of responsiveness and blindness between mothers, and at different times within each mother, as within all of us.

The seminar affords an opportunity to study these personality aspects over a period of two years, together with an opportunity to see the thrust for development in each infant, varying in strength in each case but present in all who live. One can observe the way in which trust and love and a capacity to form object relationships grows in the child through recurrent experiences of being understood. In these ways the student has the opportunity to introject selectively an experience which he can continue to draw on as a model and source for his own development as a therapist with patients.

The observation experience helps the student to endure 'living in the question' (as Keats put it) with his patients, to struggle till he can discern the implications of his first-hand, detailed impressions rather than to flee to premature application of theory. It helps him to see the infant both in the child and the adult, and in his analytic work to stay with that infant and aid him in his arrested or distorted development. It helps him to distinguish movements that are leading towards healthy rather than spurious or superficial growth. It helps to alert him to the significance of minute behavioural indicators and signs of emotion which, when taken into account, add dimension to the quality of his later work.

I think observation also helps some of us in our analytic work to avoid premature, anxiety-ridden interpretation and intervention. It helps relax undue therapeutic zeal, allows us to learn to feel and to respect the drive towards development in every patient, as in every baby. It cannot be hurried. It can be facilitated, encouraged and protected, but it canot be created or forced. One acquires something of this feeling from observing the wise mother who has learned not to push the baby on prematurely. She knows that it is illusory to believe that, if she is good enough, she can help him to grow up without any frustration. She therefore allows him to struggle with what is within his compass.

It is possible to note and discuss in this seminar the general tendency at times to find fault with the mother. (Or, in another context, the other therapist or caretaking person.) To believe, surreptitiously, that one could do so much better oneself. One may see how this tendency lies behind the recurrent urge to find psychopathology in everything, the voyeuristic eye that looks to criticize rather than to emphasize. One also sees the defences against this same tendency — the projective identification with and idealization of the mother-baby, and blindness to the difficulties with which they are struggling or failing to struggle. These impediments to accurate observation manifest themselves in every group at times. They are important to note and to be taken into account as material for the seminar. As in other working groups, their full significance for the individual student and his contribution towards them are matters for further comprehension within the privacy of the personal analysis.

One further point about this seminar. As it is a discussion of observations, not of *work* undertaken by the participants, a standard not only of detailed but also of freer and more honest reporting is facilitated. In seminars and meetings where individuals present clinical work and results, there is tremendous pressure to trim up, to leave out longueurs, confusions, mistakes, and to organize presentation in a way that pre-empts criticism. The opportunities for mutual learning can be restricted by this desire to present oneself as above reproach. One cannot do away with competitiveness and the need to appear well in the eyes of authority, whoever that authority may be. We are all so tempted. But this seminar focusses attention on the material itself, rather than upon that comparison and measurement of individual performance, which so inhibits honesty and spontaneity in describing one's own work.

Training in Psychoanalytic Psychotherapy

The heart of the course, although not its ultimate goal, is the training in the techniques of psychoanalytic psychotherapy. Three cases — a very young child, a child in the latency period and an adolescent — are seen on an intensive basis, optimally five times a week. During this part of the training the majority of the students have a sessional appointment at the Tavistock within the National Health Service. Very few spend all their time at the Tavistock, however, as most are working also at some other clinic, where they usually have been given a full-time post and seconded by the Authority concerned for training at the Tavistock. In this way we are able to train more people than the imitations of space and paid establishment at the Clinic itself would permit.

For their three intensive cases students have three different supervisors. This arrangement helps to give them some experience of the ways in which different therapists think and work. They also see a number of children and young people whom they treat by the same general techniques on a less intensive basis. They have the opportunity to learn casework with parents and in some instances to conduct analytic psychotherapy with them, when this seems appropriate.

This brings us to the often asked question: what is analysis and what is psychotherapy? Is analysis treatment of a patient on a four or five times weekly basis? And is what one does less intensively while using the same basic approach termed psychotherapy? One could use an arbitrary definition, and say that analysis is the method of treatment practised by members of psychoanalytic societies when they say they are practising analysis — however varied their ideas of this may be, and indeed are. I myself shall call analytic psychotherapy the analytic technique which our students are helped to grasp and to apply five times weekly or less. This is the analysis of the processes set in motion by interpretation of the transference relationship, enriched by private attention to the therapist's counter-transference (Meltzer, 1967). Its essence consists in the provision of a setting in which the patient is encouraged, through attention to and interpretive descriptions of his total behaviour, to bring to the therapist increasingly unknown and hitherto unacceptable parts of himself. These are experienced in the relationship with the therapist. They are scrutinized together, and hopefully understood and integrated. This brief statement, as will be appreciated, is necessarily an oversimplification of a complex process.

On the whole, the therapists at the Tavistock employ this analytic technique whether the patient is seen five, four or even one session a week. The criteria for frequency of sessions remain a matter of constant debate and exploration. One of the simplest criteria is that of sheer expediency. If a therapist has a vacancy for an intensive case at a particular time, and if parents are willing and able to bring the child so frequently, or if it is a question of a child or adolescent of an age and sufficiently

269

motivated to bring himself, the intensive help may be offered. I think this proves a better criterion than it may seem, especially if it turns out — as it sometimes does — that the patient's willingness to attend indicated a willingness also to invest in analytic work. Nonetheless, there are some children who receive five times weekly therapy who could have benefited significantly from less. On the other hand, there are some who for a variety of reasons cannot be seen more than once a week — but for whom one may feel this is totally inadequate. There are many fewer of these children, I suspect however, than is generally believed by those who have not had experience in working under clinic conditions.

There is general agreement that, whether therapists after their training wish to work intensively or not, the training work on a five times weekly basis is a necessary and valuable core experience. In it students discern and gain conviction of the intensity of infantile transference to the therapist in analytic therapy. As a rule the transference manifests itself most clearly in the rhythm of the five days sessions and the two days week-end. A recurrent experience is afforded of time with the therapist, then time away. When the infant in the patient comes to trust the experience of being closely held by the therapist's attention, he then has to cope with the break, the absence. We then see what he is able to retain of that previous experience of togetherness. The situation gives the student the most leisurely possibility of being able to study in the analytic therapy what has been glimpsed earlier in infant observation: how the infant may learn to trust, to love and to let go, optimally and desirably through gradually introjecting and assimilating the experience of togetherness which he is given.

It might in some ways be more accurate to state that analytic therapy is very largely concerned with studying in the transference the factors which militate against the possibility of internalizing — 'learning from experience' (Bion, 1962). This study always includes oneself as well as one's patients, for no development in therapeutic skill can take place without continual re-examination on the part of the therapist.

In a field where resources are infinitesimal and need is great, the criteria of selection for frequency of sessions, or indeed for analytic treatment at all, concern all psychotherapists. We have come to realize increasingly that participation in diagnosis and assessment is an essential part of the therapist's training. It is likely to play an increasing part in the work he does and in which he can usefully co-operate with psychiatric and other colleagues, utilizing the experience that is accumulated over the years from investigating in depth the developmental potential of the individual.

In the later stages of their training, or after qualification, psychotherapists are given the opportunity to be supervised on short-term consultative work with self-referred adolescents in the Young People's Consultation Centre and thereby begin to gain some experience of the possibilities and the limitations of this kind of work.

Supervision of Clinical Work

During the first part of the course there is, as a rule, no individual supervision of students' work unless it is specifically requested. Students, however, may go to their personal tutor to discuss general work problems and programme. If it seems vital that they should receive more support than can be given in the work discussion seminar groups, attempts are made to supply it. During the second part of the course, however, in addition now to individual supervision, students have three weekly clinical seminar groups. Here they have the opportunity to present, and to listen to others presenting, material from the treatment of children, young people and parents.

Throughout the second stage students are recognized as being responsible for the cases with which they are working, in conjunction of course with the relevant senior colleagues in their place of work. The role of the supervisor in this training is similar to that of the seminar leader, but more personally oriented. The personal supervisor helps the student to think about and better understand the material he is presenting. Equally, to understand the processes of communication, or failure to achieve communication, between him and the patients with whom he is working. The supervisor aims to help the student to sketch tentative maps of the patient's personality and development. He encourages him in alternative ways of thinking about problems, and sometimes raises questions when all seems too clear or pat.

As teachers we ask ourselves questions. How much should we

271

feel we have to tell the student what to say? How far should we go in teaching him to make actual interpretations, and how far should we encourage him to formulate these for himself? It can be appropriate to do both at different times. Even if one is quite convinced that a student recurrently fails to comment upon or even see material that is asking for attention, one can be useful only by trying to approach the material again and again — by describing it ever anew from different angles as it recurs in different contexts. Just as in working with a patient one has to do precisely that when trying to illuminate some blind spot. Undoubtedly the attitude of the supervisor can affect the attitude of the student-therapist to the particular case. A mother who is having trouble with her baby is often confirmed in her own inadequacy by some 'well meant' advice *de haut en bas*. In the same way the student struggling with his own inadequacy in practising therapy can be crushed by over-knowledgeable interpretations of the supervisor, which take no account of his feelings and his struggles.

A supervisor can do much to strengthen or melt away the illusion that there is a 'way' which those who have inside information know about. One may arouse feelings of envy and inadequacy, not by genuine and useful attempts to link material together meaningfully, but by hinting rather nebulously about areas where the student is not in touch and 'hasn't got it quite right' — yet without offering a helpful alternative. In short, in implying a criticism without being able to document it clearly or to teach otherwise. I suspect that when we so act we are failing to shoulder our own uncertainties. We are failing to recognize or admit how we all have to struggle in the dark towards some glimmer of light.

On the other side is the problem of the student who cannot bear to be wrong. He is touchy about being taught and having his work illuminated by someone else. That is his personal problem, with which he has to wrestle in his analysis. The supervisor may discern it and may have to take it into account. I do not think it is necessarily his job to draw attention to the student's attitude, unless it is intractable. We have a constant task in trying to improve our methods of supervising, just as the student has his in learning how to remember, to record, to present material and ask the questions which can help supervisors to be useful.

Written Work

We try to present students with the opportunity of describing and evaluating what they are learning and the teaching they receive. They are required to write descriptive papers on their observation and work experiences in each of the first two years of the course. If they go on to take the second part of the training they are asked to prepare further presentations and to write papers on some of their cases.

The Place of Theory

During their training and general reading the students encounter a variety of theoretical approaches and orientations. They are encouraged to make for themselves meaningful links between the work they are doing and the theories they study.

The basis of formal teaching in the course is that of psycho-analytical theory, as developed by Freud in his clinical work and writings and his own self-analysis, which helped him to evaluate this more accurately and to deepen the field of his enquiry — in short, to explore the unconscious in himself and in others. In addition, students study in particular Karl Abraham and the theories developed by Melanie Klein and her followers. If Freud discovered the child within the adult, then Melanie Klein revealed the possibility of seeing the infant within the child and the adult. Her work has contributed to our depth of knowledge of ways in which development, through truthfully based object relationships, may proceed in a healthy form. And, of course, of ways in which perversity and psychopathology originate and distort or impede growth (Klein; Meltzer, 1973).

The Tavistock course is one which is inevitably known as the Kleinian course in child psychotherapy. Yet it seems a disservice both to the pioneer spirit of Freud and of Melanie Klein herself to label it such. As the years have gone by, many of us who have been intimately involved in the work have come to feel increasingly that the future of psychoanalysis depends not on the learning and propagation of even the most valuable or 'respectably' documented theories, but on attention to the conditions in which the observations may be made. These allow each student of human nature to realize, and to note in others and in himself, the phenomena on which theories have been based. The furtherance

273

of the work of Freud, of Melanie Klein and of other inspired contributors to the science or art of psychoanalysis, depends on each student living through in his own way that path of discovery — of the interaction between the internal and the external world, the influence of the unconscious upon conscious activities. The journey is made a little easier by using the maps of those who have crossed the wilderness before. But maps read in the cosy safety of home are no substitute for the journey itself. Such cosiness prevents not only further inroads into unknown territory, but the maintenance of ways that have already been cleared.

The Personal Analysis

Personal analysis is a requirement for every student who decides he wishes to proceed with the second part of the course. He is asked to have about a year's experience of analysis himself before undertaking analytic cases of his own. Some candidates may have had a personal analysis before they apply, but we do not require students to be in analysis during their first year with us. This is a time of mutual exploration and selection between tutors and students. Our experience over the last few years has shown that many people are able to develop in themselves to varying degrees an enquiring approach of considerable imagination and depth towards the work they are doing, without the experience of being analysed themselves. Many people, when given encouragement to utilize and examine their own emotional responses rather than discard them as unscientific, probably improve greatly the quality and range of their work in the field of personal relationships. Some people who have never had a personal analysis may indeed already be richer and more subtle human beings than others who have. The analyst cannot *create* the individual, any more than the parents create the baby in that sense.

Nevertheless, even the most gifted individuals, capable of extensive learning from experience, do have unknown areas in themselves which can prevent them learning from experience in particular areas. These unknown or hived-off areas may be discovered and integrated by analysis. The analysis is not part of the course in the way the seminars and discussions are. It remains a private affair. Its purpose is to put the student more fully in possession of himself. Hopefully it will give him the courage to submit himself more completely to observations and experiences from which he may learn, while tolerating degrees of anxiety and pain which he could not tolerate before.

Analysis should increase the student's fellow-feeling for the children with whom he works. Many of these will be quite crushed and stunted in their growth: in order to proceed in their development they need compassion and understanding from an adult, who knows what it is to be in pain or fear — but, importantly, also knows how to struggle through it.

During the personal analysis it is hoped the student will experience more fully the infant and the child in himself; learn step by step how to contain and educate them; and resolve residual infantile grievances and distortions of perception. He should eventually be more free to fully address himself to his patient's similar problems but unique personality.

Qualities Desirable in the Therapist

The qualities of the good therapist are notably hard to define. In the past we have tried a variety of methods of selection for the course. These included group procedures, individual interviews and reference to people who know the applicants well. We have never been entirely happy about the effectiveness or fairness of any method. Because of the inherent difficulties of selection we have tried, by dividing the course into two parts, to give individuals the opportunity for self-selection. In this way the candidate can obtain gradual, realistic experience of the kind of work he will be expected to do, the kind of training offered and his own responses to it. However, there has unfortunately still to be some selection even at the preliminary stage, as the demand for training in child psychotherapy continues to grow. Up to a point we work on the basis of first come, first served. Nonetheless, there is no objection to anyone not finding a place making a further application in a succeeding year.

Many applicants come in their early twenties before they already have an established profession. Others come at a later point in their careers, when they envisage this training as furthering the development of interests arising from their

275

previous work. Any group of students profits from the inclusion both of younger and of more mature individuals from a variety of backgrounds. It is especially enriched in the present case by the inclusion of some from fields outside that of mental health — the humanities, for instance. An education which has afforded the opportunity to specialize in imaginative literature encourages a dimension of perception which may be dismissed as unscientific in many courses of academic psychology. That training takes cognizance of the reality of the inner world of feeling, imagination and values, with which psychoanalysis must be concerned. Such contributions help psychoanalysis not to surface into shallower fields of behaviouristic description, nor the aridities of Talmudic precept and argument over theory. The future of psychoanalytic work depends on the unswerving realization that the inner world of feeling and imagination is also a matter for scientific study and description.

It is important for the profession that it should contain a living core of workers who are devoted to the study itself, but who bring into their consulting room a depth and wisdom from the accumulating experience of their own lives. From the private existence — both external and internal — comes the individual richness of experience. This enables one to be aware with greater sensitivity and precision of the more subtle shades of the patient's communications and behaviour, more likely to bring about a meeting of minds than an explanation derived from a library of previously learned interpretations.

It is equally important for the quality of the therapist's work, however, that he should live in it and be fed by it, as well as by his private and personal life. It is doubtful whether, in the long run, any fundamental benefit can be derived from a contact between two people which does not benefit both parties. The child psychotherapist, nevertheless, has to acquire the capacity to delay, or rather to refrain from asking for, immediate satisfaction from the patient himself. He has to learn to contain and to struggle with just such qualities which militate against contact and comprehension, both in himself and in the child.

In order to be able to learn from experience, and to be able to utilize that wisdom to help others to bear themselves better, a reasonable degree of intelligence is necessary. As a rule, the acquisition of an honours degree guarantees the presence of this.

But the possession of intelligence by itself is not enough. Method and motivation for using it are vital. We all use our intelligence, to some extent, to find ways of managing ourselves and the world, ways which help us to avoid feeling small and inadequate. It is a more serious and questionable matter, however, when we use it to make ourselves big at the expense of others.

The child psychotherapist has to be able to tolerate feeling small and in the dark, because this is the way a child often feels. This is what the child in *us* must often feel if he is to remain alive to the wonder and adventure, as well as the hazards, of the world.

Although the therapist's private and professional life need to feed each other, at times they seem to interfere with each other. For instance, although there is now an increase in the number of male applicants, and increasing recognition of satisfying career prospects for men in child psychotherapy, work with children and young people is likely to continue to have particular appeal for women — especially, perhaps, for young women already married, or likely to marry and have children themselves. It is not, however, enough to love one's own children. One needs to have enough feeling and generosity to extend this to other people's children (who represent in the depths of the unconscious one's mother's babies). For a time, when one's own children are young, it may be difficult to find the emotional resource to make the necessary extension. It is, however, an extension which needs finally to be made in the field of work itself. It is not enough, and not in the interests of our own patients ultimately, if our preoccupation with them is so exclusive and intense that we ignore the existence of many others — those others, that is, who do not have the benefit of our special attention, however imperfect that may be.

If the benefits of psychotherapy as an art-science are to be shared, it must concern itself with society as well as the individual. As analytical psychotherapists we must realize that it is a privilege, as well as a task, to be able to offer or receive an educational resource so rare and so costly in time and money. It is therefore an obligation, if we have so benefited, to continue to consider how the attitudes which we have found to be essentially life-promoting may be encouraged in others, especially those who have a hand in the rearing of children. For this reason students are encouraged during their training, or shortly after-

277

wards, to take part in a teaching or consultative project, provided by the Tavistock for workers in the social and educational fields. Many participate in small group discussions in the course for teachers and others engaged in aspects of education.

The Philosophy of the Training

My own preference is to regard this course not as a training where students are encouraged to model themselves like apprentices on their teachers, even on the best of them, but to see it as an opportunity for education in the field of inter and intra personal development. In this the students are encouraged to work from their own observations of themselves and of the young people with whom they work. They can be helped to organize their observations by psychoanalytical theory; but they must find and draw upon their own style of working within the psychoanalytical technique.

We try to follow an approach which enabled the study of links between intra psychic development and inter personal family and group relationships. We try to consider the extent to which the individual child seems able to develop by introjecting, assimilating and growing from within — as distinct from the spurious progress made by projecting oneself into unassimilated persons and knowledge. The difference, that is, between the three-dimensional creative growing which proceeds from introjective identification: as opposed to either the two-dimensional socializing, or to the 'being grown-up' which stops at projective identification. The latter is the 'living in someone else's shoes'; the former the still more impoverished mimicry that clings to surfaces and the appearance of things (Klein, 1946; Bick, 1968).

Our method of teaching, as I have already indicated, is essentially through small seminar groups and individual supervisions. These aim to direct the attention of the student towards increasingly close observation of the details of interaction between himself and the individuals he is studying. The course intends to increase the student's capacity to tolerate uncertainty; to contain, to think about and to use his counter-transference, thereby becoming more sensitive to emotional as well as cognitive communication. It aims to help him respond in

278

practice with less certainty of ever having the final answers, but with greater hope of learning, with the help of the patient or client, the direction in which to proceed. This attitude with patients will tend to take the form of interpretations that describe and bring together data in a way that leads on to further enquiry — and not to the kind of explanations that are conversation stoppers.

Theoretical teaching and seminar discussion would aim to present theories not as sacred or final, but as convenient. They should illuminate methods of organizing observations, of naming and generalizing, and bring order out of chaotic experience — yet leave the space and freedom to admit new data.

At the end of training one hopes that the student does not emerge feeling 'qualified' with a certificate giving him the right to practise psychotherapy, or armed with a method and technique that gives him the edge over the other trainings and techniques. One hopes, certainly, he has learned something tangible. But more importantly, that he has learned how to bear uncertainties and difficult questions. One hopes he retains a deep sense of wonder at the infinite diversities of human nature, together with a great fellow-feeling for his patients. I would hope he has gathered some experience of the ways in which he may continue to explore the split-off or repressed aspects of mental functioning; how to bear the pain of struggling, sweetened by hope derived from hard-won experience.

Some of the former students of the course have extended the age range of their clients to work also with adults, an extension which is increasingly taking place within the course.

We are also concerned with the wider issues of personality development in families, schools and societies. We hope as therapists to do something towards breaking down the barriers of resentment about the privilege enjoyed by those who receive and practise psychoanalytic treatment. These barriers are erected, understandably, by some of those workers who have responsibility for the many needy not in a position to be helped in this way.

We see the training in analytic psychotherapy as a foundation rather than an end, a foundation from which further researches into the infinite variety and complications of the individual and his relationships may proceed. We believe that it is necessary for a stream of analytic work to continue more deeply and more widely, not only because of its therapeutic value but because of its necessary fertilizing effect on all studies of human relationships.

Post-Graduate Developments

Ours is a course which owes its existence to the discovery of psychoanalysis. This, however fallible its practitioners, is essentially concerned with the self-realization and striving after truth in every human being. The quality of the teaching and of the work done by anyone who undertakes training in the psycho-analytic method ultimately rests on the way in which he con-tinues to maintain that striving in his own heart; and further tries to foster it in the patients whom he treats and the colleagues with whom he works. It can be kept alive only by the individual working as best he can, not by his following precepts set by supposedly superior authorities, not by remaining a child who wishes to please the parents, but by working through the crisis which any truly developing adolescent has in finding his own mind, identity and style of life. To do this he has to question himself as well as what his parents have taught him, in order to find his best way of realizing in practice the values and experi-ence that stand the test of scrutiny . . . of promoting and protect-ing what he loves.

In saying this I am aware that it is the exceptional individual who is able to stand alone, who is confident enough about what he thinks and feels in the light of his own experience. The quality of his judgement reflects the capacity to internalize selectively, based upon some fairly clear discrimination between true and false. For most of us it takes a long time to reach a position of relative independence fortified by inner strength; we are often tempted lazily to give up the stuggle and settle for our equivalent of the ten commandments, which give at least a sense of knowing how to avoid giving offence to whatever our particular represen-tatives of God or Authority are — feared or idealized, or both.

Most of us need help, support and stimulation long after we are trained and 'qualified' to practise psychoanalytic therapy. This is not necessarily the help of further personal analysis — which has its parasitic temptations. We do need the protection of some group within which work may be discussed with colleagues of varying degrees of seniority and experience. It seems to me that such groups should see themselves as gatherings to promote mutual exchange and development, rather than to monitor or judge. Otherwise they may become, as the families of adolescents sometimes do, a restriction, rather than a nurturing resource that allows for and tolerates mistakes made in the struggle for identity and self-responsibility.

Analytical work inevitably brings the therapist into continual close contact with the relationships and constitutional factors which impede growth. To wrestle with these he has to tolerate the projection of a great deal of frustration, pain and sometimes hatred and reproach from his patients. Like parents who care for their wayward and troublesome children, therapists are also very vulnerable to criticism from the 'neighbours' — that is, their own colleagues.

It seems to me that as a professional group our health and strength depend upon the capacity of each one of us for self-scrutiny as well as devotion to the work. When we are genuinely able to shoulder the burden of trying to keep our own house in order (a never-ending task), we are more likely to be able to feel for, and to be good neighbours to, our colleagues. There is no group solution for work which is essentially individual. It is also a problem in this field, as in others, for a professional group to maintain an *esprit de corps* without becoming élitist or heresy-hunting.

The problems with which psychotherapists struggle are likely to be slightly different at different times in their careers. As practitioners and teachers we are, in growing older, bound to face encounters with our younger colleagues and students. These are the kind of anxieties that middle-aged parents face when threatened by the growing-up of their children, and by their challenge. Such threats may encourage a dangerous tendency to shore up uncertainties by the collecting of followers or admirers, by using them to further one's ideas through variations of the patronage system. Anxieties about the future of one's work and profession can increase fear of change, and promote that kind of conservatism which looks always to be reminded rather than informed.

The psychic demands of this work can make it difficult to steer between the narrows of complacency and self-righteous criticism

281

and the whirlpool of disorganization. If we are able to face the demands however, it seems to be me that the work may continue to be rewarding in a personal sense into old age, and always conductive to strength and wisdom. As long as we do not surface into clichés, we are continually wrestling with 'the enemies of promise', with the foe within. Where else, as Shakespeare so well knew, can death be defeated but in the inner world? (Sonnet 164)

[1] From *The Child Psychotherapist,* ed. D. Dawes and M. Boston, 1977.

2   Consultation Project in a Comprehensive School

1968

Two experienced child psychotherapists were appointed for one session a week each to work in a mixed comprehensive school of about thirteen hundred pupils. One of these continued for one session during the second year. The aim of the school was to see in what way it might benefit from their specialised knowledge of child and personality development, in dealing with some problems in the school. The aim of the child psychotherapists was to become familiar with the range of problems in a school, and to see in the immediate event what light they might be able to throw on these. They wished also to consider in what way their training and that of members of their allied psychological professions could be utilized and improved to co-operate with those teachers who, through particular interests and responsibilities, are likely to be more concerned with the general social and psychological welfare of the pupils. One of the child psychotherapists (Martha Harris) was responsible for training child psychotherapists at the Tavistock Clinic; the other (Edna O'Shaughnessy) was engaged in teaching and tutoring experienced teachers in a child development course at the Institute of Education.

Approach to the School

The project was in the first instance mooted by the Deputy Head, then discussed between two child psychotherapists and the Headmistress. There were then informal meetings between the therapists and senior members of the school staff, in particular the senior house-staff. Not until some positive interest in the project was shown by these staff was there a formal approach to the relevant administrative officers concerned in the Inner London Education Authority. The Headmistress then arranged a meeting with the Divisional Educational Officer the Divisional Inspector, the Chief Psychologist at County Hall, senior members of her staff, and the child psychotherapists in question.

283

It was then agreed that they should be appointed as temporary part-time members of the school staff, responsible only to the Headmistress, for one year initially. The two child psycho-therapists then went to see the staff of the local Child Guidance Clinic to inform them about the project, with a view to clarifying roles and finding possible useful connecting links with the clinic. The initial document setting out the aims of this project was distributed to the people involved.

The child psychotherapists were introduced to the staff and children as specialists helping the house-staff. Throughout the rest of the report they will usually be referred to as specialists or consultants.

Work done in the two years in the school fell under the following headings:

A. Work with the staff of the school

The Headmistress, the house-staff, house-staff and parents, house-staff and children.
Staff of the Remedial Department.
A weekly group of six to eight teachers.
Various staff members concerned together with a member of the house-staff with particular children.
Incidental work with staff.

B. Work with the pupils

A group of five problem children from Remedial classes.
Some prefects and members of the sixth form.
Some discussions assisting a member of the house-staff, with small groups of children evincing particular problems.

C. Liaison with the local child-guidance clinic

Meetings with the Headmistress were irregular and took place usually when some appraisal of the work and of relationships with the staff was indicated, and when consultation about some new development was appropriate. For instance, one of the child-psychotherapists was asked to give two talks to sixth formers on the nature of her work, in a series of talks on careers by representatives of various outside professions. Arising from this some of the prefects asked if they could come and talk about their problems as prefects. This was a welcome request, but one which obviously needed to be cleared first with all relevant members of the staff in order to avoid treading on any sensitive toes.

Discussions with the house-staff occupied the greater part of the time throughout the two years. Each consultant was attached as a matter of convenience to two of the four houses of the school (each house having two staff in charge, a man and a woman, a senior or junior in each instance) and was available at a certain time each week for consultation about any child who had emerged as needing special attention. In the second year the remaining consultant was available in the too-brief time for all four houses. In many instances she was present while the teacher interviewed a child in the semi-private conditions of the house-room, on matters maybe connected with some particular culminating misdemeanor or difficulty that had arisen during the previous week, or as part of the routine of selecting courses of study or choice of career. These interviews often took place during the lunch-hour and at times were joined by some other member of staff concerned with the case in question. Pressure of time was very often a great handicap in having a really thorough discussion before and after the interviews and on numerous occasions fuller discussion had to be postponed till the next week. Sometimes a longer time was set aside and the parents of the child were interviewed and worked together with the house-staff and the consultant to gain a better insight into the problems involved.

During the first year one of the consultants was more especially connected with the Remedial Department, and the special problems of the backward child and the Remedial teacher. She was for several weeks present with one of the new teachers with one of his Remedial Classes. As a result of this the teacher picked out five of the most difficult children to work each week in a separate group for discussions with her.

Teachers' Discussion Group

This group had an abortive start in the third term of the first year. It was formed from a heterogenous collection of teachers interested in discussing aspects of child development and problem children, some very junior staff and others carrying greater responsibility. The difference in experience and in aims of the various members made it difficult to establish agreed topics for discussion, and to keep the group working together in a fruitful way.

Another group was formed in the first term of the second year from experienced teachers (who were free at that time) and who were selected by the senior house-staff and deputy head. They were offered the opportunity of attending if they wished. They met regularly for thirty minutes each week before lunch — too brief a time, which often extended into the lunch hour with those who were not involved in duties. Discussions with this group ranged from queries posed by particular children to general problems of child development, the influence of social and environmental factors, the teacher's own part in relationships with groups and with individual children, and the influence of the school structure and hierarchy on the teacher's own capacity to function well.

(As the group grew more familiar with the consultant and with each other there was much discussion of the particular emotional stresses and strains in teaching, of ways in which teachers could be trained to cope with them, and to help younger colleagues, encountering difficult classes for the first time.)

Work with groups of pupils

The group from a Remedial class has already been mentioned. The children were selected by the teacher with the help of the consultant who had already been for some time an observer in that class. They were chosen as the most difficult and taken for a double period for about half a term. The time was chosen to help them think about themselves, their feelings and their reactions to each other, a novel and difficult task for them. The class teacher and the consultant then discussed these occasions afterwards. As a result the teacher found that the children settled rather better in class and that he himself was aided in his own handling of them.

A group of five persistently defiant adolescent girls was taken by two of the house-staff for about twenty-five to thirty minutes in the lunch hour with the consultant present and taking part, helping to guide the discussion back to the examination of the children's own problems in fitting in with school life and life in general. One of the children in this group had been referred to a clinic but could not be offered treatment because of the unco-operative attitude of the parents; another girl who could well have benefited from child-guidance treatment had not been referred as the outcome would likely have been the same.

Another group of six children, three boys and three girls from the third and fourth years met at fortnightly intervals for half a term with one of the consultants and their housemaster. These were children presenting no behaviour problems, law-abiding and conforming but obviously inhibited, either in work, social relationships and general appreciation of school.

A third group of seven or eight troublesome second and third year boys also met with the same teacher and consultant. There was a plan to form another small group of intelligent girls whom teachers had hoped would stay on at school after the age of fifteen or sixteen to train for a profession, but who had elected to leave as soon as possible. One or two of these girls were enthusiastic about the idea of meeting to discuss what they felt about school and why they thought that they had had enough. Pressure of commitments and timetable difficulties made it impossible to arrange in the time available.

The discussions with some of the sixth formers were also informal, held in the lunch hour. There were never more than four and never less than two pupils. No teachers were present; the theme and tone were set by two of the senior boys who were having great difficulties in their role as prefects, sensitive about their inadequacy, conscientious about their duties.

Liaison with the local child-guidance clinic

The therapists from the school went to meet the whole staff of the child-guidance clinic during their first term's work at the school and followed this with occasional individual meetings with the child-guidance worker connected with a particular child. Contact with the clinic was, however, much less frequent than was perhaps envisaged at the beginning due to pressure of time and the need for attention of numbers of children in the school who might be unsuitable for clinic referral for various reasons. The main effect on the local clinic as a result of the presence of the consultants in the school was probably in the greater readiness of the housestaff to contact the clinic about children referred there and, related to this, more tolerant and realistic expectations of what could be expected of a child guidance clinic.

* * *

MORE DETAILED COMMENTS ON WORK DONE IN VARIOUS AREAS

Work with the housestaff

The staff varied considerably in their readiness to avail themselves of the consultants. Attitudes varied initially from perfunctory politeness which could cover hostility towards yet another chore, another person to keep happy, or the resentful 'Who on earth is this trying to teach me my job?' — to a very warm welcome and interest in trying to see what they could make of it. This was accompanied by pleasure in talking about the children and pride in their own work and that of the school in trying to do the best possible for the pupils. As one might expect it seemed to be those who enjoyed the actual work and contact with individual children most were those who were the least hampered by omniscience and boredom and were prepared to entertain fresh ways of thinking.

Clarification of the consultant's role, with acknowledgement of unrealistic hopes on the part of the staff and disenchantment when these were disappointed, was an immediate and often an ongoing task. Some of the more enthusiastic teachers half-hoped to be relieved of their most pressing problems or to be given the entrée to mysterious means of solving them. Pressure for spot diagnosis, for advice in partially understood situations had to be resisted. In discussing different cases the aim was to link together information coming from different sources, of historical and current events in the child's family and school-life, observations made by different teachers including the house-teacher and often the consultants themselves when present at an interview with a child. The possible significance of these various data was then explored. Sometimes relevant courses of action were explored together but these always remained the responsibility of the teachers.

288

Some examples of children discussed

These are carefully disguised for reasons of confidentiality. The consultant, for greater ease of expression, refers to herself throughout in the first person.

Ronald

Ronald was a fourteen year old boy of rather more than average ability whose work had throughout school been erratic, unpredictable and his homework usually late. His parents were conscientious professional people, anxious that he should do well and had been in touch with his housemaster on a number of previous occasions. A recent consensus of reports about Ronald's neglected work motivated his housemaster to review his situation. Mr A. had told me the boy was well-mannered and polite and that he would be tempted to join in the general verdict that he was simply bone-idle and just needed a very strict eye kept on him, but somehow this view did not entirely satisfy him.

He interviewed Ronald one lunch-hour when I was present, telling him of the complaints about his work, trying to find out what he felt about various subjects, his interests at school and his views about his teachers and classmates. Ronald, a remarkably solid healthy looking boy, did his best to respond to this friendly mixture of concern and admonishment. He clearly felt the kindliness of the teacher, was aware of my presence in the room, but curious rather than incommoded by it. His reactions were slightly puzzled and slow and he seemed to have great difficulty in concentrating, especially when asked for his opinion. My impression as a result of this interview, and taking into account also the housemaster's story, was that the boy was chronically depressed rather than lazy, and was worried in an apathetic way about his failure to come up to standard. The housemaster agreed at once with this view of the matter and we discussed the implications. He decided to ask the parents to come to see us both, with a view to encouraging them to go to the local child-guidance clinic. Mr A. thought that Ronald was like his mother, sensitive and easily discouraged. He believed that she would welcome some psychiatric treatment although he doubted whether the father, who was a brusque, good-hearted, unimaginative disciplinarian, would take kindly to the idea.

We had an interview with the parents the next week. I found them to be in essence very much as described by Mr A. The father was on the defensive to begin with, fearful of being blamed for being soft with Ronald — his wife might be soft, but not he — and for taking no interest in his career at school. He was at pains to show how he chased his son up, punished him when necessary and tried to get him to take an interest. He said that he was quite a good boy, not disobedient but just lazy and always had been quite unlike the other children, who took after himself and his activities. His wife sat near tears listening to him, but when encouraged, began to fill in the father's account with her own feelings about Ronald. She said that he had always been quiet and easily discouraged like herself.

In the course of the interview father, sensing that Mr A. and myself were concerned to understand rather than to reprimand, became less defensive and hectoring, and kindlier to his wife. The idea that Ronald could be preoccupied by worries which he could not understand or express but which slowed down his ability to function optimally, was eagerly accepted by the mother who also applied this to herself. She would easily have embraced the idea of consulting the local child-guidance clinic, but father rejected this firmly, as the housemaster had predicted, despite our attempt to elicit and to counter some of his anxieties about psychiatric treatment. We left this suggestion in abeyance and continued then to talk about Ronald as he appeared both at home and at school, encouraging the father to foster and to encourage rather than to punish, allaying some of his guilt about his failure as a disciplinarian and giving the mother some hope that the school was really concerned to understand and to help. We agreed with father that it was important to see that Ronald did his homework regularly as continual failure would only increase his sense of inadequacy, but put the emphasis on support rather than forcing. When the parents left mother was bright and very grateful, father less defensive and less ashamed of listening to his wife.

The gist of our discussions about Ronald was shared with the teachers most concerned. Some weeks later one of those came to me and said that she didn't really understand how it had happened, but his work for her had improved considerably. Before our discussion she had written him off as a confounded nuisance and had resigned herself to having to nag him perpetually about unwritten work. After our discussion she had felt quite differently about him, thought that he sensed this and had become less hopeless about his work with her. This was a teacher who until then had been quite bluntly opposed to the idea that any possible help could come from talking about her pupils with someone who did not know and teach them herself.

Ronald and his mother could no doubt have benefited from more extensive psychological help — it is even conceivable that he or she may seek this in the future. Nevertheless some consideration and concern for him and for his parents at this point has resulted in a more hopeful turn to what was a chronically unsatisfactory situation.

Mavis and the geography refusers

Mavis had done very badly in her geography exam one year before she was due to take the subject in G.C.E. The geography master informed her housemistress that Mavis had driven herself into a quite unwarrantable state of anxiety about this. She had become the centre of a group of three other girls who were all in a panic about the geography exam, and had come to ask him if they could drop the subject and change to another course. It was difficult to do this at such a late stage and unnecessary in his opinion, because they were all capable of passing the exam. The housemistress told me that Mavis was a friendly, intelligent, helpful but over-emotional girl who two years previously had caused some anxiety — she showed me her file in which the matter was well-documented.

At that time Mavis had been devoted to another girl, Judy, who was always getting into trouble with the staff. Finally her form-mistress had decided very perspicaciously that Mavis was the instigator. When Mavis was accordingly tackled, this had solved the problem of Judy, but Mavis then started to stay away from school, became really school-phobic and it had needed a great deal of work on the part of the house and form teacher with Mavis and with her mother before she could attend school again regularly. They felt that this had been achieved eventually by getting her parents to buy her a little dog. For a month or two the dog had accompanied her to school, until Mavis had finally settled back there once more.

The housemistress was therefore afraid of putting too much pressure on Mavis to continue with geography lest she panicked and started to stay at home again; on the other hand the geography master was afraid that if Mavis were allowed to drop the subject the other three would want to give it up as well.

Mavis then had an interview with the houseteacher at which I was present. She was an attractive, soft-looking girl, out-going, voluble and flushed in her effort to explain herself. She seemed puzzled at her own attitude; failing to understand why she should find this subject such a difficult one. Miss A. encouraged her to express in detail her views about different aspects of it, to think how her worries about it had developed, and tried to discover if they were related to any particular teacher. Mavis praised her teacher who she felt took a great deal of trouble with them all, and had given them a fair exam paper, but said she had known beforehand that she wouldn't be able to do it even though she had spent hours on revision, totally failing to learn anything.

She kept repeating that revising for the subject ate into the time she should have spent on other subjects, especially biology. As the latter was a subject she could usually do she neglected to revise for it at all, thinking it better to spend the extra time on geography. As a result she had failed in biology too and that had really shaken her. She said that she could understand her teacher in class and also the book when it was in front of her, but that she forgot afterwards; and she instanced as an example the way in which islands were formed and suddenly appeared above the water. Maps she could not keep in her head and, when asked by Miss A. to draw a map of Africa, drew it back to front, realising that it was wrong as she looked at it but unable to say precisely why.

It was finally suggested that she should come back in a week's time to talk about it to Miss A. again together with the geography teacher. In the meantime it would be better for her not to get too involved in talking about it to the other three girls, thereby increasing their anxieties, as their difficulties with the subject were likely to be of quite a different sort, and better settled separately with the staff concerned.

Miss. A and I then pooled our impressions about Mavis. We

oth agreed that she was distressed and puzzled by the strength f her reactions. I suggested to Miss A. that geography appeared o have become a phobic subject for her as a couple of years ago he school had become a phobic place. The confusion about the naps and the formations of islands would on an unconscious evel be related to adolescent anxieties about her changing body, exuality, and babies, guilt about masturbation or masturbatory antasies that she feared would eat into, invade her preoccu-ations to the detriment of all rational learning.

Miss A.'s immediate response was to say that this view of the natter made some sense to her. She recalled that there had been omething peculiar in Mavis's attitude to the dog which her arents had bought. She used constantly to accost Miss A. to tell ier about its sex life, when it was in heat, its association with ither dogs and the sort of pups it might produce. After a few nonths she had lost interest in it and the dog was given away. We liscussed the dog's use as a more mentionable repository for her exual impulses and curiosity.

This discussion of her behaviour and its possible inter-retation was presented to Miss A. as a tentative map of the ituation, not as anything one could say to Mavis in a helpful or neaningful way. If there was a possibility of her having treat-nent she would have an opportunity to understand and work hrough these unconscious preoccupations in the relationship vith her therapist, but I thought that in the present situation it vas helpful for her to be able to express her anxieties in so far as he was able to formulate them, to have them taken seriously, nd to have the real though irrational nature of them taken into ccount when planning what to do about her course of studies. The giving-up of geography would not mean that the source of he fears was removed, but could lead to a reduction in their xacerbation at a time when she seemed to find it particularly lifficult to cope.

The next week Miss A. and I shared with the geography naster some of our considerations about Mavis before discuss-ng further with her whether, and at what point, she should give p the subject and change to another option. He could not nderstand her failure in the exams as she had always been a ood pupil in that subject, more so than the other girls who vanted to drop it. Miss A. made it clear to him why she

293

considered that Mavis's failure in this subject had to be considered more carefully than that of the other girls, that it was the result of a disturbance in relation to the work which had its roots in unconscious sources difficult to resolve in ordinary discussions. She was able to reassure him that her difficulty was no reflection upon his teaching, although we considered it conceiveable that her reaction to him as a man might have played some part in it.

When we saw Mavis again together she was much the same as the previous week; earnest, emotional, voluble and much concerned to explain to Mr R. that her worry about geography had nothing to do with him. She went on to say she thought it had something to do with her inability to find her way around anywhere new, even if she had full instructions and a map with her. She always needed another companion to accompany her to new places, or she would be put into a state and unable to find her way back home. Her parents thought that she was silly about this at her age, just as she was silly to think she couldn't do geography. Her father argued about it with her and tried to get her to see how easy it was to read maps. This just put her in a state again and made her feel more hopeless than ever. Miss A. let her talk, listened to her seriously, prompting with questions. Finally she said that she was prepared to consider changing Mavis's course but this would take a little while as it involved timetable discussions with the deputy-head. Mavis was immensely relieved and expressed her gratitude.

In discussions afterwards we decided it would be well to keep a watching brief on Mavis. Miss A. arranged to see her parents to get a more complete picture of her current activities and frame of mind and to indicate that this course had been taken because of her genuine distress, springing from sources which were not easy to understand or to tackle directly. Referral to the child-guidance clinic was to be borne in mind if this seemed feasible. I had little doubt that, were treatment available and were the parents ready to accept the idea and to cooperate, Mavis was the kind of adolescent who was likely to make use of psycho-analytically oriented therapy.

This idea was not acceptable, however. Mavis settled down to her new course. With her own anxieties somewhat allayed by this opportunity to have them considered seriously, her involvement with the other three girls as the instigator of the geography revolt was reduced. They were helped to decide that extra work would make it possible for them to continue with the subject and did so without any further fuss.

Ann, aged twelve years

One of the houseteachers consulted me with some bewilderment about Ann who was in the middle of her second term at the school. Her mother had said that Ann, who had always been very happy at school and who still said she liked it, had begun to weep every morning before coming. She would also begin to cry quietly at different times during the day. Her mother and Mrs X., who had talked to Ann, could get no idea of what was the matter. Mrs X. asked me to sit in with her the next time she interviewed Ann to see if I could pick up any clues which might help her to solve this mystery. Ann was never in any trouble about her work or conduct, was generally liked both by teachers and pupils.

When I met her I found a friendly, expansive little girl, eager and pleased to talk again to Mrs X. and to include me in her confidence. She had seen Mrs X. a week ago, said she still began to cry without warning and without knowing why and it was worse when she came back to school after the week-end. She had no complaints to make about anybody at school, said it wasn't because she didn't like school, and she wasn't unhappy at home either, except that sometimes she found herself crying after she'd gone upstairs to bed. The only time she could remember being like this before was when she first went to the infants' school, not at the very beginning but during her first year. But, she said, after a while she just forgot about that.

As she talked easily and eagerly about her friends at school and her family, I could find no more specific clues than Mrs X. had found as to why Ann was in this weepy, easily upset state. We talked afterwards of how girls at the onset of puberty often became more emotional and clinging and subject to recurrence of earlier infantile states of dependence and uncertainty. Ann's only sister, she had told us, was six years younger than herself, which would mean that during her first year at primary school her mother was pregnant and the new baby was born. It seemed

295

then that she might be undergoing a repetition of this separation difficulty in her first year at her new school in adolescence. Mrs X. was reassured to find that I could find no evidence of any obvious reason for Ann's unhappiness which she had over-looked. As Miss A. had with Mavis, she too decided to keep a watching brief. A week later she told me that a few days after this second interview, Ann had come to see her to say she thought she knew why she kept on feeling like crying. It was because her mum had, since the beginning of the term, taken a part-time job in the afternoon and wasn't at home when she returned from school. Half an hour after she came back her dad came home and then about an hour later her mum. Mrs X. then said 'What shall we do about it then Ann? Shall we tell your mum?'

'Oh no Miss', said Ann, 'I wouldn't like my mum to know, she'd give up her job and she enjoys it so much'. It was then left that Ann should come back again and talk to Mrs X. if she felt too upset.

Here the consultant agreed with Mrs X. that she had intuitively responded with the most helpful attitude. In her more mature and adequate self Ann wanted to consider her mother's interests, to become more independent herself and to allow her mother more freedom. It was her more infantile self with separation problems, re-evoked in the stresses of puberty and also in the problems of adjustment to a much larger school, that threatened to overwhelm her growing independence. With a sympathetic ear from a teacher who had heard these two opposing needs in her, she was given some support for her more infantile anxieties and a better chance of achieving some degree of independence. Had the teacher identified too hastily and completely with the weepy little girl who was missing her mummy, implicitly or explicitly blaming that mother for going out to work, and had she put pressure on the mother to give up her job, Ann would very likely have felt guilty and ashamed at letting down her more grown-up self as well as her mother.

Staff Group Discussions

Topics for discussion in this group were brought up by members from week to week. These ranged from individual children, types of children, group formations and relationships, teacher-pupil relationships in varied situations and stages, to interstaff relationships and the teacher's role in the community.

The group consisting as it did of teachers who were working together daily in positions of varying seniority and responsibilities, inevitably imposed certain strains and inhibitions which were brought into the open in the early weeks by one of the more outspoken members — 'We realise that in talking about the children we are often talking about ourselves and giving ourselves away'. There seemed to be as much anxiety about betraying inadequacy to certain fellow teachers as to the consultants.

The consultant took the line that these discussions were likely to be of value primarily in stimulating new lines of thought, enlarging fields of interest, sharpening and exchanging perceptions, and only secondarily in conveying theoretical information. Differing opinions about individual children for instance were accepted as equally valid for scrutiny in attempting to get a more complete view of the child's personality. Members were encouraged to examine and to bring out into the open their own reactions, to make use of them in understanding the nature of the children under discussion.

This encouragement and freedom of emotional expression undoubtedly has its dangers, evoking upon occasion some prolonged over-emotional outburst from a particular member of the group for whom some topic touches too keenly upon a particular personal problem. When this was the case the consultant attempted to align himself implicitly with the member who felt that he's given himself away too much, and to consider in general human terms the way in which this response threw light upon the problem under discussion rather than the light which it might throw upon the individual speaker's psychopathology.

One example follows of a case that illustrates first, the problem of keeping a child or topic under discussion, one of general interest and involvement of the whole group without leading to undue self-revelation, and secondly, the kind of tension which can be evoked and which has to be dealt with when a selected group of responsible people in an organisation meet to discuss matters of concern to other responsible people who are not present and may, therefore, feel excluded. Again to facilitate expression the consultant will refer to herself in the first person, and again this example is disguised.

297

Examples of work in teachers' group

One of the members, Mr Q., brought as a problem in the course of one meeting a boy Martin who had always impressed him as strangely different from the others, intelligent but moody and erratic in his performance and given to outbursts of protest against the government, religion and established conventions. Mr Q. had been particularly concerned because the day before, Martin had stayed behind in class after school with two or three other boys to continue a discussion that had started during the lesson. He said bitterly to Mr Q. and the others that he could not understand what people got out of living at all; for himself he could see no enjoyment in it and he had nothing to look forward to. Mr Q. had felt compelled to stand up for life, but felt that as far as Martin was concerned he made a very lame job.

Most of the other members of the group who were also acquainted with Martin had their comments and observations to make. He emerged as a source of unease and puzzlement with a general consensus of agreement about the description of his external appearance and behaviour, but with opinion sharply divided about the interpretation of this and about the best method of handling him. One view was that he was a born trouble-maker with the agitator's gift of the gab, who needed to be kept firmly in his place; that too much attention paid to him would merely inflate his sense of importance and encourage him to subvert the system. Others said more sympathetically that he was unhappy and very disturbed, probably misunderstood at home and also at school: why should he for instance be asked to have his hair cut? Why should his unorthodox political opinions be given less serious attention than they deserved?

At the end of the meeting devoted to Martin we were left with two interlocking topics, both of which the group wished to continue to discuss: that of Martin himself and the reason for the unease which he evoked; and the more general theme of adolescent rebellions and deviations together with the teacher's involvement in these as influenced by his own adolescent experiences. We decided to continue first with the primary focus on Martin and to consider all relevant observations of him, gathered during the intervening week by all the teachers in the group concerned with him.

As it happened before continuing the discussion of Martin in the teachers' group the next week, I had to deal with an accumulation of resentment in teachers outside the group, that his name had arisen as a topic of discussion at all. Neither his form nor his house-teachers happened to be in the group at that time. A member of the group had approached them, saying that we would be talking about him the next week, and asked if they could let her have some information about him. It was known only to the housemaster at that time that Martin had just become involved in difficulties outside school, in which his family was also concerned. The housemaster became very indignant, felt slighted, afraid that decisions were being taken behind his back, anxious lest confidential information would be irresponsibly divulged and discussed.

Helped by the senior houseteacher, I was able to sort out with those concerned outside the group that the purpose of our discussion was not to reach conclusions that led to decisions, or indeed to the definitive diagnosis of any child discussed, but rather to enlarge interests and to encourage second thoughts, to broaden the base of understanding from which any teacher concerned would act when appropriate. The reluctance of Martin's housemaster to disclose confidential information was respected.

This led later on in the teacher's group to discussion of the value of detailed and current information about children's background and out of school activities in order to understand them better. The unanimous feeling was, naturally, that the more information known, the better the understanding possible; hence the tensions arising at times between houseteachers and other staff who had to deal with problem children — not only because of confidential information deliberately withheld, but because of lack of communication, due maybe to pressure of time and numbers — e.g. 'How could I be expected to know that Norman was so insolent to me in class today, because his mother had just died?'

I then suggested that the group consider that, although in general we might all agree that more information confers greater advantage, our heated emotional conviction of unfairness at the withholding of information might have its irrational sources, dating from early childhood days when our parents were still the kings and queens and magicians of the fairy stories, all knowing and all powerful, and often seeming to us too miserly about that power. We proceeded to consider then that something of that ambivalent idealisation of power and of secret knowledge is probably endemic in our attitudes to authority figures of various kinds, or specialists in subjects that very nearly touch upon our welfare, e.g. the medical and psychiatric professions, even teachers, if we are outside the profession! It depends upon our own personality and upon our attitude to the particular authority in question whether idealised expectation or resentful suspicion is to the fore.

This brought the group back to consider Martin 'the born agitator', against established authority, but, some thought secretly conspiring to establish rival power groups of his own. Although the housemaster had not wished to divulge details of the recent out-of-school crisis, it was generally known among members of the group that Martin's home life was unhappy, that he was an only child, his father often away, and his mother subject to bouts of severe psychiatric illness, and that he himself had begun to be involved in an ideological anti-government group with which his father was concerned.

We discussed the possible aspects of his involvement in this group: the attempt to find a positive identification with his father; the attempt to find companionship with others knitted together by a common purpose — anti-establishment though it might be; a rebellion intensified by anxiety and disappointment at the failure of his first parental government to provide him with security.

The merits of giving him a hearing in appropriate lessons and discussions was then discussed. Doubts were raised by some about the wisdom of allowing adolescents of this kind too much rope — they didn't appreciate kindness, just thought that you were too soft, and used that to impose upon you. Then, with particular reference to Martin and details of the experience which various teachers had in dealing with him, we discussed the ever recurring problem of how to keep the balance between freedom of expression and discipline; the value of allowing verbal expression of grievances in the hope of modifying them, by insight, thereby lessening the likelihood of delinquent action; the kind of talking that is, on the contrary, designed and likely to stir up and foment grievances and justify deliquency. We talked of

300

he problem of curbing this 'rabble rousing' for the sake of the
dolescent himself, and also in order to protect the rest of the
lass or group from the need or greed of one member for extra
ttention.

One teacher made the following point that the trouble was not
eally the children but the parents: 'by the time we have them
hings have gone too far to be altered'. While acknowledging the
alidity of the parents' responsibility to a large extent for the way
n which their children grow up, I suggested that the wisdom also
f considering the responsibility which the children themselves
arry in the total situation, the responsibility, however small
vhich they might be encouraged, either explicitly or implicitly to
ssume to improve it, bearing in mind the demoralising effect of
eing regarded merely as a victim of circumstances. I suggested
hat in some instances information about bad family background
ould in fact be used not to give additional insight, but to carry all
lame and to distort one's opportunities to learn from actual
bservation of the child. This was linked with the unconscious
ivalry with the parents operating to some extent in all workers
vith children, which may intensify censoriousness of the parents
t the expense of clarity and impartiality of judgement, a factor
which also enters into rivalry with colleagues and the wish to
riumph over them by managing better with the children than
hey are able to do.

Notes on incidental work with staff

Because the consultant was not a teacher, she could be felt to
stand outside the framework of the school. This made it possible
or members of staff to voice anxieties and air grievances they
night not have been able to do with a fellow teacher.

For example, one young teacher who was in his first term at
he school, found out in conversation in the staff-room what the
onsultant's work was in the school. He began to tell her about
imself as a teacher, whether indeed he would ever make a
eacher. He said he couldn't hold the discipline in his class and he
elt the scores of experienced teachers around him must have so
ong forgotten what it's like to be new and inexperienced that he
id his difficulties from them. He talked also about his mother
vho was a teacher too. The consultant said people might really

301

remember their young days more than he thought and told him that she too was new in the school. They talked about some of the feelings raised by being new to a job. When they parted the teacher said in a sincere way that it had been a real relief to talk to her.

On another and more urgent occasion, a member of staff approached the consultant asking if he might talk to her. He told her he had been feeling the strain of work lately, and that this seemed to be getting worse. He said in fact he was feeling terribly distressed because the day before in class he had lost his temper with a child and struck him. He felt the housemistress who had dealt with the affair had been secretly very reproving of him, and concerned herself only with the boy and the school's good name. *His* situation was ignored — what was he supposed to do? He poured out some details about things in his personal life which were worrying him too. The consultant listened attentively saying almost nothing. The teacher finally apologised for flooding her with his troubles, but wondered — if she could stand it — if he might seek her out next week when she came, as he felt he really needed to talk to someone at the moment. The consultant said she would be glad to help, and over the following weeks he regularly sought her out in the staffroom. Gradually there was a lessening of intensity until the personal nature of his communications gave way to general talk about the school.

The consultant felt that because she was available in the school she had been a support to this member of staff at a moment of temporary crisis.

Work with groups of children

a) *With a houseteacher*

The two houseteachers who assembled these groups were surprised at the degree of enthusiasm shown by the majority of the children, who were not in fact missing any lessons, but were giving up part of their lunchtime recreation. Each child was currently, or had been, a source of particular concern to his houseteacher for one reason or another. Grouping was roughly according to age, and very approximately and arbitrarily according to the type of problem which the child presented at school. The majority of the children, but not all of them, were

302

known to have more than usually difficult family backgrounds, ranging from collusive sub-delinquent parents, unhappy or broken marriages, to parents with gross psychiatric illnesses. The children were not asked to talk about their homes and family relationships although some did so, both explicitly and implicitly. There was a deliberate avoidance of anything which might have been perceived by the parents or by the children as an attempt to pry into private family matters. They were encouraged to express their views about schools, their attitudes to their teachers, to lessons, their friends, their recreations. At the first meeting the teacher said to them that as they were all aware things were not always going too smoothly at school for them, and the purpose of these meetings was for them to exchange points of view with him and with each other, to get to know each other a little better, to see if this would help matters. The consultant was introduced as a specialist there to help the house-staff in their work.

When possible after the group had finished each week, the houseteacher and consultant discussed the session, compared impressions of individual children, tried to assess what had been going on through considering the underlying implications of the discussions, and also considered how to handle it the next week.

In these groups as one might expect, some children spoke up much more rapidly than others, but the more timid and withdrawn, and sometimes even the more sullen, encouraged by the teacher, were also quite pleased to join in and express their points of view. The little group of second and third year boys, who were all to some extent prone to truancy from school, evasion of work and responsibility, and some of whom were without particular friends and ties in the school, all admitted to spells of boredom which they had no special interests to alleviate. Led by one lively small boy who seemed to suffer from undirected mischievous energy, rather than any serious antisocial or emotional maladjustment, and who had outspoken and genuinely appreciative feelings towards the school and his teachers, they took up a suggestion from the housemaster to organise themselves into a little club to visit places of interest within reach of the neighbourhood. The housemaster told them of just such a miniature travel organisation which had been run for a year or two by a group of boys by that time in the sixth form, and asked the leading spirit by then a prefect, to come and talk to them about it and give them some advice on how to set about matters. The sixth former came, was greeted by slightly embarrassed but flattering attention, and sufficient impetus was given to enable the little group to carry the idea into action.

b) *Group of five remedial children*

This is an account of the group of children, already mentioned, that was formed from the Remedial Class the consultant had been visiting for six weeks. After discussion with the class teacher a small group of 5 children was chosen, for their own benefit, and also to give the class teacher a little relief from them. The children were told they would be seeing the consultant for two periods each week; they were to go with her to another room, and they need not bring any books with them.

The children came with alacrity, in a mood of 'We're getting out of lessons'. The consultant began by confirming they were there, not for lessons, but for something different. It was meant as time for them to think about themselves. One of the children responded to this by saying 'You must be joking', a cry which was then taken up by the others, and she was told to 'Come off it'. When asked why they thought she wasn't serious, one said 'It's not worth it, Miss', and another anxiously suggested that she hear them read instead. She pointed out that they even seemed to like lessons better than her plan that they should think about themselves, and she suggested they talk about why they didn't like her idea. The children were not articulate, nor much able to concentrate, but with persistent and considerable encouragement, their fear of being mocked by the enterprise as well as their anxiety about self-reflection did emerge.

As the meetings went on these themes were often enacted in the group itself. For example, one child would derisively jeer at another trying to enlist the consultant's support, saying 'He's just a dope, Miss. Don't bother about him', and this could be made an opportunity for the group as a whole to talk about the attitude of not 'bothering with a dope'. The consultant would also ask the question of why the one had called the other a dope in such a hostile way. She found the group had the answer to this one, 'Because he's an even bigger dope himself!' Indeed, the

304

tendency of all these children to disparage others to avoid the pain of self-disparagement emerged clearly and became something the children felt they understood and could recognise, though always more easily in others than in themselves.

Looking away from, rather than at, themselves was a marked general feature of every child in this group. As an example, one child was telling the rest how he couldn't get on with his work and that it was very blotty. The consultant enquired why it was like that and he said 'It's my neighbour, he jogs me'. His neighbour, a fellow member of the group repudiated the blame for bad work that was being thrust on him. An intense exchange took place, during which the neighbour told him he should blame *himself* first and not find excuses like him jogging him. The boys' tempers flared and they began fighting each other and had to be separated. Slowly, through incidents of this kind, the children got some glimmering that their chronic feeling of being badly treated came partly from blaming neighbours, teachers, prefects, instead of blaming themselves. They realised, a little, how hard it was to look to yourself and also that this was the only hopeful way.

There was constant pressure from the group, once the children became less suspicious, to get the consultant to join them in criticising other teachers or to be on their side against the school. This took various forms, open invitations to run down the school, or blandishments like 'It's nicer being here than having maths with old Mr X.'. Of course, their feelings sometimes veered swiftly, and when reluctant to go with the consultant, they would slyly say to Mr X. that it would be more use to them to stay and do work with him, wouldn't it? The consultant at such moments needed good-will and a sense of common purpose from the class teacher, and she in turn was careful that the children didn't go away with the idea that she could be used against their teachers.

Another difficulty was the violation of school rules. For example, the children openly chewed gum in her periods, something they knew no teacher would allow. In the beginning the consultant was not certain what to do. After a while she decided to insist that rules be kept. This was to prevent the children viewing her as an indulgent figure they could oppose to the harsh image they had of their teachers, as this would interfere with the possibility of their modifying their sense of grievance against the staff.

The consultant felt it was important not to raise unreasonable hopes in the children, or in the class teacher and herself too. The consultant and class teacher met often to talk about the children in the group and this led to useful discussions of the burden of teaching so many disturbed and backward children. The class teacher confessed that he always had the guilty feeling he should be able to do more for the children. This led to an effort to distinguish appropriate goals from impossible goals, and to discussions of how, in deluded omnipotence, one either blamed oneself, or else became irritable with the children for failing to achieve the impossible.

Sometimes the consultant found it necessary to protect one of the group from making too intimate disclosures. One child was afraid he would die in the night. Between the children in the group there were not sufficiently strong affectionate bonds to make such disclosures possible without risk of hurt by ridicule in the group or leakage to other children in the school. When a child verged on telling too much, the consultant intervened and suggested he keep that to tell her later. As the weeks had gone by a pattern of using these double periods had taken shape. The first period was spent in talking, the second was more for individual work and attention. The children each had a writing and a drawing book in which they did what they wanted while one of them had his private ten minutes or so with the consultant. In the beginning the wish to read or do spelling was mainly a manoeuvre to avoid self-reflection. However, the consultant felt to persist with 'no lessons' would deprive them of the chance to convey to her their most pressing problem in the school — their illiteracy. So in the short private time they had with her the children could try to read to her, or spell, or simply talk to her.

It must not be thought that this group went smoothly. Some days, one child, or even all of them, would try to obstruct anything being done. Sometimes they could not be drawn from their disconsolation. Sometimes they were bored. Nonetheless the children at the end thought it had been worthwhile and were sorry when it came to a premature end when the consultant stopped work in the school.

Discussions with Sixth Formers

These emerged most explicitly as the need of many of the senior boys and girls to talk to the staff and to have some help in finding their role as budding adults, to have the opportunity to express their opinions and to get a better understanding of the contradictions in their feelings and their attitudes. As one boy said, 'All through the school you tend to look at the forms above you and to copy them. When you get to the top there's only the staff above you and you know that you're not really one of them but it helps sometimes when they talk to you on a level . . . often it feels as if you're given a lot of duties of the staff to keep order, but none of their real authority . . . you feel a silly fraud when some little squirt that you're ordering back into line, turns and cheeks you, and asks you who you think you are . . . Mr B. or Mrs G.?'

Had the time been available, and the school timetable allowed an ongoing free discussion group with sixth formers and with fourth year leavers, this would undoubtedly have been one of the most fruitful and necessary areas of work.

Reflections on the work done and on possible growing points

This project had to end after the second year as neither consultant had enough time to continue — it was not in any case envisaged as long term. Both consultants felt that this experience of working within a school as part of its staff was invaluable in giving them a first hand experience of the difficulties in finding the time and appropriate setting within an organisation to deal with individual problems, in underlining the great number of children and families who present these problems, of a critical or more chronic nature, who either would not or could not be dealt with in a clinic setting. On the other hand it brought home to them the exceptional possibilities of the school situation in detecting and modifying some of these problems (which usually have to be carried willy-nilly), of the school as a potential therapeutic as well as an educational institution, since it has care of children over a number of years, as well as during a large part of the day.

There was no attempt to make a quantitative survey of the population of children requiring attention during the two years work. Without a good deal of investigation, involving every

307

child in the school, numbers would be meaningless, and the number actually seen or discussed with the consultants was also limited by the amount of time, and the time of day when they happened to be there each week.

The establishment or mutual confidence between the consultant and the staff with whom she works must be emphasised as of primary importance. This is possible only when the head teacher is in favour of such a project and has sufficient confidence both in her own teachers and in the consultant to allow them to get together without forcing matters, and to take a positive attitude in helping to resolve any discords that may occur.

In this school the Headmistress had established a well-developed system of pastoral care around the houseteachers whose functioning largely covered many of the areas for which school counsellors are being trained (personal, educational and vocational guidance). The consultants continued to work largely through these houseteachers — in effect to function as consultants to the counsellors — to broaden their perceptions and help them to assess more accurately the significance of the data which they acquired about their children, and thus to increase the sensitivity of the way in which they were responding to it.

As their aim was to establish an easy working-colleague relationship with those members of the staff who wished or who were able to have contact with them, the consultants were available to discuss cases brought forward by the teachers rather than to be directly involved in selecting children who needed special attention. As one might expect the children who first emerged were those presenting some obvious problem in school — such as unruliness, truancy or unsatisfactory work. On the other hand it is extremely unlikely that any child who is unhappy, antisocial or developing in an impaired fashion, will fail to show signs of this in the course of his school life — they are there if the teacher is receptive enough to detect them, if she has some acquaintance with what she is looking for. A number of these children were considered.

Whether the houseteachers would have been able to function so efficiently as counsellors had they not first been trained as teachers and were they not still spending quite a proportion of their time in teaching, is a matter for debate. Certainly those who were most deeply concerned about the responsibilities and potential opportunities conferred by their special role, entailing continuity of care and some degree of global concern for the children in their houses, were constantly dogged by pressure of commitments that often curtailed the amount of attention they felt they should have been devoting to particular children and at times also to their parents. It was also stated that so much time had to be taken in dealing with the crises and matters of immediate urgency that there was not enough left to spend in developing over a period of months and years the relationship of confidence and trust with the bulk of their children, which might sometimes have led to the forestalling of the crisis before it came to a head.

On a number of occasions relief was outspoken about the opportunity to discuss questions and decisions with the consultants: 'Even though it turns out that there is nothing more that we could have done, at least it's a relief to know that we've done the best we could in the circumstances, and to see the picture a little more clearly'.

Such part-time consultation work is likely to be useful mainly, or only, when there is a basis in the school organisation to receive it. It could be considered as a kind of in-service training in certain aspects of counselling, on the dynamics of interpersonal relationships between individuals and groups, children and adults, both parents and teachers, and in personality development. There is little doubt that a school of the kind described could usefully employ as a full-time member of staff a specialist whose initial and primary function would be that of consultant to the housestaff and others concerned with pastoral care, but who would also become involved in working directly with individuals and groups of both children and parents. Although the consultants in this project were impressed by the freedom with which the children responded to their teacher's interest in personal matters, there are undoubtedly cases and situations when the role of teacher, concerned with action and discipline as it is, can impose inhibitions on both parties in an intimate personal interchange with a pupil.

At the present time, given the great scarcity of psychological workers trained in therapeutic techniques and in the dynamics of interpersonal relationships and child development, and the scarcity of teachers with such training, the writers envisage the possibility of demonstrating their appreciation of those who cooperated so willingly with them in this project, by making some use of their experience in the school to conduct seminars with interested teachers on the lines described in this report.

With Edna O'Shaughnessy. (Some of this material appears in 'Teacher, Counsellor, Therapist: Towards a Definition of the Roles'.)

This eventually became the School Counsellors' Course at the Tavistock Centre.

3

Teacher, Counsellor, Therapist:
Towards a Definition of the Roles
1972

I am going to start by raising questions which are likely to recur to most of you many times during the year, and which I know have in previous courses been debating points in most of the small groups. What is counselling? Can a teacher be a counsellor as well — are the roles compatible? What is the difference between a counsellor and a therapist? It is often assumed that the approach of a teacher to children must of necessity be a directive one; that of a counsellor less directive; and that of a therapist quite non-directive. I would like to consider what we mean when we talk of 'directive'.

But first of all it is worth stating in brief but general terms the requirements for providing a good environment in which to bring up a child or young person, to bring out and develop the potential in its various forms which is within him. To begin with, he needs a place where he feels contained, where he is known, where he has an opportunity to become aquainted with people and, from their responses to him and his reception of their impingement on him, to get to know himself. Although his mother initially and his family, provide their first place of containment, the next in time and ordinarily the next in importance is provided by the school. At school he will not usually receive from his teachers — and as a rule will not need to receive — the same closeness and detailed attention which he required from his parents in the first formative years. But probably every child needs throughout his years of growth some degree of individual attention and respect from some of his educators, as well as opportunities to feel that his questions and opinions are of interest, are valued. Having a chance to express himself with freedom in different ways, is not the same as indulgence.

The child will feel free to do this only if he can trust the adult world which has to take ultimate responsibility for him until adolescence. Then the emphasis begins to shift, so long as he can trust his caretakers to provide a framework which will protect him in time of need from the dangers of his own ignorance, from

311

his own destructiveness and from the destructiveness of others. Within such a framework he needs the opportunity to acquire facts, information about the world; and to learn and develop skills which will help him to be useful and to make a place for himself in the world, along with the social skills for getting along with other people in order to share in activities with them. And in the midst of all this he has to learn how to manage his emotions. But before he can manage those in a way leading to any kind of creative development, he has to be able to contain and tolerate them a little: to be able to feel them without immediately evacuating them in action or speech. It is in this area that our educational system, both formal and informal, is probably at its most deficient.

Throughout our lives we all, to some extent, have difficulty in tolerating emotions which cause mental pain. From infancy onwards, we develop numerous defences against experiencing these emotions. Painful emotions centre on two areas: primarily, danger to the self, and then danger to people, objects or values that we care about. These two areas are not always easy to distinguish, and they do in fact often overlap; but it is important, when trying to assess the quality of a child's anxiety, to consider whether it seems to be mainly persecutory (i.e. fear of danger to himself) or depressive (fear of doing harm or of harm coming to someone or something he loves). The greatest bar to protecting oneself or people whom one loves from the many external danger situations that arise, is the difficulty in disentangling those from the other dangers deriving from one's own destructive impulses. The destructiveness from within is the one danger from which we can never escape — physically speaking it kills us all in the end — yet it is the danger which we spend much of our energy in trying to escape, to deny, to project outwards. In so far as we have to do this, it clouds our perception of ourselves and of the world. It causes us to be unduly fearful; to look for other people to blame; to take up positions of inferiority from which we can feel above reproach.

When we are unable to perceive and to manage the destructive aspects of ourselves and to tolerate the recurrent failures connected with these, we are likely to have difficulty in bearing these in the children — in having a fellow-feeling for children who have and who cause difficulties. It is only through fellow-feeling that we can help them to direct their aggression (for instance) into more profitable channels, or to relax the inhibitions against experiencing those areas of the personality which are found terrifying and therefore unacceptable. There is an immense difference between identifying with the child in difficulty from some common basis in experience, while recognising his separateness in age, situation and total individuality, and maybe even feeling some degree of dislike or distaste; and the patronising attitude of the directive approach: 'Oh, I've come across this before — when you're my age you might understand better, that this is how it should be dealt with . . .' For all growth and development is attended by mental pain and discomfort to some degree: the pain which always accompanies uncertainty, however much it may also be mixed with the excitement of adventure. If growth is to continue, one needs to be able to persevere in putting out new feelings into the world, despite the uncertainty of outcome. However the stress of the adventure needs to be mitigated from time to time — as every good teacher knows — by some measure of enjoyment and the possibility of success.

The role of the good teacher has, I would imagine, as its central core, the task of encouraging the child or young person to reach out to seek information about the world — circumscribed only too often, alas, by the demands of the exam syllabus — and to help him to see the relevance of this information to himself and to the culture in which he lives. The child needs guidance in thinking about the information which comes within his compass, in evaluating and organizing it. And here I would think that the teacher's own personality and attitude to his subject is often of great importance to the child as a model, sometimes perhaps an inspiration, hopefully never a wetblanket. But the teacher's primary task is to orient the child to the subject, information or skills operating in the world outside. However, he has to take into account as best he can the stage and state of each child, and their readiness in the process. Since the teacher works with groups, sometimes large groups, his personal involvement with individual children in his teaching role, is of necessity curtailed. The larger the group, the more distant is the relationship. Which is not to say that he may not often have a profound and lasting effect on many children, who observe his way of handling the class: of dealing with the disruptive, the clever, the slow, the

313

flatterers. Some may imperceptibly identify with him, admiring or criticising.

But nearly every teacher takes on an informal counselling role from time to time with individual children, and when the emphasis shifts to investigating the children's attitudes and openness: maybe about a piece of work, maybe school affairs or some project that is occupying them out of school. This is 'counselling in the corridors or on playground duty', as one of the people on a previous course called it. There are also those occasions, maybe towards the end of term, when the requirements of the syllabus are relaxed and a lesson becomes a free exchange of opinions about officially irrelevant topics, yet dear to the preoccupations of the children themselves. In many schools of course there are lessons variously called social studies, current affairs, or something of that kind, which are in effect designed as opportunities for the children to discuss with the teacher their views and attitudes to life: lessons which are akin to group counselling sessions.

I would think that the essence of the counselling situation, is in eliciting and valuing the expression of emotions, opinions and aspirations from the pupil; in helping him to recognise the implications of what he expresses; and in linking these together in a more meaningful way so that he can act a little more rationally and with better judgement. In a small group situation, the task of the counsellor would be to bring together and mediate between different voices; perhaps to clarify the difference between various points of view; to keep the vociferous in place and perhaps make active attempts from time to time to bring in the silent minority. I would not, myself, in a counselling situation, regard personal opinions, information, or even from time to time tentative advice from the counsellor, as out of place; but it should be offered for consideration and for discussion with the child or young person, and preferably linked to some active attempt on his own part to think about his situation.

This kind of counselling situation is possible, I think, in more informal moments of protected time between teachers and pupils: between a pupil and a teacher who may at other times be acting in a disciplinary role. It is comparable to the kind of discussions that parents may have with their children when the relationship between them is basically affectionate and trusting;

although at other times there may be struggles and resentments because the parents hold ultimate responsibility for checking antisocial action. But this combination of roles becomes more difficult with adolescents: who, as part of their stage in development, are struggling against authority, and touchy about any suspected attempt to make them conform or sell them into slavery to the older generation. It is probably most difficult of all in areas connected with sexuality; a great deal of the adolescent's sexual sallies and phantasies are involved with conscious and unconscious feelings of grudge and competitiveness against the parents. A suitable climate for approaching touchy subjects like sex, may perhaps sometimes be created through group discussions, where the more timid may take courage from the expression of controversial opinions by the bold. The shy young person then has a chance to see how the others react, and how the teacher/counsellor accepts what has been said. He may then feel encouraged to make a more personal and private approach himself, to express his own feelings.

Now, how does this role of a counsellor differ from that of a therapist? Again, this must be my attempt at a personal definition; though one which most people trained as therapists at the Tavistock would probably in the main agree with. Both therapist and counsellor have the task of helping the child or young person to look at and tolerate the anxieties connected with undescribable parts of themselves, derived from infantile levels and experiences of the personality: parts which are interfering with their current functioning and development. However, the methods for approaching the maladaptive elements, differ. In the one-to-one counselling or therapy relationships, the young person brings his hopes and fears to us, expressed verbally but also in more intangible ways which evoke in us feelings and impressions, maybe impulses to action, or ideas of direction which may be premature. In addition to current conflicts, he transfers to us attitudes, aspirations, emotions, and aspects of his personality, that derive from the past. He is likely to evoke in us the same emotional responses which he has evoked from his parents in the past, and from others in similar positions in the present. It is important to become aware of the nature of the feelings he is transferring, by examining our countertransference — that is, our own response to his transference — before

315

responding to it. The appropriate response is likely to differ in the therapy situation from that in the counselling one. I will take an individual case to discuss how a child was helped on by counselling attitudes, and then suggest what the approach of the therapist would likely have been, had psychotherapy then been undertaken.

Ronald was a fourteen-year-old boy of rather more than average ability, whose work throughout secondary school had been erratic and unpredictable, and his homework usually late. His parents were conscientious professional people who were anxious that both their sons should do well, and who had been to see his housemaster on a number of occasions. The housemaster consulted me because a recent consensus of reports indicated that all his teachers were feeling more than usually hopeless about him. He wondered whether the verdict should not be that Ronald was just bone idle and needed a stronger crack of the whip; but somehow that view of the matter did not seem to satisfy him entirely. He asked me to be present one lunch hour when he was interviewing the boy. He told Ronald of the recent complaints about his work, and tried to encourage him to say what he thought about the different subjects, his teachers, his other interests at school, his classmates. Ronald, a remarkably solid-looking, healthy, red-cheeked boy, did his best to respond to this friendly mixture of concern and admonishment. He clearly sensed the friendliness of the teacher. He was aware of my presence in the room, but seemed curious rather than incommoded by it. His reactions were slightly puzzled and slow, and he seemed to have great difficulty in concentrating, especially when asked for his opinion, though he was clearly trying to think of a response. My impression as a result of this interview, taking into account also the housemaster's story, was that the boy was chronically depressed rather than lazy, and was worried in an apathetic way about being unable to meet the demands upon him, for he would really have liked to oblige. The housemaster agreed immediately with this view of the situation; he capped my description of the effect which Ronald produced on me, by saying that he reminded him of the Chekhov play *Ivanov*, where the main character — a middle-aged man in a state of depression — says he feels like a strong young workman who once lifted a huge sack that was too heavy for him, so that something inside him broke, and from then on he lost all his strength and dwindled away.

The housemaster decided to ask both the parents to come to see us, with a view to seeing, possibly, whether they might consider Child Guidance treatment. He thought that Ronald was very like his mother, easily discouraged, and that she might welcome the opportunity to have more help than the school could provide; but doubted whether the father, who was goodhearted but an unimaginative, brusque disciplinarian, would take kindly to the idea. We had an interview with the parents the next week. I found them to be in essence much as the housemaster had described. Mr R. was on the defensive to begin with: fearful of being blamed for being soft with Ronald (his wife might be soft but not he), and for taking insufficient interest in the boy's schooling. He was at pains to show how vigorously he chased his son up, punished him when necessary, and tried to get him to take an interest in manly things. He said that he was a good boy, not disobedient but lazy; unlike his brother who took after himself and always found plenty to do. Mrs R. sat listening to her husband, in tears a good deal of the time; but when encouraged, she began to fill in the father's account with her own view of Ronald: a sort of apologia for her son, who was so like herself — not really up to the rough and tumble. In the course of the interview, Mr R. sensed that the housemaster and I were less concerned with reprimands about Ronald's poor report, than with trying to understand him better, in order to find a way of enlisting his interest. He became less hectoring and blustery and kindlier to his wife. The idea that Ronald could be weighed down by preoccupations which he could not express or even formulate, and which could be slowing down his functioning, was a new one to him, but was at once accepted by the mother, who applied it also herself. She caught on eagerly to the idea of a Child Guidance clinic, but this was rejected out of hand by the father, although we did try to elicit from him some of his anxieties and prejudices about this. We left this suggestion in abeyance, and continued to talk about Ronald as he appeared both at home and at school, emphasizing to the father that it would be better to foster and to encourage rather than to punish. When Mr R. realised that he was not being called to account before some higher tribunal, he seemed to relax his disciplinarian attitude.

317

The mother took heart and hope that the school was really interested to help. We agreed with the father that it was important to see that Ronald did his homework regularly, because continued failure there could only increase his sense of inadequacy; but we suggested that the emphasis might be on support and encouragement, rather than upon directing or forcing. When the parents left the mother was visibly brighter, the father less defensive and less ashamed of listening to his wife. The gist of our discussions about Ronald (except for some confidential material which the mother had disclosed about herself), was shared with the teachers most concerned. Some weeks later, one of those came to see me to say that she didn't understand how it happened, but he really was turning in good work on time for her now. Before our discussion she had written him off as a confounded nuisance, and was resigned to having to nag perpetually about unfinished work. After our discussion she had another look at him, and thought that he must have sensed her interest or sympathy for he had sparked up a little.

Although Ronald and his mother could no doubt have benefited from more extensive and intensive psychotherapeutic help, had this been available and acceptable, this was an instance where a counselling approach initiated by someone trained as a psychotherapist and another trained as a teacher, was at least some help to the boy and his family; also mobilising the school's resources by enlisting the interest of other teachers concerned. We were operating with limited knowledge about the factors contributing to and producing Ronald's depression. The therapeutic or mutative factor was, I suggest, the recognition of this feeling state for what it was: a recognition that left Ronald and his mother less solitary and misunderstood, and which eased the father of the nagging feeling that he ought to be flogging on a horse that was already overburdend. The source of Ronald's depression clearly lay outside the school in his family relationships, and deriving from a much earlier time, perhaps the very begining of his life. But school failure, and non-comprehension of its cause, was bound to perpetuate and increase in him feelings of weakness, unworthiness and consequent disorganisation.

Further counselling interviews with Ronald on his own might have been productive, but possibly not if he were too passive to be able to talk about himself. But regular interviews with a therapist employing an analytic technique could, I think, have been fruitful in Ronald's case, in time. Using such a technique, it would be important for the therapist to keep the regular treatment sessions a private and protective matter, so that the boy should feel that what takes place there will not be impinged upon or shared with others. In such a protected treatment evironment, the actual help in managing his external life would be left to others; while within the session itself, an analytically-trained therapist would be free to concentrate upon the minute details of behaviour and communication, indicating the deeper-than-verbal transference of primitive anxieties, wherein resides the clue to the origin of the difficulties. This treatment would not on the whole preclude or take the place of a counselling aproach. Analytic therapy involves a progressive investigation of the child's inner world, and the ways in which infantile patterns of behaviour are interfering with the mind's current functioning. The counselling role necessitates sensitivity to the child's feeling state, and an appropriate reaction to it — in the light of common sense, I would say; helping him as he is here and now, to be a little clearer about the implications of what he is doing and what is observable if he turns his attention to it. It also involves, as in Ronald's case, helping the others concerned with him — teachers, maybe parents — to reconsider their view of him, without necessarily giving away any confidential material which might be disclosed during a session.

People in a counselling role can often feel frustrated because they are not making sufficiently dynamic sounding interpretations of their client's behaviour; they feel that things might move much faster if they could do this. On the other hand, they can become very anxious when they become the recipient of floridly expressed anxieties and manifest disturbance on the part of the child: feeling fraudulent owing to being presented with all this, without knowing how to deal with it. But I think that as a counsellor, one gradually feels less fraudulent as one comes to have a more realistic conception of the parameters of one's setting, one's personality, the current state of one's training and level of competence. In due course one builds up a store of experience with young people, and of difficulties weathered in the past, which helps one to approach the next child or young person with more confidence. Hopefulness informed by experience is the

319

most precious ingredient this work requires; but also, I would think, the realisation that it is not possible to hand over one's experience *en bloc* in the form of theories or advice.

Therapeutic work of the analytic kind is narrow and specialised. It needs a considerable commitment of time and effort on the part of both patient and therapist. Extensive training and experience seem to be required in order to develop a clear grasp of the infantile levels of feeling and behaviour in each patient; it cannot be learned or applied from text books or theory. But it can, in my experience, bring about *fundamental change* in personality functioning, in the organization of the personality, in ways that nothing else can.

Now from my experience of detailed analytic work with children and with adults, I would feel justified in making the general statement that Ronald's depression and apathy will be connected with an incomplete awareness of his own hostility, and therefore of its management. The fact that it would also seem to reflect his mother's depression would not contradict this, for every child at depth feels omnipotently responsible for any defect in his parents. It is only in the course of favourable development that this area of omnipotent responsibility and guilt becomes mitigated by a more realistic grasp of his responsibility, not only for external happenings, but also for the state of relationships as they exist in his own mind. This statement about the connection between depression and aggression is a theoretical one: true in general, in my opinion, but not an interpretation that could be made in any meaningful way at the time to either Ronald or his parents. Indeed an attempt to do so would have been wild anti-therapy. But in the framework of analytical therapy, evidence would gradually appear in the transference relationship with the therapist, which could be interpreted meaningfully — communicated via action, drawings, words, dreams. Interpretation of such evidence, which is initially unconscious to the child, will tend to enable him to open up further and give the therapist the opportunity to penetrate into the origins of his maldevelopment; but such penetration demands an absolute concentration on the transactions between patient and therapist.

In the counselling situation, such depth of penetration is not possible; but as I have just pointed out, it has other advantages. There is the possibility, even necessity, of the counsellor mobilising and helping to put the child in touch with other resources in his environment. So it does then involve a willingness to work together with other teachers in the school, and maybe other agencies who may sometimes be concerned with the family of the child in question. Any sort of competition in well-doing would be counter-productive; on the contrary, the counselling situation requires a sympathetic attention and respect for the difficulties that these other workers may be having with the child or family.

Some of this material appears in 'Consultation Project in a Comprehensive School'.

4   The Individual in the Group: On Learning to Work with the Psycho-Analytical Method
1978

This paper attempts to convey some of the ways in which I see Dr. Bion's work as raising questions and throwing light upon problems of organizing training in pyscho-analytical method and attitudes. His thoughts on this topic are most cogently but, as always, often obliquely stated in *Attention and Interpretation*. There he pursues further his ideas about the relationship between the container and the contained; the nature of the transformations effected by the quality of their interaction; the subtle proliferation of mythology and lies which in differing degrees obstruct the search for truth. There he continues the preoccupation which runs throughout his writings, with the relationship between the individual and the group, and, as befits a historian, the relationships between different groups.

It is hardly possible to be complacent about the history of psychoanalytic groups or of psycho-analysis in groups. The tension between the pressures of the group and the thrust of the individual for development, is a theme which runs throughout Bion's work: between man as a social animal dependent upon, and with obligations to society; and man as a developing individual with a mind that grows through introjecting experiences of himself in the world, impelled to think in order to retain internally relationships with needed and valued objects in their absence.

Those of us who are concerned with training and the establishment of psycho-analytic work cannot afford to neglect his ideas. The vertex from which I shall be speaking is that of one who has been concerned for over twenty-five years with the practice and training in psycho-analysis in public institutions as well as privately, and in particular with the expansion of the Tavistock training in Psycho-analytical Psychotherapy with Children, Parents and Young People. This is a four year training based upon on-going work and is divided into two parts. Part I is concerned with the development of psycho-analytical observation and attitudes in various settings, while Part II is specifically concerned with learning to apply the method of psycho-analysis to treatment, ranging from once weekly to five times weekly. This training qualifies people to become members of the Association of Child Psychotherapists and to join what was initially a somewhat nebulous and almost unrecognized profession, which has now expanded to achieve a salary and career structure within the British National Health Service. This professional respectability carries with it the necessity of conforming to certain minimal criteria changeable only by the agreement of the appropriate committees. These are by definition bound to be fairly conservative in their operation and undoubtedly inimical to 'catastrophic change'. And yet change and expansion needs to be facilitated so that psycho-analytic ideas and attitudes can travel and take root among workers who are ready to receive them, so that their usefulness may find homes in which to flourish.

So how does one keep the mystical idea of psycho-analysis alive within such a formal structure? How can a structure remain adaptable and be used to protect, perhaps even to promote the development of the individual worker within it? How can one create a group of professionals, of psycho-analytic workers who are able to function with and among other groups of professionals in a way that reduces interference (is 'commensal' in Bion's terms), and may even be beneficial? To quote from *Attention and Interpretation*:

> In the symbiotic relationship there is a confrontation and the result is growth-producing though that growth may not be discerned without some difficulty. In the parasitic relationship the product of the relationship is something that destroys both parties to the association. The realization that approximates most closely to my formulation is the group-individual setting dominated by envy. The envy cannot be satisfactorily ascribed to one or other party; in fact it is a function of the relationship. . . .
>
> In a symbiotic relationship the group is capable of hostility and benevolence and the mystic contribution is subject to close scrutiny. From the scrutiny the group grows in stature and the mystic likewise. In the parasitic association even friendliness

323

is deadly. An easily seen example of this is in the group's promotion of the individual to a place in the Establishment where his energies are deflected from his creative-destructive role and absorbed in administrative functions . . . the dangers of the invitation to group or individual to become respectable, to be medically qualified, to be a university department, to be a therapeutic group, to be anything in short, but *not* explosive. . . .

'The institutionalizing of words, religions and psycho-analysis — all are special instances of institutionalizing memory so that it may 'contain' the mystic revelation and its creative and destructive force. . . . The function of the Establishment is to take and absorb the consequences so that the group is not destroyed. (pp. 78-82)

Perhaps one could transpose this into a lower key and say that the function of the psycho-analytical training group or establishment is to provide a sufficiently protected and organized place in the world within which students are given the opportunity, facilitated by their own personal analysis, to study and to experience development and change, in themselves and in their patients; to study and to work with the elements and configurations which impede that process. If psychoanalytic work, transcending the urge to cure, has an appeal for them, this will be prompted by the emotional impact of the close scrutiny of the children and adults with whom they are concerned.

As described by Bion in *Elements of Psycho-analysis*, the evolution of the transference in the psycho-analytic relationship, involving passion rather than violence (as for example in the form of action by either analyst or patient) is essentially creative-destructive for both: destructive of existing states of mind and constantly creating others. It may not always be apparent whether the new state of mind is — so to speak — a step in the right direction. It is hard for the teachers and establishment of any group that begins to meet with some success in the world, to bear in mind that they may not know the right direction, that there may not be a right direction, without being formless and disintegrated. It is difficult to allow the individual workers to find their own style and voice in a language and in a setting which enables them to carry on some meaningful discourse.

324

Some of the applicants for the Tavistock Course have already sought analysis for their own personal problems. They may be motivated to become psychotherapists themselves partly through projective identification with their analysts, fundamentally still children who believe that to have children/patients, will make them grown-up like mummy and daddy. This is a ubiquitous phenomenon and we all probably retain vestiges of it within our personality. Others, however, may wish to learn to work with patients, following some more genuine introjection and appreciation of the attention and understanding from which they have benefited and which they would like to share with others.

Observation as a prelude to analysis

As Part I of the course is concerned, not with the application of the psycho-analytic method to the patients, but with the development of psycho-analytic modes of observation and thinking in varied settings, students are not required to have had some experience of analysis themselves before they begin.

We attempt to give them a disciplined experience of close observation of the week-by-week development of an infant in a family, of a young child or children. Such detailed observation has inevitably an emotional impact upon the observer which is likely to disturb complacency and to lead to the kind of self-questioning that evokes an interest in personal analysis in those whose desire to get at the truth of themselves is likely to be stronger than their wish to preserve the status quo. The same kind of closer observation of the details of interaction and the responsibilities involved in the work with children, families or young people which students are also doing in this first part of the course, also alerts them to the mental pain as well as to the developmental thrusts in their charges. It enables them to be more receptive of the projections of this which come their way and to see that personal analysis leading to self-analysis is a method for being able to bear this better.

These infant observation seminars were initiated by Esther Bick in 1949. They now form part of the curriculum of the British Psycho-analytical Society and have proved to be one of the best preparations for developing those qualities of perception which

Bion describes as essential in the psycho-analytic consulting room, The mother-baby couple, initially the baby-breast, can be perceived as a model for the psycho-analytic couple, exemplifying the relationships, for instance, which he categorizes as parasitic, symbiotic or commensal. The discussion of these observations within a small group in which theoretical preconceptions are relegated as far as possible to the background, can be a model for the work group where the task is to study the aspects of material described and to look at them from different angles until some pattern emerges which speaks for itself. The discussion relates to a situation in which the observer has no responsibility other than to notice what there is to be seen while remaining unobtrusively friendly and receptive. As the impulse to action has to be noticed and restrained, the task of the group is to follow, imagine and think about the observations, including the role and effect of the observer, and notice the difficulty sometimes in refraining from taking action to 'improve' the situation.

Thus one has the leisure to note how relationships develop and change without interpretation or formal intervention. This helps towards the orientation described by Bion in which the analyst realizes that he is observing phenomena from which it is possible to construe mental processes. If one is truly observing configurations which are there and is describing them well enough, unimpeded by theoretical preconceptions, other people with a different theoretical background may, if they can also free themselves from their preconceptions, make similar findings. As it is difficult to free oneself from one's background and the expectations and modes of thinking established by that, it is a help in seminars which focus on detailed observation to have members who come from different backgrounds. There is no university course which prepares one for psycho-analytical thinking and observation. People may be facilitated, but are also limited, by the vertex from which they begin to describe human behaviour and interaction. To have in a seminar people who approach it from different vertices is an enrichment, even if at times one has to reckon with those whose previous training may have positively blocked their spontaneous vision.

Let us assume that detailed observation, and that the increase in awareness of the children's emotional life in their work settings which ensues, brings the student into greater contact with mental pain and the devices used to avoid experiencing this. He may feel the urge to understand the turmoil and disturbances evoked in himself, a state of mind which is likely to prompt him to seek analysis for himself. This may be necessary for his training and is essential for those who wish to proceed to Part II. The link between analysis and training is, however, an unfortunate one. Experience indicates that the more the former can be seen as an entirely private matter, a process which will hopefully give the analysand a new experience of hitherto unapprehended parts of himself, the freer he is likely to be to have such an experience, which will incidentally add to the equipment he can bring to his work. If the analyst is required to make judgements about his progress, this undoubtedly encourages the analysand to keep an eye on the expectations of analyst and teachers, to make transformations in K (learning about) rather than in O (becoming). It is difficult enough to become the person one is without positive encouragement from the establishment towards conformity and deception.

Relationship between student and teaching group

To recount a personal recollection of Dr. Bion when confronted with the anxieties of a candidate with a first training case: 'What do I do if the patient asks me if I am a student?' 'What *are* you when you *cease* to be a student of psycho-analysis?' Every teacher must be continually learning or he has no immediate experience to share. Every therapist must be learning something in the heat of every session or he has nothing of interest to say. One of the ways in which senior practitioners can continue to learn, apart from their own direct experience, is by trying to share the experience of younger people and by trying to look at material from their vertices.

In a psycho-analytically oriented framework, the work must be done by the individual on his own, whether he be concerned with the meaning of the behaviour of another individual in an intimate individual, family, or small group setting. In order to work well, to think about relationships involved, most people for a while do need the support of some group of colleagues as well as of teachers and supervisors, who are learning with them.

According to Bion's premises, all groups are subject to basic

327

assumption activity which interferes with the capacity of the members to work severally and together. We must assume that no training group or society of psycho-analytical workers is going to be free from these phenomena, or that one can ever afford to relax one's vigilance in trying to spot their recurrences. Perhaps the pairing groups produce the messianic hopes whether substantial or false, which tend then to become invested in a dependent group or groups relying on these new or apparently original messages. Then in turn these are inclined to become the fight-flight groups ready to flee from or to attack enemy ideologies. The dependent group structure so often manifests itself in the reliance upon a crystallized selection of the theories of Freud (the original Messiah), sometimes pitted against a similar extrapolation from Melanie Klein (a latter day saint). Bion is unlikely to escape the same fate. Their theories in such a climate of polarization are suitably selected and presented to eliminate the essential questioning, contradictions and progressions inherent in the formulation of pioneers who are constantly struggling to conceptualize the clinical observations they are making. Bion's postulation about the impossibility of knowing or describing truth, about the existence of thoughts which do not require a thinker (and of psycho-analysis as one of these thoughts) may help us to try to relinquish the idea of owning our own particular brand of psycho-analysis.

One can hope to promote a relationship between fellow workers, students and teachers which might be described by Bion as symbiotic for some, and for the rest at least commensal: co-existent if not mutually profitable. Thus the therapist's relationships with his patients, objects of study, may take place within a framework of teachers or colleagues who are all dedicated to the task of enlarging their field of observation and of self scrutiny. In such an atmosphere, hopefully, senior colleagues instead of being content to rest upon positions earned by past achievements, or longevity, may be able to continue or to allow others to continue that process of mental and emotional growth whose infinite possibilities are released, according to Bion, by putting aside memory and desire in order to have a better apprehension of the present moment.

Recruitment for training

A group or training is either kept alive or ossifies, by virtue of the quality of the new members it recruits. These may be attracted by the power or status which membership is supposed to confer upon them; they may be attracted by the possibility of partici- pating in some interesting learning experience connected with the work which they are already doing or which they would like to do. The senior members forming the establishment which selects the new trainees tend to become increasingly exclusive as a training acquires a reputation and attracts more applicants. Sheer numbers may make exclusion necessary. The tendency in a genuinely well-meaning establishment concerned with preserving standards of work is to use experience of past mistakes to play safe. The establishment of a group in which envy pre- dominates, as described by Bion, may tend, under the guise of protecting standards, to proliferate regulations which do the choosing and end up by including a preponderance of people who have come to join an élite profession which they have a vested interest in restricting.

If one has to limit recruitment, how can this be effected with- out producing an élitist atmosphere? The best way of selecting would seem to be to give candidates an experience analogous to the work which they wish to do, which will also allow them an opportunity for self-selection, and place the decision as far as possible in their hands. The most obvious course is to encourage prospective students to have a personal analysis. If they find they can stay with that and with the revelations of themselves which unfold in its progress, then hopefully they should have a better basis for supposing they may be able to help others to undergo a similar experience. This is the usual procedure in most psycho- analytical societies and in principle can hardly be bettered as an initial method of selection.

One must allow, however, for the likelihood that some analysands will return having fairly successfully resisted a real experience and grasp of their more unpleasant parts (the un- wanted O), perhaps having learned *about* them and become cleverer consciously or unconsciously in disguising them. These may return filled with enthusiasm about analytic work and training, having achieved some sort of collusion of mutual

329

idealization with their analyst — enthusiasm about analysis for others, not for themselves.

If one can sometimes deceive one's analyst and go on deceiving oneself, one can surely also deceive one's tutors and teachers. It seems necessary throughout training to allow work and study experiences which as far as possible encourage students to test the results and capacities which they have. It seems important not to collude in the idealization of being a psycho-analyst or a psychotherapist. For that reason we hope that students in Part I will already be working professionally with children, families and young people in a job that may be seen as valuable in itself and potentially more interesting and rewarding as the worker's perceptions increase. The aim is to make it easy for students to leave after the first part of the training, or to develop more satisfactory roles and methods of working in the fields where they are already employed. The basic aim of the course is not to create a certain number of trained professionals, labelled 'child psychotherapist', but to offer an education in psycho-analytical attitudes and ideas which will lead to some people learning to practise the psycho-analytical method, and to others learning to practise these attitudes and modes of thought in related fields: as in social case work, pastoral care in schools and colleges. The present Part II of the course is likely in the future to be one alternative, alongside others which may be devised to try to meet the need for further development in related fields.

Teaching methods and continued self-selection

Students who do proceed to the second part of the course — the application of the psycho-analytic method, in the playroom and consulting room — need support to bear the exigencies of the work, but also sometimes towards selecting themselves out of it if the burden seems likely to be greater than the pleasure and profit derived from it. The attitude of the teaching group can surely do much to promote or discourage honesty in the individual.

If seminars are used too much for monitoring and judging the progress of cases or of the students presenting the cases, their potential usefulness can be obscured by the evocation of feelings of inferiority, defensiveness and the urge to produce less than honest work: to bring to a seminar, for instance, only those sessions in which the therapist thinks he appears to advantage. The primary function of a seminar leader, as of a supervisor, is surely to help the therapist after the event to think about the experience of clinical interaction which he is describing, and to recapture imaginatively the events described. Thus he may be able to think about them better and become more able to shoulder the burden of clinical responsibility and more open to receiving the patient's projections. This, I imagine, is an aspect of what Bion is describing when he talks of experiencing O, involving always a further penetration in the direction of the unknown. I would be inclined to think that the most fruitful seminar or supervision is one in which participants are left, not just satisfied with a piece of good work done, dazzled by the brilliance of pupil, teacher or patient, but with the impetus for further exploration in their own work, and encouraged to persevere in the face of difficulties.

In supervision (surely one should try to discard the name and concept of 'control'), the tendency of the non-omnipotent student who is anxious to learn and who respects his supervisor, is to look for explanations, clarifications and good interpretations which he is sure the greater expert can offer. Bion has repeatedly emphasized that however inexperienced and uncertain the candidate, no knowledge and experience on the part of the supervisor can equal the actual experience of being with the patient in the session. The supervisor is always working with the student's reports.

This perhaps brings us to the usefulness of Bion's advocacy of the abdication of memory and desire. It is a difficult concept for the inexperienced student to grasp. When one is conscious of having so little information about psycho-analytic theory and personality development to remember, it is particularly difficult to put that aside rather than to cling tenaciously to the scraps that one has. But it seems to me essential to proceed and to encourage students to proceed on two fronts: they need to acquire and evaluate information which I suspect must mean in earlier learning days the writing of some very detailed notes on cases and observations as an exercise in remembering and in producing something which can be studied sufficiently closely in seminars or supervisors to throw into relief what is *not* there. But yet the

331

encouragement towards the putting aside of memory and desire, that 'willing suspension of disbelief' as described by Coleridge, would seem to me a state of mind essential to try to cultivate in the psycho-analytic sessions. When achieved it can, for instance, relieve the boredom and frustration of apparently interminable unchanging sessions with a latency child who sits everlastingly drawing similar geometric patterns. The recollection that so it was yesterday and the desire — somewhat hopeless — that it should not be thus tomorrow, can so cloud one's perceptions that they are unable perhaps to receive some intimation of anxiety or emotionality peeping out from the confines of the pattern today.

It is perhaps especially difficult for people working analytically in clinics to achieve the necessary state of sequestration to direct the beam of darkness on the here and now; to put aside expectations arising from yesterday's session together with whatever information may have percolated from some other worker about the family or crises at school. It is helpful as an exercise in studying what may be drawn out of the immediate session to concentrate occasionally in clinical seminars upon the presentation of a session in detail without any history, to work in the dark to find out how much food for thought there is when not flooded with information.

If one has to guard against institutionalizing psycho-analysis, one must beware of using past experience in training to limit future as yet un-thought-of developments. Bion's comments on the limitations of relying upon memory and desire have some applicability to the field of training as well as to the consulting room; to one's wish for instance to keep up standards which may alas tend towards reproducing paler copies of oneself. The more one has to delegate to committee judgement the more one is likely to flatten out into a group of social and well-adjusted banality consisting of those who have learned to adapt successfully to the system.

However, as a tutor or supervisor one cannot abdicate entirely the responsibility which greater experience confers, both to the patient and to the student, for trying to see that some reasonable match of capabilities takes place between a particular case and a particular student with regard to his stage of development. Experience is likely to bear out the fallibility of these assessments and certainly one cannot judge from the apparent progress of the

332

reatment alone the capabilities of the worker who is undertaking
t. Some patients have such an urge to grow and to understand,
hat they do well with attention but limited comprehension on
he therapist's part. Others need infinite patience and test to the
imit the therapist's capacity to bear negativism and the projection of frustration and pain.

It seems to me that during training one must allow situations
which give students the opportunity to test and live through some
of the stresses to which they must inevitably be subjected sooner
or later in psycho-analytic work, to find if they can struggle with
them and even enjoy that struggle. As Dr. Bion once remarked:
one may not necessarily have to be outstandingly intelligent to be
a psycho-analyst, but such intelligence as one has must be
available for use under fire; and this is especially true in work
with certain children. Baptism under fire at some point is an
essential part of the development of a child psychotherapist, and
it can be a help towards recognizing the same configurations
occurring in a subtler form in the adult.

If we cannot and should not protect our students from difficult
and frustrating experiences and we should probably be loath to
rescue them too soon even when the going becomes very rough,
yet support may be necessary and required: support of the kind
that shares the burden of thinking and worrying. This may
alleviate but can never remove the loneliness in difficult clinical
situations, for no supervisor can relieve one of the burden of
deciding how to respond in the immediacy of the session.

As, obviously in this field, teachers must continue to be
practitioners, continued experience with patients — especially
when these are not all aspiring analysts or psychotherapists —
keeps one closely in touch with the pains and unpredictabilities in
becoming an individual, and more able to empathize with the
problems of fellow practitioners who are less experienced in
years. The humility which this should engender is the only way
of hoping to create a profesion that will not be idealized as an
élite, and of hoping that it will not attract recruits for this reason.

Written work

In the Tavistock training we have found that it helps students to
think about what they are doing and learning, by writing

333

accounts of their work at different stages. We seem likely to extend this as an additional method of self selection, to ask for descriptions and distillations of sequences of observations, work experiences, case presentations and comprehension of theory. Encouragement to present honest accounts of experience, rather than scholastic essays including references to all the right authorities, may contribute to producing a group of workers who do not proliferate the kind of theories described by Bion as characteristic of the lying group dominated by envy. Probably one of the ways of mitigating the envy of the achievements of others, the passively dependent attitude which sees the strength and expertise in others, and which is moreover unable to describe between true and false achievement, is the attempt at least to do and to take stock of what one is managing to do oneself, to use language as a prelude to further achievement.

Theory

There is a question as to how to teach theory in a course which aims to encourage students to learn from a genuine experience of themselves in close contact with others. The collection, the manipulation, the evaluation of theories are traditionally used in the field of mental health as bulwarks against disturbing uncertainties endemic in the work. But yet one needs theories and 'models', to use Bion's term, as a notation or mythology to bind constant conjunctions. They are necessary as tools to help one to organize thinking about experiences in order to proceed further. In Bion's definition 'Theory not as a solution but as a model which may prove convenient and useful' (*Attention and Interpretation*).

Over the years with the help of Donald Meltzer, a selection of reading has been evolving which aims to orient students to the study of psycho-analysis as a developing art-science of a descriptive kind, essentially useful as it illuminates the experiences and furthers the method of working with the transference within the consulting room. It is studied from a historical point of view as a series of pioneering adventures in the mind. We begin with Freud's attempts to free himself from a nineteenth-century physiological view of the mind, to evolve theoretical models which could account for the phenomena he encountered in his patients. We follow the development of his theories of psycho-pathology as he attempts to reconstruct from his patients their childhood neurosis and to account for what went wrong. The work of Melanie Klein centering round the *Narrative of a Child Analysis*, is studied from the point of view of her attempt to observe how the child builds up from infancy, his inner world, and the way in which this influences the kind of adult that he will become. Finally Bion's work is studied as an attempt to evolve a model of the mind providing a method of studying linkages between emotionality, truth and lies; an attempt which is in the vanguard of psycho-analysis.

Working in institutions

The emphasis in all of this has been on how the establishment may foster the development of individuality and individual responsibility. Yet we are training people to work in institutions that are likely to contain rival groups and forces that are inimical to psycho-analysis. We must hope to create a friendlier climate in some of these institutions.

The practice of the psycho-analytic method requires a degree of sequestration so that the patient may be protected from the impingement of unnecessary external intrusions which could interfere with the evolution of the transference. The therapist himself needs to find a place in his institution so that he too can deploy his attention during the treatment in a relatively un-cluttered way.

This sequestration and preoccupation lends itself to being perceived by other less psycho-analytically involved colleagues as a mystique and as a claim to special consideration and position. Therapists in a clinic can attract to themselves only too readily an ambivalent transference, as to parents who evoke curiosity by obtruding evidence that they are engaged upon some mysterious intercourse, but who tantalize by performing it behind doors. They may take refuge from the attacks of the critical by forming a close-knit little group, a mutual protection society which, however much in possession of the truth it may feel, is bound to be essentially persecuted at core; or they may try to deal with these transference phenomena by denial and placation of differences. The tendency to revert to basic

335

assumption behaviour enters into and between every group formation, in an institution or clinic which can readily split itself, and give up the task in hand in favour of defending respective positions or ideologies. The most pervasive basic assumption perhaps in work with children is the dependency one. Close work with children in pain, and accountability to rivalry with their parents, tends to bring out feelings of inadequacy and unresolved infantile dependence in ourselves. If we cannot manage to deal with those by introspection, and introjective identification with valued internal parental figures, how can we deal with them in the children we treat? Surely there must be someone who can provide a better answer than we can? — Our supervisors, our analyst, or — supporting these — some excellent theoretical formulation into which all clinical data most ultimately fit? There are tendencies even (perhaps particularly) in the most progressive groups to rely upon the latest findings and formulations to provide the answer for every problem. Hence the polarization in so many psycho-analytical groups between adherents to different psycho-analytical theories, rival loyalties to the different flags where unresolved hostility and envy underlying the dependence is split off on to the rival group. There is something to be said for working in an institution which contains a section of workers who are simply ignorant of or hostile to psycho-analysis. This gives one the impetus to have another look at essentials.

Dr. Bion's studies of group behaviour have continued to be the germinal impulse for the recurrent group relations conferences held by the Tavistock, an impetus to institutional groups to study themselves and their behaviour to one another. There is one psycho-analytical tradition that regards the study of group behaviour as almost disloyal to psycho-analysis which is concerned with the internal world, the internal grouping. Yet the study of the transferring of this internal grouping to the therapist in the psycho-analytic couple is surely complemented by the study of the behaviour of the individual in a group, of the impingement of group pressures upon him. The departure from analytic attitudes occurs when the study of group behaviour becomes the kind of group therapy in which a cure is effected through an abdication of responsibility, by fragmenting and losing parts of oneself in the group, by regressing to proto-mental activity, carried along by the stream of unconsciousness or the mythology jointly engendered.

Work groups and establishments

To return to that early distinction made by Bion between the basic assumption and the work groups. Without continual and rigorous examination of group activities in the realm of training and of practice with colleagues, the activities of the establishment group are only too easy to talk about when one is an outsider but to overlook when one becomes a member. *Knowing about* groups and being aware of the nature of one's emotional participation in a group activity are two different things; again instances of the distinction between transformations in K and *becoming* O, where experience is transformed into growth and learning through experiences takes place.

In order to prevent oneself from becoming the spokesman of some 'advanced' psycho-analytic group perhaps one should consider the following quotation from *Attention and Interpretation*:

> The individual himself must be able to distinguish between himself as an ordinary person and his view that he is omniscient and omnipotent. It is a step towards recognition of a distinction between the group as it really is and its idealization as an embodiment of the omnipotence of the individuals who compose it. Sometimes the separation fails and the group is not only seen to be ideally omnipotent and omniscient but believed to be so in actuality. The individual's realization of a gulf between his view of himself as omnipotent and his view of himself as an ordinary human being must be achieved as a result of a task of the group itself as well as in individual analysis. Otherwise there is a danger that a state of mind is transferred (by projective identification) to the group and *acted out* there — not altered. (p.76)

Despite all the emphasis upon training people to be as far as possible individuals within their group it seems likely that for most of us the continuance of a group or an establishment within which we can work is a necessity. 'The function of a group is to produce a genius: the function of the Establishment is to take up and absorb the consequence so that the group is not destroyed.' The International Psycho-analytical Association is the Establishment within which the work of psycho-analytic geniuses, rare as always, but including surely Bion, must be preserved and utilized. But when an establishment becomes too vast and monolithic the tendency is to increase committees and legislation in ways that do not allow for individual developments and eccentricities. 'Dislike of the onus of decision, or awareness of responsibility for the decision, contributes to the formulation of selection procedures by which selection, like dogma and laws of science, is made to act as a substitute for judgement or a scapegoat for the guilt attendant on overtly acknowledged exercise of responsibility' (*Attention and Interpretation*).

There is room and, it seems to me, a necessity to allow for a number of establishments within which the psycho-analytic ideas of genius are contained and within which students may become acquainted with them and learn to apply them from different vertices. The vertex from which one looks when nourished by close observation of child and of infant development would seem to be a fruitful one for discerning later on the presence of the child within the adult, an essential nucleus of analytic work with adults.

How does a parent who wishes to have his child psychoanalysed or a person who wishes to have a psycho-analytic experience himself, know how to set about it? Bion in *Experiences in Groups*, indicates that in this field the label on the bottle can be no guarantee of the contents. 'Psycho-analyst' like 'Psychotherapist' is a trade name; the former more exclusive than the latter and carrying with it probably the guarantee of a more formal training. But neither name is any guarantee as to whether the individual in the role designated has some competence and capacity to go on struggling to improve that competence by practising the psycho-analytic method. Prospective clients or patients will have to continue to use their other known professional advisers, their friends, the grapevine, and sometimes — if available — their own intuition in the last resort when they wish to find their way to having psycho-analytical treatment. But a variety of training establishments which are attempting to cultivate a psycho-analytic attitude and to follow the psycho-

338

analytic method must, hopefully, make this more available to patients — who exist everywhere, and not only in our capital cities. To quote Bion's comments about the growth of the personality, applicable also to institutions which are concerned with this: 'What is required is not the decrease of inhibition but a decrease of the impulse to inhibit; the impulse to inhibit is fundamentally envy of the growth-stimulating objects.'

5   Bion's Conception of a Pyscho-
     analytical Attitude
     *An Obituary Appreciation of the Work of W.R. Bion
     (1980)*

In considering Bion's contribution to clinical work, much could be said of how he used and extended, in his own inimitable way, some of the theories of Freud and of Melanie Klein in so far as he found that they illuminated the observations which he was able to make in the consulting room: thus carrying on the great tradition in psycho-analysis. A number of people have been studying his work at the Tavistock Clinic during the past few years with Donald Meltzer, and this has been expounded in the third volume of *The Kleinian Development* (1978).

I would like to select what is, for me, the most inspiring and liberating aspect of his conception of psycho-analysis. Although he believed that there is no substitute for undergoing an analytic experience in the sequestered but turbulent milieu of the consulting room, if one is bent upon exploring the mysteries of one's personality, Bion sees the discipline of psycho-analysis for analyst and patient alike, as aspiring to continue that great tradition of thinking in art, science and philosophy, which investigates not only the nature of the world in which we live, of human beings in that world, but also the mind of the observer, the thinker himself.

The following quotation is from the last of the lecture/discussions he gave in New York in 1977. It follows upon some query about the way to approach a dying patient. Bion is aware that in a sense we are all terminally ill, and the problem is how to learn to best use the unpredictable time that we have available:

'What is your assessment of the job of a psycho-analyst?'
'I have already suggested that it would not be much use being invited to tell various forms of agreeable lies, nor would I want to terrify anybody by telling him frightening stories about his possibly having a fatal disease. Although it may seem theoretical, or even philosophical, I find it easier to fall back on the feeling that I am called upon to make the person

340

familiar with a particular aspect of truth. I know that is an unsatisfactory statement; Bacon summed it up in a famous essay: "'What is truth?' said jesting Pilate, and would not wait for an answer." But I think that most people know what I mean when I say it is safest to feel that one is falling back on as near as one can get to the truth. At least one becomes part of a distinguished company of scientists, painters, musicians and other artists — they are all attempting to display some aspect of the truth — I say all, by which I mean all those who belong to the distinguished company. There is something unsatisfactory about the imitation, and if it is unsatisfactory to oneself it does not require a great deal of imagination to suppose it would be unsatisfactory to a patient who is in a desperate situation.

'The *truth* — what does it look like? — Who wants to be confronted with a trompe l'òeil representation of Paradise? Such confections are pardonable to an agent selling us an earthly home, but not for our eternal home — our *Self*.'

Years earlier in *Learning from Experience* (1962), Bion has referred to truth as the food of the mind, and considered that the personality may suffer from starvation of truth much as the body suffers from malnutrition if it lacks nourishing food. Lies would be linked with imitations and perversions of that truth, leading to mental malnourishment and poisoning of the mind. Like Keats and many another poet he seems to regard truth as inevitably linked with beauty, and became in later years increasingly concerned with the problem of giving some fitting expression to the poetry of intimate personal relationships:

A scientific paper should remind you of real people; it should not be so boring, so unaesthetic that it becomes a pain in your mind to read it. We have a difficult job — even the impromptus in the analysis, the interpretations that we give, would be all the better if they stood up to *aesthetic criticism*. I hope that this is not too much like Satan rebuking sin — I am well aware that my own interpretations, spoken or written, cannot pass these tests, — but there is no reason why yours should not. You do not need to be confined by the limitations of your lecturers, teachers, analysts, parents. If you are there is no room for growth.

341

Leaving room for growth, promoting development, becoming a mental midwife: these are functions which Bion attributes to the analyst, the parent, the educator, who is concerned with enabling the patient, the child, the pupil, to develop through having a genuine experience of himself: an experience of feeling, of thinking based upon that feeling, and of attempting to formulate or take action upon these thoughts.

How does one help a patient, or child, to have a true experience of himself? Bion, as you remember, has used Keats's term 'negative capability': the ability to refrain from irritably reaching after fact and reason, to restrain the impatience that reaches for the answer which stifles further questioning; 'La réponse est le malheur de la question', as he quoted. *Negative capability* implies readiness to accept, to allow the impact of meeting another person. In his last paper to the British Psychoanalytical Society, 'Making the Best of a Bad Job', he describes this meeting of two personalities at close quarters, between analyst and analysand, as giving rise to a disturbance which he called an *emotional storm*. Throughout this, 'storm-tossed but not shaken, the analyst must go on thinking clearly, from which the more disciplined reaction will build up and the troops will not run away but will begin to stand fast.' At first, the analyst is ignorant of what is happening: but 'if we stay, do not run away ... go on observing the patient, after a time a pattern will emerge.' Discernment of that pattern, the wresting of some order from chaos, may result in mutually beneficial growth for both analyst and patient.

Those of us with some experience of child analysis, and even of child rearing, may be aware how too intense an encounter with their hidden selves may be avoided by paramnesias, as he describes in his paper on evidence. There are patients who may be successful in avoiding that unpleasant experience of 'break-up, break-down, break-through', of catastrophic change; and with whom one may be seduced into carrying on that unsatisfactory imitation of an analytic encounter in which the truth of an immediate experience is by-passed.

In order to achieve that state of negative capability or readiness to receive and think about the patient's projections, a state of intuitive awareness, Bion has advocated the abandonment of memory and desire. This, of course, does not mean the abandonment of such mental equipment as our experience has enabled us to cultivate. But it would involve a wariness of being clogged by paramnesias, of space-filling facts, of loyalty to theories that have served us well in the past and which we may become committed to defend as the expense of noticing inconvenient new facts. It would mean forging goals both for ourselves and our patients. 'What we *ought* to be is of no importance in the practice of psycho-analysis or in the practice of *any part of real life*. It does matter what we *are* . . . The analytic procedure is an attempt to introduce the patient to who he is, because, whether he likes it or not, that is a marriage that is going to last as long as he lives.'

Bion, indeed, has been at times irritating to some of his admirers who have struggled strenuously to understand his concepts: as for instance, on those occasions when — questioned as to his meaning — he would often indicate that he had moved on from there. An example of this occurs in the New York lectures where, when questioned about the Grid — his famous attempt to categorize the movements in thought — he says: 'As soon as I had got the Grid out of my system I could see how inadequate it was . . . He put in his thumb, and pulled out a plum, and said "what a good boy am I!" — but the satisfaction does not last long.'

His attitude would be that truth can never be attained, or possessed; it is never static. Glimpses of aspects of truth occur fleetingly, on the way to becoming more experienced. This entails the ability to live in the present, bringing one's experiences from the past constantly into the present to link up with the perceptions of the present. The Self grows in experience and in the ability to express itself.

By 'Yourself' he means the total person, body and mind, with its whole history, pre- and post-natal. His perception of the modes of expression of the Self became increasingly sharpened by observations which led him to his imaginative conjectures about the relationship between these two selves, pre- and post-natal, within the same body. Bion's thinking about this remained still in the realms of imaginative conjecture, despite some later evidence of states that could be linked to it.

Thinking he regarded as a human activity still in its absolute infancy. The development of a capacity to think creatively, which might harness human passions in the service of development and wisdom, appeared to him as something of a race

343

against time. His own intuitive thinking was so far in advance of anyone else's in our field that its seminal effect can only begin to be felt. Such is the impact of *A Memoir of the Future*, which traces the complex mind in action, talking from many vertices, from the whole gamut of his years — the foetus in the womb to the 77-year-old (as he was when he completed 'The Dawn of Oblivion'); it presents the living drama of his internal history; amusing, argumentative, profound, puzzling, always unexpected, sometimes blindingly, obviously true.

Those of us who had the privilege of listening to his mind in action in seminars, groups and in conversation in these last years, feel very cheated that his pen could not continue to glean from his still teeming brain; but we are very grateful for what remains, both published and as yet unpublished, to stimulate our attempts to think about ourselves and our work.

As Bion says at the end of 'The Dawn of Oblivion', we must become more expert in discrimination: 'There are no labels attached to most options — there is no substitute for the growth of wisdom. Wisdom or oblivion — take your choice. From that warfare there is no release.' This is the Bion who sees analysis in the consulting room not as a refuge, but as a preparation for the real thing: for a richer and wiser mode of living in the world.